Harvard Historical Studies, 112

Published under the auspices
of the Department of History
from the income of the
Paul Revere Frothingham Bequest
Robert Louis Stroock Fund
Henry Warren Torrey Fund

The Conversion of Henri IV

Politics, Power, and Religious Belief in Early Modern France

Michael Wolfe

Harvard University Press
Cambridge, Massachusetts
London, England
1993

This book is printed on acid-free paper, and its binding materials
have been chosen for strength and durability.

Library of Congress Cataloging-in-Publication Data

Wolfe, Michael.
The Conversion of Henri IV: politics, power, and religious belief
in early modern France / Michael Wolfe.
p. cm.
Includes bibliographical references and index.
ISBN 0-674-17031-8
1. Henri IV, King of France, 1553–1610—Influence. 2. France—Politics and government—16th century—Religious aspects.
3. France—Church history—16th century—Political aspects.
4. Monarchy—France—History—16th century. I. Title.
DC122.3.W65 1993
944'.031—dc20
92-24881
CIP

To Dr. Ruth Emery, whose love and
wisdom have always sustained me

Contents

Acknowledgments

COUNTLESS DEBTS to friends and colleagues have been incurred over the past ten years as I've struggled to understand what Henri IV's conversion meant to his contemporaries. Whatever I might manage to say by way of thanks to them will perforce fall short. But perhaps that's how it should be. Orest Ranum has taught me—and continues to teach me—new ways to untangle the peculiar, yet so familiar, behavior and mindset of those early moderns who intrigue us. Nancy Roelker has guided my understanding of sixteenth-century France since my days as an undergraduate at Boston University. My love for all things early modern was sparked by John Gagliardo, whose selfless attention and affection will always inspire my labors. My heartfelt gratitude goes to all three of these fine scholars and friends. Other great teachers who have left their mark on me are Robert Forster, John Baldwin, and Mack Walker. Fellow graduate students, now all accomplished historians in their own right, lent me their ear on many a long and now fondly remembered night. My thanks to John Theibault, Lisa Rosner, Alison Smith, Marian Matrician, Larry Ellis, and Jim McNaughton. Lionel Rothkrug, Lloyd Moote, and Ed Perkins also gave me invaluable assistance as I worked through the seemingly endless revisions. I would also like to thank the staffs at the Bibliothèque Nationale, Bibliothèque Mazarine, and Archives Nationales. Patrice Higonnet, Elizabeth Suttell, and Christine Thorsteinsson at Harvard have all helped in the final crafting of the book. Crucial support has also been received from Penn State University–Altoona and the National Endowment for the Humanities. I am grateful to the editors at *Historical Reflections/Réflexions historiques* and *French History,* where portions of this study, since revised, appeared earlier as articles. Whatever merits this book may have belong by right to all of the above; its defects I must claim as my own.

My only wish is that my mother could have seen the results of the work that occupied her son so this past decade. My wife, Amy, read the innumerable drafts, always suggesting the more elegant turn of phrase. She tolerated Henri's presence in our lives lo these many years even though—to paraphrase Fats Waller—she's always been the only one for me. Our children, Ross and Adriana, may find it a little easier to play their computer games now that Daddy has finished, at least for the time being.

The Conversion of Henri IV

Introduction

HENRI IV'S LEGENDARY quip that "Paris is worth a Mass," with its mocking irreverence and jarring sense of political realism, is often cited to characterize the growing secularism of early modern politics. Yet how many today know that when they utter this facile remark, they repeat not Henri IV's words but those of his Leaguer enemies? This otherwise curious footnote, if examined closely, may force us to reconsider the achievements of France's first Bourbon king by focusing on his conversion to Catholicism in 1593. The emergence in 1584 of the Protestant Henri de Navarre as presumptive heir to the Catholic throne of France dominated contemporary thought as did no other issue during the early modern era. It also touched off the most serious challenge to royal authority in France prior to the Revolution of 1789. Pamphlets, treatises, letters, and memoranda all resonated with the burning question of the king's faith during this tragic *fin de siècle*, sparking among some an acute sense of eschatological dread and anticipation, while eliciting from others an urge for stoic withdrawal from the chaos that seemed to engulf them.

The conversion of Henri IV in 1593 marks a crucial stage in the development of the French monarchy and early modern political culture. In retrospect, it provided the key to ending thirty years of war and rebuilding the crown's shattered authority. Thereafter, Navarre's successors gradually refashioned the monarchy and the society it governed in a process we now call the growth of absolutism. What made Bourbon absolutism so distinctive is a question which has troubled historians for many years. Some have gauged the expansion of royal power by reference to new instruments of rule, giving particular emphasis to the *conseil d'état,* the venality of office, and the intendancy.[1] Others have shown how royal fiscal policies divided provincial elites in ways which allowed the crown, through the use of clientage and law courts, to insinuate its authority at the expense of regional liberties.[2] Historians of political thought have stressed the earlier, crucial changes that had taken place in ideas about kingship and the law during the sixteenth century.[3] Recent work deciphering the intricate patterning of royal ceremonies, such as funeral rites, *lits de justice,* coronations, and royal entries, all confirm the emergence over this period of more dynamic conceptions of the royal office and its prerogatives.[4]

Unyielding in theory, yet collaborative in practice, these innovations in royal government developed in response to the many sources of tension present in French society. International rivalries with the Hapsburgs, the startling growth of Calvinist dissent, and a worsening economic outlook proved a volatile combination that quickly overwhelmed Henri II's sons and wife, Catherine de Medici, after 1559. During the generation of war that followed, Huguenots and Catholics from all social classes—nobles, townspeople, judges, crown officials, clergymen, artisans and peasants—mounted at varying times and with varying success strong challenges to the crown's new legislative claims. Asserting special rights derived from customary law and Christian belief, these groups helped give rise to new theories justifying resistance and tyrannicide. These potent appeals to tradition and conscience occurred first among Huguenot thinkers such as François Hotman and Théodore Beza, and later among Leaguer Catholics such as Jean Boucher and Rossaeus. During the 1570s and 1580s, economic collapse and growing social misery exacerbated this battle over France's future, plunging the country into a deep crisis that lasted into the next century.[5]

The struggle over the conversion of Henri IV has often been seen as part of this ongoing debate over French kingship, as a constitutional clash between Huguenot, then League proponents of elective monarchy and *politique* advocates of an absolute king who commanded the unquestioning obedience of his subjects.[6] Overreliance on these party tags may run the risk of reductionism and partisanship, however. After all, these names had originated as epithets defined by the propaganda needs of the opposition, and as such often distorted rather than clarified the aims of the party concerned. Charges of anti-royalism and irreligion, however false, became common currency in polemical literature; equally confusing is the fact that each group saw itself as the true embodiment of the patriotic *bon françois*. Despite their disagreements, Leaguers and *politiques* shared many assumptions about French kingship and religion. Sixteenth-century political designations must also be used cautiously because they often fail to account for the critical divisions within each group. As will be seen, these divisions played a crucial role in the genesis of Henri IV's conversion to Catholicism.

Reducing the conflict over Henri IV's faith to a constitutional contest offers only a partial explanation of the issues at stake in these last and perhaps most violent of the Wars of Religion. Until 1559, constitutional discussions had largely been confined to the sophisticated writings of legists and humanist scholars, or enmeshed in codes of royal ceremonial. These rather speculative reformulations of monarchical theory and practice only began to excite public concern as the crown's ability to preserve order crumbled during the 1570s and 1580s. Even though constitutional language colors much of the polemical literature, as in the controversy after 1584 over the Salic Law and Law of Catholicity, it hardly explains why so many different groups across France took up arms over the king's faith. Closer attention must instead be focused on the extraordinary character of the conversion problem and the unusual passions it raised among Huguenots and Catholics alike. They fought each other not over constitutional differences, but because they shared the conviction that the salvation of both France and themselves depended on the resolution of the conversion question.

The extent to which language and behavior coincide during any period can vary enormously with each individual and group. Several considerations complicate the attempt to comprehend the role of public opinion in the struggle over the king's religion. Public opinion was not the broad impersonal force we think of today, but rather an expression of the collective mentality of the established elite. Elements of an older oral culture, which stressed personal idiosyncrasies and face-to-face encounters, became amplified and gradually transformed through the increasing use of print. Discursive differences defined in print helped readers to articulate—and legitimate—their level of engagement in the struggle. Literacy allowed the educated individual to trace, introspectively, the boundaries between *honnêteté* and deviance. The garbled murmurings of the lower classes represented either a threat to the moral values of privilege or, more rarely, a potential tool to be used against the opposition; that is, of course, if they were heard at all. However myopic, these attitudes helped to shape how elites at the time responded as individuals and groups to the struggle over Henri IV's religion.

Discerning an individual's particular stance can be difficult because documents from the period do not always vouchsafe the precise connection between a person's ideas and subsequent actions. Letters, for example, whose privacy is today backed by law, were then considered highly public records to be circulated and copied. This fact naturally affected their contents. Attempts to encode or obfuscate a letter's meaning could signal but not necessarily delineate the author's political affiliations. Moreover, the standards used to justify public conduct at that time differed greatly from those used today. During the early modern period, public avowals of moral purpose often overlay the private search for emoluments, offices, and advancement; the adage that virtue is ultimately rewarded frequently meant that personal gain signified public merit. Although often elusive, these perceptual dimensions of the conflict must be investigated if we hope to understand the shift to Bourbon rule after 1589.

Historians who, like Aristotle, seek reasoned consistency in people's thoughts and actions will be sorely disappointed by the French Wars of Religion. The public shocks occasioned by the Saint Bartholomew's Day Massacres, the Day of the Barricades, the murder of the Guises, and the assassination of Henri III, deeply affected individual judgments and positions during these years, giving rise to political theories and personal anxieties which might otherwise not have emerged. The unpredictability of events also gave people a more acute sense of both the demonic and sacred elements present in the world. This palpable lack of control which contemporaries sensed helped sustain the conflict over Henri IV's religion. The key here is not to try to reconstruct what Henri IV actually thought when he made his "perilous leap" at St. Denis; that question which so agitated his contemporaries will never be satisfactorily answered by modern historians.[7] The more important question is how French Catholics, after years of acrimonious dispute and armed aggression, eventually came to believe him sincere and thus acceptable as their king.

The conflict over Henri IV's faith had its deepest roots in the great debates over faith and grace prompted by the Protestant and Catholic Reformations. Both reform movements had compelled French men and women to grapple with the dynamics of religious change and belief. The tremendous interest that Henri IV's contemporaries took in matters of faith not only fueled the rise of new forms of devotional literature and penitential practices, but also shaped how they responded after 1584 to the explosive clash between the king's conscience and the dictates of his royal *dignitas*. Although politics certainly had its place, as did questions of social interest and economic competition, these bitter conflicts were primarily religious wars. In the final analysis, it was the struggle over eternal verities that gave the wars their special dynamism.

Commitments proved so uncertain because contemporaries knew that at any time Henri IV could radically alter the situation by deciding to abjure Protestantism and embrace Catholicism. This apprehension reveals one of the most enigmatic dimensions of the French Wars of Religion, namely the enormous impact that individual decisions such as Henri IV's could have on the tragic course of events. His contemporaries knew only too well the determinative influence one person could exert on history. How different it all would be, the French frequently lamented after 1559, had Henri II not insisted on that last, fatal joust with the Sieur de Montgomery. These cries reached a crescendo after 1584 when Henri de Navarre emerged as presumptive heir to the Catholic throne of France. This fearful sense of what was to come revealed the special concerns and assumptions held dear by French Catholics as they struggled for security and order. This deep foreboding arose from the belief that the malignant forces behind the conflict, if victorious, could undermine the essential moral bases of French society. When we join these concerns with the conviction that all might depend on the slender thread of one man's life, we can begin to appreciate the magnitude of the crisis posed by the conversion of Henri IV.

1

The Search for God

WHAT IT MEANS to be a Christian, though perennially asked, elicits a different answer in every age. In early modern Europe, this question affected individuals as well as essential traditions and institutions. And perhaps in no instance was it of more concern than in the struggle over the conversion of Henri IV. The roots of the problem of the king's religion can be traced back to the days of the Apostles and the early Church. Despite Christianity's ongoing historical evolution, a simple fact about the faith has never changed: no one is born a Christian. An individual only becomes a member of the faith through the sacrament of baptism which, by cleansing the taint of original sin, allows the initiate to begin a new life in Christ. This first, baptismal meaning of conversion as an act of consecration marked Christianity from the very start, and has since served all confessions as the principal sign of inclusion among the faithful who form God's church.

The rise of infant baptism in the fourth century, though perhaps necessary for Christianity to become a mass religion, in time made the problem of backsliding a grave one for the early Church. Church fathers responded by formulating another meaning of conversion, one that gave the sinner an opportunity through repentance and forgiveness to renew personal faith. This second, more complex notion of conversion, developed during the Middle Ages, lay at the heart of the dynastic crisis brought about by Henri IV's accession in 1589. What Henri IV's experience meant to his Catholic subjects and how they could come to accept it as sincere therefore merits close attention.[1]

The Catholic Concept of Conversion

A number of traditions, not all of them religious, informed Catholic ideas about conversion during the sixteenth century. In sacramental theology, for example, the conversion of the Eucharist into the body and blood of Christ, with only the accidents of bread and wine remaining, closely resembled hermetic notions of conversion as physical change.[2] Baptism brought about a similar inner transformation of the individual without altering external appearance. Interest in conversion as an ongoing ethical commitment to Christ's teachings shifted the emphasis from theology to morality, from the science of God to the emulation of Christ's life. The tendency to view conversion as a new way of life had become particularly pronounced in early medieval monasticism, when conversion had meant literally to become a monk. In the fifteenth century, Thomas à Kempis, among others, opened the pathway to perfection to the laity in his *Imitatio Christi*. Catholic penitential practices during the late Middle Ages also stressed this new concern that conversion be a conscious restoration of God's image in humankind. Conversion could thus mean a miraculous transformation of physical property, a commitment to moral probity in everyday life, a spiritual flight from base illusion to a higher truth, and a vigilant observance by the individual of sacred duties that afforded membership in the community of the elect. By the sixteenth century, dying to sin and living anew in Christ no longer remained confined to the act of baptism but instead had become an experience that many Christians tried to reenact to deepen their faith.[3]

The Church's official attitude toward conversion revolved around its basic teachings on grace and free will. According to Augustine, intellectual awareness of sin could lead to the threshold of salvation, after which a believer needed an act of will aided by grace to merit God's forgiveness.[4] This view of free will as only free insofar as it conformed to God's intentions was not without ambiguity. Centuries later, Thomas Aquinas reformulated the complex relationship between human free will and grace in his *Summa Theologica*. He stressed good works and obedience to the Church as the principal signs of the individual's sincerity. Yet while good works allowed individual Catholics to participate in salvation, Aquinas defined participation sacramentally by channeling it into the penitential system of consolation and forgiveness that underpinned the Church's efforts to control lay society.[5] The delicate balance between an individual's search for eternal life and God's saving grace thus compelled the sinner to turn to the priesthood to effect a reconciliation with God. Thomist salvation theology, which was adopted in 1563 at the Council of Trent as the official position of the Roman Church, reinforced the Church's authority over the faithful as it began to face the Protestant challenge.

Protestant reformers, beginning with Luther in 1517, had harshly criticized the monopoly claimed by the Catholic clergy over God's mercy. For Luther, the faith of the individual believer, not sacramental penance or good works, provided the key to salvation.[6] Calvin carried this critique of Catholic salvation theology a step further in his doctrine of predestination, arguing that the fate of every soul had been determined at the moment of Creation. Whereas Luther emphasized the compassion of the Son, Calvin held that the individual's search for righteousness rested entirely in the inexorable judgment of God the Father.[7] Despite their differences, Luther and Calvin each believed that a sinner's conversion reaffirmed human abjectness, not greatness, before God. The professed words and accompanying gestures of Protestant conversion directly challenged the sacramental system upon which the Church's authority depended. Therein lay the essence of the Protestant revolt against Rome.

The Protestant Reformation forced Catholics to redefine what it meant to be orthodox. This monumental task fell to the Council of Trent (1541–1563) and the generation of reformers it inspired. Trent reaffirmed rather than recast the fundamental tenets of Catholicism, particularly the controversial doctrines of good works and free will. The Council worked to bring the different traditions of conversion— as transformation, mystical union, and election—more in line with sacramental penance. The potentially destructive inward tendency contained in many of these traditions had to be modified, not discarded.[8] Mediated by words holy and human, a public conversion had long served to promote a special sense of spiritual unity with God and social cohesion in the community by dramatizing the sinner's formal reintegration into the body of the faithful. After Trent, Catholic authorities in France added to the individual's quest for spiritual perfection the pressing need to fight Protestantism. These propagandistic concerns often obscured the complex motives behind an individual's decision to change confessions. Reasons for conversion could range from a desire for salvation or fear of bodily punishment to considerations of social status and family interests. Conversion accounts often accompanied the public prayers and processions that many French bishops organized in their dioceses for the extirpation of heresy.[9] Conversion ceremonies staged in local churches showed the faithful the efficacy of their supplications. They also gave the community an opportunity to celebrate its righteousness in God's eyes. As a result, official images of Catholic conversion during the sixteenth century rendered it more a public spectacle than a personal search for God.

This collective aspect gave Catholic conversions in France a new polemical importance during the religious wars, since Catholic authorities considered the conversion of even a common heretic a signal victory in the struggle for people's souls. The stakes became staggering when the heretic in question also happened, by the hazards of dynastic succession, to become king of France. The clash between Henri IV's royal dignity and heresy greatly heightened the public consequences of private piety because, according to Renaissance political thought, the faith of the prince shaped his subjects' beliefs. French Catholics therefore saw Henri IV's stubborn adherence to heresy as a threat not only to their own search for God, but to France's unique role in sacred history.[10] Two jolting visions of France's future, one hopeful and another despairing, thus lay behind the question of Henri IV's susceptibility to conversion. If sincere, the king's conversion held the promise not only of an end to the wars that ravaged France, but also of the reunification of Christendom under the eldest son of the Church. If insincere, however, Henri IV's conversion would pose dangers to France and Mother Church too horrible to imagine.

The Road to God

Fascination with the interior life was by no means confined to intellectuals and ecstatics during the sixteenth century. Thousands of pious tracts, most of them modestly priced, along with new forms of devotional practice, exposed French Catholics to new currents of belief when they confronted the king's faith as well as their own.[11] Although differences existed, most writers averred that a fallen person's return to God began with the knowledge of personal sin. This explains why Catholic instruction held such an important place in discussions about true conversion and played such a critical role in the controversy over Henri IV's religion. Such instruction ranged from sacramental theology and dogma to proofs of the Church's unity and authority. The Council of Trent had reorganized the catechism to make it more teachable and thus better able to combat Protestantism. The exchanges made between the penitent and the spiritual director during instruction usually formed the body of the convert's later profession of faith and abjuration of heresy. Delivered publicly before God and the convert's fellow Christians, these two declarations documented the penitent's decision to abandon error and embrace divine truth as revealed by God's ministers.

An intellectual awareness of sin meant nothing unless accompanied by a change of heart.[12] Preachers constantly stressed the need for sinners to approach the confessional in a spirit of remorseful shame, or contrition. Although Trent had made allowances for attrition, an attitude which arose from the fear of divine punishment, many Catholics viewed it as evidence of the sinner's own conceit, not humility.[13] This issue arose during the conversion of Henri IV when some Leaguers questioned his sincerity by stating that he went to Mass out of fear of Catholic rebellion, not love for God.[14] Contrition prepared the penitent to make auricular confession to a priest. To receive absolution without contrition greatly reduced the psychological, though not sacramental, effect of priestly forgiveness and consolation. The Catholic Church insisted that such mortal sins as heresy be fully enumerated by the penitent for conversion to be complete. Venial sins, such as lying and disrespect, could be omitted without offense and expiated through voluntary fasting and acts of charity.[15]

During the ceremony of Catholic conversion, the act of confession was public insofar as the congregation saw the convert enter the confessional; the contents of the confession, however, could not be divulged by the priest on pain of excommunication. As a Calvinist, Henri IV had denied the sacramental nature of confession; by consenting to enter the confessional during his conversion in 1593, he offered a public sign of his new faith. Absolution enabled the penitent to receive Communion, thus signaling to the congregation a return to the Church and Christian society. Although performed privately in the confessional, absolution proclaimed the penitent's worthiness as a Christian. Absolution forced the congregation to accept the penitent back into the Christian community regardless of past offenses. This helps explain why so many French Catholics remained circumspect about Henri IV until the pope agreed to pardon him in 1595.

Although absolution forgave the sinner, it did not eliminate the need to atone for past transgressions. After absolution, therefore, came the final and most public stage of penance, known as satisfaction. Satisfaction enabled the sinner to become righteous through good works. Penitential manuals of the period stressed the need for satisfaction to fit the penitent's past crimes, yet not be beyond the individual's ability to fulfill. Properly determining penitential works and amendment became known as the science of casuistry. Though often attacked as a source of moral laxity, casuistry personalized the treatment of sin by tailoring penance to the special needs and character of the individual. It also further underscored the clergy's control over the avenues of forgiveness and consolation essential in a Catholic's relationship with God.[16] The Catholic Church commonly regarded fasting, almsgiving, and prayer as the best ways for a penitent to atone for sins. Prayer knit invisible bonds between the sinner and God that could benefit others when the supplicant asked God to intercede on their behalf. The public prayers offered for Henri IV's conversion, like those for the souls of dead kings, expressed a common belief in God's special favor toward the French.[17] Other forms of satisfaction compelled the convert to begin a new lifestyle after conversion. Concern with individual behavior reflected the community's stake in the convert's struggle against sin. Arbiters of public morality therefore kept an attentive eye on the convert for any sign of sin, such as sexual deviance, cruelty, uncharitableness, blasphemy, or disobedience to superiors.[18] Converted heretics also had to promise to shun friends and family suspected of irreligion. Magistrates in the courts and clergymen in the confessionals then presumably monitored these outward expressions of religious belief. A convert's lifestyle became public knowledge, allowing others to judge the truthfulness of the promised break with sin. Henri IV's royal dignity made the question of penitential works even more delicate because his Catholic subjects, once they accepted his conversion, could hardly require him to carry out acts of atonement that sullied his majesty. They did, however, expect his policies at home and abroad to reflect the sincerity of his new convictions. During much of his reign, Henri IV had to try to balance public scruples such as these with the dictates of political necessity.[19]

Trials of Faith

No more urgent problem faced French Catholics during the sixteenth century than the need to distinguish between true believers and hypocrites. Because of its hidden character, religious dissimulation threatened God's church even more than overt heresy. Church officials therefore worked long and hard to devise reliable ways to validate the sincerity of believers, particularly that of new converts. By acknowledging the new importance of individual conscience during the Reformation, Catholic authorities redefined the boundaries of early modern religious and legal culture in France.

The frustrating and—in the end—quixotic search to validate sincerity in the sixteenth century fueled persecution and inspired devotional innovation to meet the rising challenge of individual conscience. Official fears of hypocrisy bespoke grudging acceptance of the new forms of individual piety, developed since the late Middle Ages, that stressed the private as opposed to the public dimensions of faith. By the sixteenth century, silent prayer, along with reading in seclusion, for example, had introduced a new subjectivism into religious life that cut across confessional and, at times, class lines.[20] The constant efforts by ecclesiastical authorities in both the Catholic and Reformed churches to monitor individual behavior, through either the confessional or the encouragement of neighborly prying, helped foster a sense of private conscience just as they sought to eradicate it. Royal officials in France also took a keen interest in heresy trials, partly because they provided the king's courts a chance to extend jurisdiction over church affairs, but primarily because they believed religious dissent invariably led to sedition. The evolving legal definition of treasonable *lèse majesté divine et humaine,* for example, reflected the Parlement's concern that a transparency exist between an individual's thought and action. Legal punishments that called for the offender's physical mutilation by branding or piercing of the tongue, especially for "language" crimes such as blasphemy, left a permanent public sign of the deviant's true character. Witch hunts also provided ample instances of the more intrusive surveillance that resulted from collaboration between official agencies and the local populace.[21] By focusing on the inner dynamics of individual belief, legal procedures designed to root out deviance—be it religious, demonic, or political—invested conscience with more responsibility, substance, and secrecy.

How did individuals who fell under suspicion respond to what could become fatal accusations? Although many thousands courageously died for their beliefs during the sixteenth century, few went out of their way to feel the "gnashing of lions' teeth," as one second-century saint so graphically put it.[22] Faced with brutal persecution, many religious minorities chose to accommodate, whenever possible, the confessional prejudices of the local majority by refraining from public displays of their faith. Nicodemism provides an interesting example of how religious dissenters, such as Marguerite de Navarre's evangelical group in Guyenne in the 1540s or the later *nouveaux convertis* of the seventeenth century, prudently severed any direct connection between the heart and action.[23] Named after an early convert to the faith known for his discretion and moderation (John 3:5), Nicodemism rejected stern dogma in favor of a more flexible, inner piety. By downplaying the importance of religion's external aspect and stressing instead its interior dimension, Nicodemism justified outward conformity with beliefs which the individual inwardly repudiated. It was this purposeful divorce between act and belief that so worried John Calvin and later Catholic apologists who equated Nicodemism with weakness of faith.[24]

Historians have yet to uncover the full extent of Nicodemist practice, though Carlo Ginzburg's contention that it was an organized, European-wide movement does seem exaggerated.[25] Nicodemism nevertheless offered a viable option to those in France who embraced reform but not the desire for martyrdom. Like Machiavellianism, another term of opprobrium bandied about at the time, Nicodemism could be cited by contemporaries as additional proof of the widening split between individual faith and behavior during the sixteenth century. Bridging this gap seemed from the start destined for disappointments which, in turn, fed fears of religious hypocrisy. Verbal denunciations often became allied with ritualized forms of persecution and punishment during the process of unmasking the hypocrite: establishing an individual's sincerity could apparently only come as a result of these public exorcisms.

Even for its sternest advocates, persecution was at best a partial solution to the problem of religious dissent because it could encour-

age rather than repress dissimulation. Historians have long emphasized the violent aspect of militant Catholicism, epitomized in France
by the frightful St. Bartholomew's Day Massacres (August–September
1572), though perhaps more significant for the future was the
Church's attempt to bring about the mass reconversion of Protestants.
After the Council of Trent, conversion came to mean less the pursuit
of spiritual perfection and more simply a change of confessions.
Thereafter, Catholics and Protestants alike faced the difficult problem
of how to determine the sincerity of such changes. Tridentine reform
was only partially accepted in France by 1615 (articles that violated
the Gallican liberties not being followed), but it had had an immediate impact a generation before on the strategies of persecution and
persuasion devised by Catholics to deal with the startling growth of
French Calvinism. Both approaches ultimately relied on force to
achieve their ends—a force at once moral and political which the
monarchy increasingly sought to monopolize then and later into the
seventeenth century.

Conversion ceremonies usually took two forms, depending on
whether they were prompted by a court order or initiated by the
accused. An oppressive consistency characterized the crown's treatment of heretics from the days of the Chambre Ardente under Henri
II through the early 1580s. Catholic opinion generally favored harsh
policies because it considered leniency toward Protestantism a cause
of France's ills, not their solution. It took a considerable amount of
convincing by the crown at the end of the sixteenth century to persuade Catholics to accept a less brutal approach to the Huguenot
question. The hundreds of sentences handed down under Henri II set
the tenor for the years ahead by trying to secure sincerity by sheer
terror; in nearly all cases, royal tribunals used the Mass as a forum in
which to punish the delinquent and edify the congregation. The fate
of a certain Benoist Chassaigne, judged guilty of "blasphèmes et
erreurs lutheriens," was typical. Convicted on May 9, 1548, in Paris
he was sentenced to return to Riom, his place of residence, and there
to make an *amende honorable* during Mass at the church of St. Am-
able. At the portal of the church, his "feet and head bare, holding in
his hands a large wax candle," Chassaigne had to abjure his heresy
and proclaim his undying belief in Catholicism. He had to ask pardon
not only of God, but also of the king and the judges who had convicted him, thus highlighting the civil nature of his crime. While the

priest prepared the Eucharist for Communion, Chassaigne had to stand before the altar—and the congregation—as a sign of his humble submission to God. His punishment also provided the topic of that day's sermon. Another unfortunate, Pierre Briquet from Moulins, underwent much the same ordeal, though he witnessed after Mass a solemn burning of heretical books that had been found in his possession. The rehabilitations of both men were still not complete, however. Each had to suffer, as a token of repentance, floggings over the next three days "in numerous public squares . . . led about by a cord around the neck." The courts then rewarded the men's promises to remain good Catholics with banishment. Some fared worse than they, however; Jean Everet, convicted of blasphemy on October 12, 1548, went to the stake after his *amende honorable*.[26]

Although occasionally modified by the Parlements, the brutal punishments meted out by the lower courts for heretics, blasphemers, and witches—all those whose hearts harbored evil thoughts—encouraged some individuals to take the first step in making amends with the Church. Monetary awards from local *caisses de conversion* also provided an incentive to repent.[27] Protestants who chose the path of least resistance often gained acclaim in published accounts known as *récits de conversion*. These accounts became a standard feature of Catholic propaganda in the mid–1570s and 1580s—just as the crown began to adopt more "gentle" forms of persuasion—and continued to flourish well into the seventeenth century.[28] Underwritten by the Church and Parlements, these publications enlisted the experiences of new converts in the cause of militant Catholicism. Publicizing, for example, the conversion of Hugues Sureau du Rosier, Matthieu de Launoy, and Henri Pennetier—all Calvinist ministers—showed the Church's prowess in winning over leaders of the Reformed faith. As part of the ongoing war of words against Protestantism, these published confessions highlighted the role that natural reason, more than grace and spontaneity, played in the conversion experience. Affinities can be found here with the Neostoic revival during the late sixteenth century.[29] To be considered valid, sincerity had to be well informed by teachers of sound doctrine, not compelled by grim-faced inquisitors. That was, at least, the conceit conveyed in the accounts.

Sureau du Rosier's conversion in late 1572 is of particular interest because he had formerly served as a pastor to Henri de Navarre. Catholic officials probably hoped his confession, once published, would counter Protestant charges after the St. Bartholomew's Day Massacres that Sureau du Rosier, like Navarre, had converted only under duress. The joint confession of Launoy and Pennetier five years later lacked this immediacy.[30] All three nevertheless portrayed their conversions as the result of methodical learning during which they discovered the errors of their ways. A wide range of controversialist arguments, many drawn directly from the Tridentine decrees, was often used by converts to demonstrate their newfound allegiance to Catholicism. Whereas Sureau du Rosier offered a detailed critique of Calvin's doctrine of the Trinity, Launoy and Pennetier defended Catholicism against the reformers' charge of idolatry. Printed confessions often expanded on the abjuration of heresy and profession of faith required for a canonically sound conversion. Political considerations were also introduced, particularly in the frequent mentions of the apostolic succession, which gave the Church its historical unity—something the Protestants could never achieve since, according to Sureau du Rosier, they did not exercise a legitimate vocation.[31] Without legitimacy, Launoy and Pennetier added, the reformers' efforts to purify religion resulted only in violent schism, which ultimately bred political sedition.[32]

These avowals of faith showed conversion to consist of little more than acceptance of key exegetical interpretations of the Bible. In the debate over the Eucharist, for example, the convert's belief in the real presence of Christ hinged on a literal understanding of Christ's words "This is my body" (Mark 14:22). Sureau du Rosier's attack on the Lutheran doctrine of justification rested on rhetorical, not theological grounds. The legal infighting between church and crown officials could also be touched on, as when Sureau du Rosier sarcastically remarked that the Protestants used the term "justification . . . much the same as did sophists of yore and lawyers in the Parlement today."[33] Printed confessions, like controversialist argument, frequently mixed semantics with satire to defend Catholic sacramental theology. As such, the public declarations made by converts tended to emphasize philological method and humor rather than heartfelt experience. In the 1590s, loyalist Catholics refused to allow the king's instruction to become a vehicle for possible confessional reconciliation because they thought it improper—and potentially confusing to the king—to link the royal catechism to a discussion of exegesis.

The problem of verifying internal faith is especially well illustrated by the case of Sureau du Rosier, who later recanted his new faith and returned to Protestantism. He documented his decision to fake his Catholic conversion in another printed confession which revealed, much to the horror of Catholics, the insidious nature of religious dissimulation. According to this new account, published in 1574, Sureau du Rosier's hypocrisy had begun unknowingly, though in retrospect he realized he had only renounced Calvinism to avoid execution, a legitimate fear given the recent massacres. He had also thought at the time of his conversion that God might actually favor Catholicism, since the Lord's elect suffered so unmercifully. After his release from prison he had been called to court by Charles IX, who then convinced him to persuade the young princes of Navarre and Condé to abjure their Protestant beliefs and become papists. This damning avowal perhaps helped Catholics a few years later better understand why these two princes repudiated their Catholic conversions of 1572. Sureau du Rosier had fooled his captors into believing him to be a true Catholic by reducing his conversion to its most visible components, such as dress, countenance, and words, which he then used to create the illusion of sincerity.[34] His dissimulation complete, he nevertheless in time fell prey to pricks of conscience which eventually became so overwhelming that he finally resolved to end his charade and return to the Reformed church. For Huguenots, still reeling after the massacres, Sureau du Rosier's belated decision to recant his Catholic conversion vindicated the truth of Reformed religion. For Catholics, however, his relapse into heresy raised legitimate doubts about whether converts could ever be fully trusted once allowed back into the Church. They could perhaps take consolation in the fact that hypocrisy would eventually disintegrate under the weight of its own contradictions—a point later made by the Leaguer Jean Boucher in his attack on Henri IV's conversion.[35]

The case of Sureau du Rosier was not unique after the massacres and revealed the precarious nature of confessional gains achieved by force. In response, there developed under Henri III a twofold policy based on social class which remained in place over the next century. Although harsh punishments continued to be meted out to offenders from the lower classes, milder methods of persuasion—involving the enticements of office and preferment—were often used to rehabilitate higher-placed members of the Reformed religion. The French church also established in the 1580s stricter guidelines regulating conversion. For example, it enjoined spiritual directors to scrutinize the convert's motives, urging them to extend the preparatory period if they thought it necessary. Some delay could prove useful, if only to test the convert's resolve.[36] In justifying a stance on the king's religion, French Catholics often referred after 1584 to the possible risks and advantages of Navarre's delaying his conversion—concerns which again arose from the difficult problem of how to verify a convert's sincerity.

French authorities apparently thought the public ceremonies of conversion gave Catholics firmer proof of the Church's ultimate victory over heresy than the smoke which rose from the Place Maubert. The abjurations of Matthieu Grillon, a *gentilhomme*, Nicolas Lamy, a doctor from Nantes, and the pastors Geoffroy de Vaux and John Cosburn typified this new approach to religious dissent. Such *récits de conversion* usually began by providing readers with a brief summary of the essential elements in each conversion ceremony, thus lending them a journalistic quality altogether missing in the more reflective confessions considered above. Each account emphasized the voluntary nature of the convert's decision to embrace Catholicism.[37] Each gave the name of the officiating prelate as well as the date and place where the conversion occurred. The detailed narratives that often followed the printed abjuration thus conveyed to readers a clearer sense of conversion as a public event.

The ceremonies observed at these conversions, as well as at Henri IV's, reflected the emerging theatrics of baroque piety. On the day of his conversion, for example, Grillon threw himself on the church steps, where his tears and lamentations signaled to the assembled witnesses his unqualified change of heart. A few minutes later, the Cardinal d'Armagnac, who officiated at the ceremony, gave Grillon absolution and raised him to his feet. The penitent then turned to the crowd gathered in front of the church and read his abjuration and profession of faith "à haut voix." He also signed notarized copies of each, which he left with one of the clergymen in attendance. Grillon then entered the church, where he heard Mass and received Communion.[38]

The account of De Vaux's conversion adhered closely to that of Grillon. It added certain details which are of interest with regard to the ceremonies used during Henri IV's conversion. A former student of Calvin and almoner for Jeanne d'Albret, De Vaux had apparently first shown an interest in Catholicism at the conference gathered in Meaux in March 1593 to instruct Henri IV. The similarities carried over into ceremony as well. Like Henri IV, De Vaux arrived at the cathedral barefooted and dressed in the "habit de vray pénitent," that is, a white tunic—the same garb used during other acts of public censure, such as *amendes honorables*. The tunic's color symbolized the purity of his desire to submit to God, and his bare feet bespoke his willingness to undergo the rigors of penitence. Five bishops and all the canons assisted the Cardinal de Joyeuse's reception of the penitent on the cathedral steps, lending De Vaux's reconciliation with the Church great solemnity and éclat. A large crowd, estimated at close to ten thousand, awaited him in the Place St. Étienne, making his conversion an event of great importance to the city of Toulouse. This huge turnout suggests that a prior announcement had been made, perhaps through the city's parish churches the previous Sunday, or through municipal news networks such as town criers.[39]

Like Grillon, De Vaux pronounced and signed his abjuration and profession of faith before he entered the cathedral. Unlike Grillon, however, he spoke as head of his household for his wife and children. Henri IV assumed a similar obligation to recatholicize the royal family when he converted in 1593. Conversion ceremonies thus not only recognized social distinctions, but also reinforced patriarchal authority.[40] Joyeuse bestowed absolution on De Vaux and his family while the choir sang the psalm *Miserere*. The cardinal tapped the convert on the shoulders with his crozier three times as a sign of punishment by the Church. De Vaux then stood up, took Joyeuse's extended hand, and proceeded into the cathedral, which resonated with the chant *Te Deum laudamus*. De Vaux's conversion culminated in the celebration of High Mass, during which the new believer received Communion. In this way, his reconciliation with the Church became part of the dominical service that nourished the congregation's faith with the Eucharist, the Word, and the holy exemplar of a converted heretic. The effusive character of such a conversion gave the public a visible display of the emotional experiences encouraged in penitential poetry and practice.

Published accounts of Catholic conversions must in the end be approached cautiously, because they drew heavily on the literary *topoi* established in devotional manuals and Books of Hours. In this regard, conversion accounts—of which there were thousands printed—are but another genre of early modern religious literature. In traditions that date back to Augustine's *Confessions*—a text that merits further study as regards its place in sixteenth-century religious culture—conversion often came to be expressed in the mystical language of experiential religion, or the doleful verse of penitential poets such as Philippe Desportes and Amyrault Jamyn. The chaos of the religious wars, as Denis Crouzet has abundantly demonstrated in his recent book, made the theme of penitence a very popular one in late sixteenth-century devotional literature and practice.[41]

The challenge of Catholic conversion forced church authorities and royal judges in France to acknowledge more fully the new subjectivism in religion by devoting as much attention to indoctrination as to compulsion. As a result, Catholic conversion took place primarily as a series of acts—catechism, confession, absolution, Mass, and public abjuration—through which the convert passed before God and the assembled witnesses. Although these public acts could not guarantee sincerity, they could perhaps make glaring instances of rank hypocrisy less likely to occur. Yet by reducing true conversion to ritualized speech and gestures, Catholic reformers—despite their best intentions—encouraged a further split between individual conscience and outward conformity to public expectations.

Thus even as the Catholic Church began after Trent to organize its campaign for reconversion, it could never adequately devise a system guaranteed to insure the sincerity of the converted. And neither could the Protestants. In fact, individual conscience became even more difficult to monitor as the Catholic Church formulated in ritual and speech acts the essential criteria by which to judge a believer's sincerity. Conversion accounts focused on the doctrinal reasons for confessional change and their enactment through ceremony because these aspects could be most easily controlled by civil and ecclesiastical authorities. In time, concern for indwelling belief yielded to the pressing need to reestablish public order in war-torn France.

The theatricality of baroque Catholicism, with its emphasis on éclat over substance, provided a possible means by which to reabsorb the individual—and his conscience—into the fabric of the church community. Yet by measuring individual piety in terms of ceremony and language, the Church further widened the split between the inner world of belief and the public world of self-fashioning and calculated disclosure. In time, this emerging duality in post-Reformation religious sensibility and practice, epitomized in the experiences of new converts such as Henri IV, encouraged a compartmentalization of religious consciousness shaped by the modalities of language and gesture. In the end, the conversion of Henri IV forced French Catholics to confront the age-old question, now immeasurably sharpened by years of civil strife, of who should cast the first stone. Ultimately, public acceptance of a convert's sincerity rested not on proof, but rather on a leap of faith.

2

Into the Maelstrom

DESPITE RISING social unrest, France seemed remarkably immune to the sectarian disputes that rocked the rest of Europe during the 1520s and 1530s. This deceptive calm finally broke in the 1550s as a result of John Calvin's decision to evangelize France from his base in Geneva. His message of spiritual discipline and local autonomy appealed to groups such as urban artisans and the nobility, long unsettled by the corrosive effects of inflation and the crown's more intrusive presence in society. Calvin's novel ideas about church organization, which vested local communities with authority over religious affairs, and his uncompromising theology threatened to undermine the crown's control over the Gallican church. François I and Henri II recognized these dangers but could not check the spread of the Huguenot movement. Calvin's appeal for reform, much like that made by Catholics later in the century, called into question the monarchy's role in the church and society, especially after Henri II's sudden death in 1559. The startling spread of dissent, rivalries with the Hapsburgs, agitations among princes of the blood, and a worsening economy soon swept the country and the monarchy into the maelstrom of religious war. The ensuing chaos and violence only began to subside years later when Henri IV, himself a child of the wars, decided in 1593 to convert to Catholicism at the abbey church of St. Denis.[1]

Conversion and Relapse (1553–1576)

Henri IV's long journey to St. Denis began at birth and was deeply affected by the early history of French Protestantism and its encounters with an intolerant Catholic majority. His religious development as a child was guided by his parents, Antoine de Bourbon and Jeanne d'Albret, king and queen of Navarre, and cannot be understood outside this family context. Like so many first-generation Calvinists, Henri de Navarre had originally been baptized and raised a Catholic, as had his sister, Catherine, later Duchesse de Bar. This initial exposure to Catholicism later convinced some Catholics that King Henri had unwillingly left the Church because of parental pressure. The fact that Henri never received confirmation, wherein the believer professes a mature understanding of Catholic doctrine, raised questions years later about how deeply committed he actually was to the Reformed religion.[2]

Ironically, it was the Hapsburgs who helped encourage Calvinism's later success in France. The Spanish monarchy's longstanding desire to absorb the tiny kingdom of Navarre attracted many noblemen in that fiercely independent land to the Reformed faith in the late 1540s. Calvinism eventually reached the Bourbon court at Pau in 1555, when Louis de Condé, Henri's paternal uncle and Calvin's first Bourbon convert, introduced Protestant pastors into the royal household, thus fomenting that confessional split among the Bourbons that was to prove crucial in the 1580s and 1590s. The next Bourbon to exhibit an interest in the Reformed religion was Henri's father, Antoine. He attended several Calvinist services with his younger brother as early as 1556, all the while fulfilling the devotional requirements of a Catholic. This ambivalence characterized Antoine's confessional leanings for the remainder of his life, as it did his wife's until 1560. Although Antoine briefly flirted with Calvin's teachings, whether out of personal doubt or political ambition, he disavowed them in early 1562 when he joined with disgruntled Catholics who wished to undermine the Edict of January 17. The crown had hoped that this decree would avert bloodshed by conceding limited toleration to the Huguenots. Needless to say, it did not work and war soon broke out. Antoine's choice of Catholicism quickly estranged his Huguenot supporters as well as his wife, whom he had left several months earlier. He died that year, branded an atheist by Protestants and Catholics alike. Antoine's behavior was to become an object lesson on the perils of confessional change for Henri when he later considered professing another faith.[3]

Unlike the impetuous Antoine, Jeanne d'Albret gravitated more slowly, though more surely, toward the Reformed faith before she openly embraced it for herself and her children in late 1560. She spoke prematurely for Henri, however, since he soon after accompanied his father to Vendôme, leaving her and his Protestant tutors in Béarn. Henri apparently remained a Catholic until his father's death the next year, whereupon he returned to his mother's court at Pau and recommenced his Calvinist catechism, falling under Jean de Morély's influence after 1566. He regularly attended Reformed services and became more involved in confessional politics over the next ten years under the tutelage of Jeanne and the Amiral de Coligny. Henri learned from them what it meant to be leader of the Huguenot party and a prince of the blood, especially after the death of the Prince de Condé in 1569. The young Henri evidently evoked admiration from all quarters. In 1567, a high-ranking Catholic magistrate from the Parlement of Bordeaux spoke glowingly of the thirteen-year-old prince's talents, yet added ominously: "I will forever hate the new religion for having removed from us such a fine young prince."[4] He was not the last Catholic to distinguish between Henri's person and his dissident faith.

The next decisive turn in young Henri's confessional allegiances occurred when he converted to Catholicism after the Saint Bartholomew's Day Massacres. This conversion, which Henri recanted four years later, came back to haunt him and France in the 1580s and 1590s. His first conversion resulted from Catherine de Medici's befuddled attempt to end the religious strife of the 1560s with a dynastic settlement that would join her daughter, Marguerite de Valois, and Henri de Navarre in matrimony. She determined upon the marriage to reinforce the precarious peace of St. Germain (August 8, 1570) and, with it, her son Charles IX's authority as king. Aware of Jeanne's anxiety over the religious question, she was careful not to insist that Henri convert as a precondition to the wedding. Catherine's attempt to sidestep the issue of Henri's heresy opened the door to papal influence, since the proposed wedding required a dispensation to lift canonical prohibitions against mixed marriages.[5] Rome objected to the union because it and the peace of St. Germain represented a retreat before heresy and a blow to the reform program recently launched at Trent. Many Catholics at the Valois court also opposed the marriage because they feared it would only validate important concessions, such as the right to worship and to hold office, that the crown had granted the Huguenots in the peace of St. Germain. Rumors that Coligny hoped to persuade the king to invade the Low Countries to assist the Dutch rebels in their struggle against

Spain gave them further cause for alarm.[6] The Guise family fanned these Catholic fears, since a dynastic alliance between the royal house and the Bourbons forestalled any hope its members still had of recovering influence with the king. The Saint Bartholomew's Day Massacres were precipitated in part by the desire of resentful Catholics to foment an open break between the crown and the Huguenots.

These formidable obstacles at home and abroad made the royal marriage seem highly unlikely until the spring of 1572. The breakthrough came on April 11, when Jeanne d'Albret, succumbing to political pressure and ill health, reluctantly agreed to sign a marriage contract which set the wedding date for sometime that summer.[7] In it, she also arranged for the marriage of Henri's cousin Henri, Prince de Condé, to Marie de Clèves. Jeanne's death on June 9 virtually sealed the agreement since Coligny and his supporters favored a rapprochement with the crown. Catherine also continued to honor the agreement by refusing to broach the question of Henri's faith. Even the papacy modified its stance. In July, Catherine learned of Gregory XIII's readiness to grant a dispensation before the marriage, provided that Navarre make a personal request to him for Catholic instruction. She rejected the pope's conciliatory gesture, however, because rumors at court hinted that Navarre already appeared attracted to the Mass. Fearing that the pope only sought an excuse to delay the marriage, Catherine considered it safer to let the enticements of the Valois court seduce the young Navarre.[8]

The royal pair finally were married in Notre-Dame de Paris on August 18, six days before the frightful Saint Bartholomew's Day Massacres began.[9] Both events—one controlled, the other uncontrollable—reflected the frantic hopes and fears of the crown as it searched for ways to strengthen its tenuous authority. Scholars have recently devoted a great deal of attention to the massacres, illuminating both their background and repercussions in French society.[10] The role these upheavals played in prompting Henri's first conversion to Catholicism is often neglected, however. Despite the virtual disappearance of Henri and his cousin the Prince de Condé during the month following the massacres, this dark period proved crucially important in the dynastic struggle twelve years later. Everyone at the time agreed the princes were in imminent peril. One source claims that shortly after the killings began on August 24, Charles IX summoned the two young men to his chamber to assure them they had nothing to fear because he had given orders for them not to be harmed.[11] According to Claude Haton, it was Marguerite de Valois who shielded her new husband from attack when rowdy Catholics scoured the Louvre in search of Huguenot refugees.[12] Several days later when the violence began to subside, Condé reportedly swore revenge against the murderous Catholics—a statement that so enraged the king he flew at him with a knife.[13] Henri's reaction to the massacres, by contrast, apparently failed to impress his contemporaries. Indeed, he seemed much more resigned to life at the Valois court than Condé during the next three years—a difference Condé duly exploited when he later challenged his cousin for leadership of the Huguenot party.

Charles IX's contrary actions reflected his lack of control over affairs following the massacres. On August 28, for example, he declared the peace of St. Germain still in effect, then a few days later sent the Sieur de Beauville to Rome with a message in which he claimed credit for the killings—an assertion most historians now regard as unfounded.[14] The need to secure a papal dispensation for the royal marriage offers one reason why the king chose to bloody his hands—and reputation—after the fact. Charles IX and his mother considered the union even more essential to maintaining order after the massacres, because they had reason to believe that the Huguenots would soon organize a retaliatory strike against Catholics and thus reignite the civil war.[15] Although the pope celebrated the bloodbath, issuing a medal to commemorate the Church's victory over heresy, he condemned the marriage and the episcopal dispensation bestowed on it by the Cardinal de Bourbon, arguing that such cases were reserved for Rome. Gregory XIII only reversed his stance several weeks later when he learned, much to his surprise, that the princes had converted to Catholicism.

Memoirists place Henri's first conversion sometime in late September, and his cousin's a bit earlier.[16] The secrecy that enshrouded the princes' return to the Church seemed deliberate, though it later raised serious doubts about their sincerity. Traditionally, a conversion not only signified an inner return to God, but also represented a public act of reconciliation with the Christian community. Moreover, Renaissance monarchs rarely overlooked an occasion to display their glory in the pageantry of ecclesiastical and courtly ceremony. The crown's unwillingness to stage the princes' conversions in public also meant it missed an opportunity to claim credit for the hundreds of conversions that occurred in the wake of the massacres.[17] Perhaps Catherine considered the issue of the princes' sincerity to be less important than the need to reestablish peace in the provinces. After all, news of the princes' abjurations sufficed to remove them as possible rallying points for Huguenot opposition. Moreover, a public conversion performed in a church would expose Navarre and Condé to needless danger and invite allegations of coercion. This calculated silence was thereafter construed as evidence of duress, though Navarre's behavior over the next three years may force us to reconsider this interpretation.

The abjurations which Navarre and Condé made in September omitted features usually associated with Catholic conversions. These included the name of the prelate before whom the abjuration took place, its location and date, as well as the list of witnesses who had observed it. An even more crucial omission allowed Henri to avoid detailing his past errors. Navarre later claimed that this oversight invalidated his conversion because he never understood the act's full significance. Irregularities also appeared in the professions of faith sent to the pope in October. Although both princes praised God and the pope for enlightening them, they added a grim reminder of "the fear . . . they otherwise would have of the Holy Father's righteous wrath."[18] This mention of fear probably also referred to their dread of Catholics in Paris. Vague statements about the Catholic instruction they had received from the Cardinal de Bourbon and the Sorbonne only tended to confirm suspicions that they had embraced Catholicism without knowing its doctrines. The princes even pled ignorance, and thus innocence, of their past errors, attributing them to "teachings we had received from others while still young and of tender judgment without malice aforethought."[19] Henri used much the same excuse in early 1576 when he repudiated his Catholic conversion.

Despite these shortcomings, Catholics at court had reason to believe that in time Navarre would become a good Catholic. Indeed, over the next three years Henri gave little hint of regretting his confessional change. Many Huguenots certainly believed he had betrayed them. Upon news of Henri's conversion, *réformés* in Bordeaux, for example, announced that they no longer recognized Navarre's authority as protector of the faith. Although Henri asked the Marquis de Villars, royal provincial governor of Guyenne, to protect these outspoken Huguenots, he instructed him to spare no effort to convert them to Catholicism.[20] In 1573, Henri even became privy to the crown's military plans against the Protestants, yet made no attempt to pass the information along to his former *confrères*.[21] He also regularly attended Mass and participated in Catholic ceremonies at court, such as the celebration at Notre-Dame of the Duc d'Anjou's election to the Polish throne. When Anjou returned to France as Henri III after his brother's death in 1574, Navarre took part in the coronation rite and *sacre* performed at Rheims. His intrigues with the king's brother, Alençon, reflected political ambition, not crypto-Calvinism. Henri's flight from court on February 3, 1576, and subsequent recantation understandably took many Catholics and Protestants by surprise, given his past behavior.[22]

Henri's decision to return to Protestantism must be seen against the background of the monarchy's steadily diminishing prestige and control in France. The crown's wild fluctuations between harshness and leniency had demoralized a people whose historic royalism ran deep. This eroding confidence in monarchical leadership can perhaps best be seen in the sudden growth after 1572 of local self-help groups and paramilitary organizations in provincial cities and the countryside. The quasi-republican assemblies and ideologies of French *réformés*, in particular, became a constant source of trouble for Navarre after he recanted in 1576. Though bitterly opposed to each other, the various Protestant assemblies and Catholic leagues that emerged shared a common mistrust of Henri III and his mother. A group of moderate Catholics, known as the malcontents *(mécontents)*, became disgusted with the violent fanaticism of such extremists and began to rally around the king's brother and heir apparent, François, Duc d'Alençon. The *mécontents* worked out an alliance with Huguenot forces which eventually forced Henri III to grant concessions in the Peace of Monsieur (May 1576). Many of the Catholics who assembled later that year at the Estates General of Blois quite naturally criticized the crown for this retreat before heresy; the deputies refused to grant funds, however, when Henri III offered to renew the war against the Huguenots. Why allot money for the good fight against heresy if the king would not stand firm in the face of Huguenot demands? As a result, the Guise family saw its stock rise among disgruntled Catholics after 1576. By the early 1580s, Henri III had lost whatever influence over events he had had at the beginning of his reign. Unable to wage war or preserve peace, Henri III spent the rest of his life trying to master a crisis which in the end cost him his reputation and life.[23]

These years offered boundless opportunities to men of ambition such as Henri de Navarre. During his so-called captivity at the Valois court, Navarre forged ties with court Catholics which later worked to his advantage. Interestingly, however, the *mécontents* passed over Navarre when it came time to restore princely leadership over the Huguenots. They chose instead to engineer Condé's escape to Strasbourg in the early summer of 1575, whereupon he renounced his conversion, began negotiating an alliance with German Calvinists, and accepted the protectorship over the Reformed churches.[24] Both groups clearly considered Navarre to be less reliable than his hot-tempered cousin. Although Henri never mentioned it in his letters, he no doubt resented Condé's claim to a position he believed to be rightfully his. Henri's eventual flight from court in February 1576 resulted more from these political concerns than from religious qualms. That he waited over three months after his escape before officially recanting his conversion further indicates just how incidental his confessional allegiances had become to him.

Henri's conversion in 1572 and subsequent return to Protestantism in 1576 weighed heavily in the debate after 1584 over his claim to the Catholic throne of France. The decision to allow Henri's return to the Church to be conducted in private made it possible for him to disavow his conversion later without compromising his integrity as a Christian prince. Had he been more firmly bound by public ceremonies and a detailed abjuration, he might have thought twice before recanting in 1576. Whether these shortcomings rendered Henri's first conversion invalid became a matter of controversy for years to come. The fact that so many of the French questioned its legitimacy at all meant that Catholics had to exercise greater caution when circumstances later compelled Navarre to consider another Catholic conversion.

France Divided

The issue of Henri de Navarre's faith only became explosive when the king's sterility and the hazards of royal succession conspired together after the premature death on June 10, 1584, of the Duc d'Alençon. With Henri's sudden emergence as heir presumptive came a further undermining of Henri III's effectiveness as king. Militant Catholics quickly rallied to the Holy League revived by the Duc and Cardinal de Guise, while *mécontents* became increasingly torn between fidelity to the hapless Henri III and their allegiance to royal traditions such as the Salic Law, which guaranteed Navarre's right to the succession. Navarre had worked hard since 1576 to regain from Condé his leadership of the Huguenot party, overseeing its reorganization and reemergence as a force to be reckoned with in French politics. Even so, his leadership of the Reformed community did not go undisputed in the years ahead; powerful competitors, such as Condé, who died under mysterious circumstances in 1588, and, later in the 1590s, the clever Duc de Bouillon, stood ready to assume the leadership should Navarre fail to satisfy the assemblies. Foreign powers, particularly Philip II of Spain, Elizabeth I of England, and the new pope, Sixtus V (1584–1590), complicated matters even more since each used these domestic factions to play out their rivalries in France. The struggle to reconvert Henri unfolded over the next ten years in this predatory environment.[25]

Alençon's death in 1584 created a conflict between Navarre's dynastic claim and his role as protector of the Reformed churches. The calculated ambiguity of his numerous declarations in the 1580s reflected the need to encourage Catholic hopes for his conversion while allaying Huguenot suspicions about his commitment to the Protestant cause.[26] He worked hard to portray himself as a *bon fran- çois* who stood above faction and whose deepest concern was for the monarchy's welfare. This stratagem obviously impressed René Lucinge, Savoy's ambassador to France, who wrote in 1585 that "most Catholics who sympathize with Navarre do so because they think it pleases the king."[27]

Perhaps the greatest cause of worry for French Protestants was the fact that since his return to Calvinism in 1576, Navarre had never publicly rejected the possibility of another conversion. In fact, as Leaguer Catholics pushed Henri III toward another religious war in early 1586, Navarre announced his readiness to convert to Catholicism should a national church council declare him to be in doctrinal error. This astute display of openmindedness—some *réformés* called it budding treachery—afforded Navarre several dividends even though such a colloquy never met. It allowed him to keep his distance from Protestants, particularly the consistorial leaders, who saw a national church council as a way to vindicate the Reformed position. It also presented Catholics with a more attractive image of him as an errant believer who only sought religious truth.[28]

Navarre knew his call for a settlement of all confessional differences would go unanswered; it was therefore merely a smokescreen behind which to hide his indecision. The possibility of a council nevertheless created a quandary for militant Huguenots and Catholics, because both sides would measure such a colloquy's success by how well each could vanquish the other and not lose any portion of the debate. This circular reasoning had thwarted earlier rhetorical efforts, beginning at Poissy in 1561, to bring about a conciliar solution to France's religious strife.[29] The alternative to discussion was war—a course which since the 1560s had proved equally nugatory. By the 1580s, polemical strategies mirrored the confusion wrought by a generation of civil war and the hazards of royal succession. For no group involved was this more true than for the Huguenots, particularly as they confronted the dreadful prospect of Navarre's conversion after 1584.

Henri's apparent willingness after 1584 to consider another confessional change sharpened existing divisions in the Protestant community. These differences roughly corresponded to the movement's mixed social makeup and regional character. Militancy prevailed in urban Reformed churches, particularly in the west and scattered areas in the Midi, whereas moderate conciliation with the crown found adherents among the Huguenot nobility, especially in Languedoc where ties with Damville's *politiques* were strong. When these ties began to weaken in the 1590s, Huguenot noblemen tried to wrest concessions from the crown by fanning the local reformed churches' fears of renewed persecution, though never so much as to force a showdown with the by then Catholic Henri IV. A fatal contradiction thus developed after 1584 between French Calvinism's cooperative paramilitary institutions and the monarchical tradition which its princely protector hoped to inherit. Although few appreciated it at the time, this incongruous situation seriously undermined the Huguenot case against Navarre's conversion. Indeed, the latent rifts that later proved fatal to French Calvinists in the seventeenth century could only have been mended had they convinced Navarre not to convert.[30]

The paralyzing limits of Huguenot loyalism can further be seen in the well-known shift that took place after 1584 in the political writings of such Protestant luminaries as Duplessis Mornay, François Hotman, Théodore Beza, and a host of lesser publicists. Almost overnight, they dropped the radical theories of legitimate resistance and constitutional monarchy elaborated after the Saint Bartholomew's Day Massacres and became staunch champions of France's royal tradition—a tradition, of course, shorn of its overtly Catholic attributes. This proviso lent their royalism a crucial distinction which debates over France's fundamental laws simply masked with a veneer of Gallicanism rather than dispelled. At the core of Huguenot loyalism in the 1580s and 1590s lay two distinct interpretations of the monarchy's role in French society. The first, exemplified in the writings of Beza and the *consistoriaux,* stressed that Henri's claim to the throne represented a key step in the evangelization of France; for supporters of this view, the crown's sacred mission now became a Calvinist, not a Catholic one. The other, less conventional yet perhaps politically more realistic, view offered a secular justification of absolute monarchy based on natural law, not divine right. François Hotman's *Antisixtus* (1585) and the anonymous *De la vraye et légitime constitution de l'estat* (1591), for example, reflected this new tendency in Huguenot legal circles. From this perspective, the accidents of royal succession which eventually brought Navarre to the throne in 1589 began to give the monarchomach forebears of Locke's *Two Treatises* paternal claims to Hobbes's mighty *Leviathan* as well. Secular justifications of royal absolutism and religious toleration were the last things Henri IV wanted associated with the debate over his faith because they invited charges of atheism. When seen in this light, the arguments of Huguenot loyalism—whether evangelical or secular— did not have much to offer the embattled Henri de Navarre.[31]

Henri's most formidable opponents, of course, came from the Catholic League—a movement whose political and social character still baffles historians. A complex conglomeration of differing separatist tendencies, the League seemed inherently prone to infighting. Apart from a handful of well-known pamphlets and incidents, these contests rarely assumed an overt social edge until the final stages of the wars. Conflicts within the League more often than not pitted noble against noble, urban notable against urban notable, and cleric against cleric, in an incessant struggle for power and influence. By focusing on radical preachers and lesser robe officials in the municipal government of Paris, historians have reinforced the partisan contention made by loyalist Catholics and Huguenots that these groups in the capital represented the essence of the League. This was far from the case, however, since the League also attracted a significant number of *grands* as well as many prelates and judges.[32] The reasons that these groups became involved in the League often differed considerably from those motivating the radicals in Paris. The need for a thorough investigation of the League's social and ideological diversity has been suggested by Robert Descimon, but remains to be carried out in a detailed study.[33] Such a project might confirm the suspicion that the only factor which kept the League from disintegrating before it did was the fear all Leaguers shared of Henri de Navarre's heresy.

The ingrained royalism of the League has also been underestimated, though from the outset League publicists carefully promoted the Sainte Union and its leaders, the Guises, as devoted servants of the crown. As presented in pamphlets, the League existed only to defend the monarchy and the Church against heresy. The dynastic crisis, Leaguers argued, stemmed from a failure to maintain the moral purpose of governing institutions—a leitmotif that recurred in Protestant and loyalist Catholic political thought as well.[34] For the League, moral order in society began with the king's commitment to uphold religious uniformity because upon it rested the crown's ability to enforce law. The early appeal of the League, culminating in the Estates General of Blois in late 1588, derived in large part from the alluring image of the Leaguer as both *bon françois* and *bon catholique*. Those who accepted this image—and there were many— agreed that departures from the cherished Christian norms of piety and justice ultimately jeopardized the salvation of every Catholic. Engagement in the struggle against Navarre, although presented as thoroughly *bon françois catholique,* became more difficult when Henri III turned out not to be the devout monarch the Leaguers so earnestly sought.[35]

Loyalist Catholics, too, hardly formed a cohesive group which espoused a common set of beliefs. They were, rather, a loose coalition of court officers, noblemen, magistrates, and clergymen who, though united in their opposition to the League, could nevertheless differ sharply on many of the issues facing France in the 1580s. They all agreed, however, that Navarre's conversion held the key to ending the wars and revitalizing the kingdom. Rather than adopting the escha tology of Leaguers, they offered legal and historical arguments for religion's vital place in the polity. This search after 1584 for a theological understanding of political and social problems did not replace, but rather complemented earlier forays into history and law; loyalist Catholics were not, to use modern parlance, "born again." Given its implications of secularism, *politique* is therefore something of a misnomer for describing the views of most loyalist Catholics. Their new interest in religious discourse grew out of their abiding concern to reestablish the moral foundation of civil harmony in France.[36]

What critics saw as a divorce between piety and politics was in reality a reflection of growing disenchantment on the part of loyalist Catholics with the conventional forms of resolving religious disputes. As they saw it, the use of force had promoted rather than stemmed the spread of Huguenot dissent. Royal edicts of pacification had failed because, as one observer put it in 1586, the crown itself was a captive of partisan interests.[37] Loyalists believed that Navarre's conversion, by removing the pretext for Leaguer sedition, would restore the civil order necessary for a lasting settlement of religious differences. Unlike Leaguers, loyalist Catholics considered the equally desirable goal of religious unity simply unattainable as long as civil disunity ran rampant in French society.

It was the sequence of the loyalist Catholic program, the conviction that only the peace achieved by obedience to established royal traditions could lay the groundwork for genuine religious reconciliation, that led opponents to accuse them of advocating a divorce between piety and politics. In reality, the loyalist Catholics strove to combine piety and politics under the aegis of the traditional monarchy, one which retained its religious integrity by remaining Catholic and its ethnic legitimacy by respecting the Salic Law of succession. Only the conversion of Henri de Navarre satisfied both these conditions—a proposition most Leaguers eventually accepted after 1593 since they too fought for these same basic objectives. In the end, Catholic commitment to the future Henri IV turned on the belief that civil and religious peace could be achieved in France only once the king was at peace with God.

During the 1580s and early 1590s, Catholics on both sides of the conversion question experienced a crisis of faith in the monarchy as it failed to provide the security for which they so desperately longed. Yet this waning confidence in royal leadership hardly dampened the public's desire to find and then realize a more perfect form of monarchical government. Despite different assessments of Henri de Navarre's susceptibility to conversion, Leaguers, such as Jehan de Caumont and Michel du Rit, and loyalist Catholics, such as René Benoist and Claude d'Angennes, shared many beliefs concerning the attributes of ideal kingship.[38] In particular, they all maintained that certain constraints *(freins)* existed that set moral rather than political or institutional limits on the crown which the king could not transgress without jeopardizing his exercise of sovereign authority. Both sides acted on the crucial point made by Bodin in his *Six livres sur la république* (1576), namely, that a king's absolute authority in civil society had to respect divine and natural law.[39] For Leaguers and loyalist Catholics, the moral checks inherent in French kingship had to be reestablished if the crown was to stop popular sedition, the depredations committed by unruly nobles, and the spread of Huguenot heresy. They considered these contagions symptoms of the crisis that racked French society, not its causes. The ruling authority that both Leaguers and loyalists imputed to the crown was in the end a function of its moral credibility; a credibility they determined by how well it combined the dictates of piety and justice considered necessary for good government. Where the Leaguers and loyalist Catholics differed again was on the knotty question of Henri de Navarre's susceptibility to conversion, on whether he might by such an act redeem the monarchy or destroy it and French society.

Brutum Fulmen and the Debate over Fundamental Law

The League at first held out the possibility of Navarre's conversion as long as he agreed to embrace its program of total war against the Huguenots—a position which loyalists considered the surest means of forever alienating him from Catholicism. Such half-hearted overtures by the League ended in September 1585 when Pope Sixtus V, hoping to confer legitimacy on Catholic resistance, excommunicated Navarre and Condé in the bull *Brutum Fulmen*. In it, the pope nullified any right Navarre might claim to princely authority in France by declaring him a relapsed heretic. This new definition of Navarre's canonical status, which upheld the validity of his 1572 conversion, rendered another Catholic conversion impossible from the papacy's standpoint. Another, more suitable candidate for the throne had to be found to resolve the succession crisis, one whose moral integrity could ensure Catholicism's continued place in French society.[40]

Brutum Fulmen touched off a storm of protest in France. Members of the Parlement of Paris saw it as an unwarranted infringement on Gallican liberties, and legists such as François Hotman argued that no power on earth could invalidate Navarre's claim to the throne.[41] For Huguenots, *Brutum Fulmen* merely confirmed that the pope was the Antichrist; for loyalist Catholics, however, the matter was not so simple. References to the Gallican liberties would do little to forestall a disastrous shift of Catholic sentiment to the League should Henri III die before Navarre converted. To disregard the pope's wishes would merely repeat one of the mistakes made in 1572, when Catherine de Medici had willfully precluded a role for Rome in Navarre's first conversion. It also gave Henri an excellent excuse to ignore loyalist entreaties because, the issue of sincerity aside, a conversion without papal approval was almost as controversial as no conversion at all.

Brutum Fulmen and the responses it sparked disclosed the serious constitutional implications of Navarre's claim to the throne. Debates over the fundamental laws of the kingdom, France's unwritten constitution, had raged since the 1560s and largely centered on Protestant demands to invest the Estates General with more legislative authority.[42] Prior to the 1580s, jurists had given little attention to the Salic Law of succession, which some asserted dated back to the founding of the monarchy by the Merovingians. According to this venerable tradition, which vested the crown in the eldest male closest to the king through patrilineal descent, Henri de Navarre stood next in line to the throne should Henri III die without a male heir, as seemed likely. The conflict between Navarre's Calvinist beliefs and the crown's Catholic character threatened the religious sanction long enjoyed by the monarchy, but did not thereby invalidate his claim to the throne.

Leaguer Catholics considered the heretical succession an unmitigated disaster for themselves, the Church, and the monarchy as they traditionally knew and revered it. And it was not long before several thinkers translated these concerns into a theory that countered Navarre's claim according to the Salic Law. Belief that a special relationship existed between the French king and God, which dated back centuries, assumed a prescriptive character in one of the League's earliest manifestos, the *Articles de Péronne,* published in 1585. This tract proclaimed the Law of Catholicity to be the most necessary and sacred of all the fundamental laws of the kingdom. Derived from God, the Law of Catholicity naturally superseded the Salic Law, which Leaguers argued could claim only pagan origins. Moreover, how could a heretic be expected to fulfill the coronation oath to eradicate heresy? Inspired by *Brutum Fulmen,* Leaguer writers developed in the notion of the Law of Catholicity a constitutional alternative to guide their search for a suitable successor to the French throne.[43]

This search eventually settled on two candidates: Henri, Duc de Guise, and Charles, Cardinal de Bourbon. It will perhaps never be known how seriously the Duc de Guise contemplated a bid for the French crown in the 1580s. The fact that he never declared such an intention suggests that his enemies, in an effort to discredit him and the League, deliberately fabricated the Guisard plot to alter the succession. Indeed, rumors that the house of Lorraine sought to usurp the crown had first surfaced in the late 1570s from the pens of Huguenot writers.[44] The Duc de Guise publicly discounted these allegations on several occasions, though Henri III later cited them as the principal reason he ordered Guise murdered at the Estates General of Blois on December 24, 1588.[45] Moreover, no League writer ever supported Guise's claim to the throne as a descendant of Charlemagne; that was again the work of writers in the opposition. Darling and protector of the League, the Duc de Guise and his supporters no doubt realized how closely they would be flirting with disaster should they openly contest the Bourbon family's right to the throne. Such a daring new departure only came about after the death on May 4, 1590, of the Leaguer pretender, Charles X, formerly Cardinal de Bourbon. Serious candidates from the house of Lorraine appeared on the scene once the League had made the momentous decision in the early 1590s to break with the hereditary nature of the royal succession and elect a Catholic king.

In the 1580s, Leaguers found a much more viable candidate for the throne in the person of Navarre's aged uncle, the Cardinal de Bourbon. League publicists such as Matteo Zampini formulated a battery of arguments in advancing the cardinal's cause. The cardinal's candidacy, for example, belied any suspicion that the League opposed the Bourbons' right to the succession, thus maintaining the *bon fran-çois* credentials of the League.[46] The cardinal's claim also drove a wedge between Navarre and Catholic members of the Bourbon family, particularly Henri's impetuous cousin the Comte de Soissons.

These reinterpretations of the Salic Law were not without precedent in the annals of French royal history. Even Henri III, frustrated by Navarre's refusal to convert, conceded Charles's prerogative in mid–1588, though he soon after disavowed this imprudent admission.[47] The League's case for the *droit de proximité* logically meant, however, that Navarre stood next in line for the throne should Charles predecease him without male issue. Such an eventuality seemed likely given the cardinal's vow of celibacy and his advanced age.

To avert such a turn of events, Leaguers eventually fell back on the medieval theory of suitability recently resurrected by Sixtus V in the bull *Brutum Fulmen*. Stressing personal piety as the key to suitability, Leaguers contended that Navarre's relapse into heresy in 1576 rendered him unfit ever to assume the French crown. Charles, however, was a prelate noted for his kindness and devotion—qualities that made him, above all others, eminently suited to rule Catholic France. Leaguers saw Charles's character in terms of their ecclesiological conception of the monarchy; for them, he was to be a new Melchisedech, the priest-king of Israel, who would lead the people of France to the kingdom of God.[48] In sermons and pamphlets, Leaguer preachers frequently contrasted the personality of the "gentle prelate" with that of the "wily heretic" from Béarn. They realized, as did many of Navarre's supporters, that emphasis on the cardinal's personal piety touched French Catholics more deeply than the arid and inaccessible legal reevaluations of the Salic Law. The League's campaign for the Cardinal de Bourbon thus combined arguments based on his dynastic legitimacy and others, more polemical in tone, designed to elicit popular support.

Important questions remained about who determined suitability, however. Some Leaguer writers ascribed this power to the Estates General, which, in conjunction with the pope, could transfer the succession to a more worthy candidate. Deputies at the 1588 Estates General of Blois, in fact, approved such a resolution when they permanently barred Navarre from the throne.[49] The theory of suitability nevertheless had its potential weaknesses, however remote these seemed in the 1580s. By making personal piety the litmus in determining eligibility, the Leaguers left themselves open to the almost unthinkable possibility that Navarre would one day convert with the pope's blessings. This was canonically possible because what could be done by one pope could be undone by another. Loyalist Catholics tried to exploit this flaw, but soon discovered it was impossible to coax support from Rome so long as Navarre remained a Protestant.

The cardinal's candidacy put loyalist Catholics in a difficult position because they could not deny the image of the "gentle prelate" without putting their own religious credibility on the line. Loyalist Catholics therefore treated the competing claims of Navarre and his uncle with great caution in the 1580s lest they too be branded heretics. Tact was also essential if they hoped to persuade Charles to give up his claim and join other Bourbon Catholics, such as the Duc de Montpensier and the Comte de Soissons, who declared for Henri in 1586.[50]

The Law of Catholicity was more than a legal device which the Leaguers used to change the succession. At a deeper level, it reflected the League's conviction that the French monarchy was a civil expression of divine order. For Leaguers, to be *françois* necessarily meant to be Catholic—an equation which held true for both persons and laws of the realm. Even Catholics otherwise opposed to the League in the 1580s, such as André Maillard and Nicolas de Villeroy, found it hard to deny this correspondence between civic identity and religious faith. Like the Leaguers, they drew a connection between the king's profession of Catholicism and the legitimacy of his rule.[51] The crucial difference again lay in their contrary views of the conversion question. Whereas loyalist Catholics held out the possibility of Navarre's return to the Church, Leaguers had concluded with the pope that Navarre was a relapsed heretic beyond salvation.

Henri III and the Protestant Béarnais

Henri III decided to follow the path of least resistance as regarded Navarre's faith, but not out of religious indifference, as his Leaguer critics so often charged—indeed, the king frequently expressed his aversion to heresy and its seditious tendencies.[52] For Henri III and loyalist Catholics, toleration—if it can be called that—mixed the need for order with confidence in the power of gentle persuasion, not persecution. Using the lure of office and royal favor to back up his policy of *douceur*, Henri III won a number of converts from the Reformed religion in the 1580s.[53] Loyalists had every reason to believe similar efforts to convert Navarre would also be successful. After 1584, royal overtures to Navarre, however futile, also kept alive the

possibility of an alliance with the Protestant leader. Such a rapprochement, particularly after the League seized control of Paris in May
1588, led Henri III and his mother to minimize the role of conscience
in their arguments for Navarre's conversion. This oversight lent substance to Huguenot warnings that Catholics cared not a jot for Navarre's sincerity or personal reputation.

Henri III's decision to use *douceur* in winning the presumptive heir
back to the Church entailed other drawbacks as well. His relations
with his cousin from Béarn often had to be compromised to appease
Catholic militants; at other times, his own frustrations with Navarre
led him to adopt a sterner attitude. The king's ambivalence toward
Henri became more marked as the crown's prestige disintegrated after
1586. Official efforts to convert Navarre should therefore be considered apart from those undertaken by individual Catholics in the
1580s. At the time of Alençon's death in June 1584, Henri de Navarre
was at his chateau in Pau, located in the Basses-Pyrénées. He had just
had a serious falling-out with Henri III over Catholic violations of the
latest cease-fire, and hoped his absence from Paris would move the
king to make amends. Shortly after news of Alençon's demise arrived,
Henri III quickly sent word to the Duc d'Épernon, who happened to
be on his way to Pau to discuss the recent edicts of pacification with
Navarre. The king told him to drop that topic and instead begin talks
on the crucial question of Navarre's religion. Henri III's choice of
Épernon is revealing because he, unlike other *mignons,* refused in
later years to become involved in the resurgent League. Épernon had
also knit bonds of *amitié* with Navarre which might prove critical if
the crown hoped to win Navarre back to the Church. In fact, Épernon
became so friendly with Henri that some Catholics thought he might
be in the secret employ of the Béarnais.[54]

Talks between Épernon and Navarre began in late June and lasted
nearly a month. The former appealed to Navarre's love of country,
urging him to convert lest he jeopardize the king's authority and the
welfare of the realm. Coupled with the tangible benefits of conversion
was the king's threat to declare Navarre guilty of *lèse majesté* should
he stubbornly adhere to his heretical beliefs. Although a prince of the
blood and heir to the throne, Henri de Navarre's status in the eyes of
the king and loyalist Catholics still remained that of a subject, whose
principal duty lay in obedience to his sovereign. Henri III thus
brought to bear on the conscience of Henri de Navarre the same stern

language of *service du roi* that the crown had long employed in dealing with the Huguenot party. Needless to say, it had the same ungratifying results. The king's overture to Navarre only aroused Henri's suspicions and inflamed militant Catholics who dreaded such a rapprochement. Épernon warned Navarre of the king's readiness not to recognize him as heir should he not convert. Even this menace left Henri unmoved. Henri III's apparent willingness to abrogate the Salic Law eloquently testified to his own fears of a heretical succession.

Épernon's interviews that summer were the first in a series of royal attempts to coax Navarre to convert. Each encounter saw the crown reiterate these same basic arguments about obedience and love of country. Henri III grievously miscalculated, however, if he thought closer ties with the League would induce Navarre to abjure Protestantism. A month after he had signed the Treaty of Nemours with the Duc de Guise, in which he agreed to repeal all previous edicts of pacification, Henri III sent the Cardinal de Lenoncourt and other dignitaries to Navarre to tender another offer to convert. Henri simply laughed it off as he planned for the brewing conflict known as the War of the Three Henris.[55] The conferences held at Saint-Brice in late 1586, which briefly reopened the talks, ended in such acrimony that Catherine de Medici urged her son to redouble his efforts against the heretics.[56] Another war broke out the next year which eventually climaxed in Navarre's overwhelming victory at Coutras (October 20, 1587), which dispelled any hopes of crushing the Huguenots militarily.[57]

The year 1588 marked a crucial turning point in the struggle over Henri de Navarre's faith. Condé's mysterious death on March 3 greatly strengthened Henri's position because it rendered the Huguenots even more dependent on his leadership.[58] Huguenot military successes then demonstrated to Henri III the need for him to break with the League and begin reconciling with the Protestant heir. His overtures to Navarre, however, only prompted militant Catholics to take matters into their own hands when radicals in Paris, known as the Seize after the city's sixteen arrondissements, engineered a coup in May which drove royal officials out of the city.[59] Despite later rifts with the Seize, the Guises initially benefited from the Leaguer takeover of Paris, since it allowed them to pressure the king into renewing his alliance with the Holy League and, in June, to convoke an Estates

General to settle the dynastic crisis. The Edict of Union, issued by Henri III in July, required all crown officials to swear an oath of allegiance to the Holy League as well as to recognize the Duc de Guise as *lieutenant général de la couronne*. The League's control over the king and royal policy had never seemed firmer than during the summer of 1588.

The Estates General of Blois (October 1588–January 1589) brought together the many strains of Catholic discontent that had arisen since the 1570s. The list of grievances the deputies carried to Blois was long and included protests against the crown's recent military setbacks; rising taxes and fiscal profligacy; governmental corruption, especially the venality of offices; the breakdown of local law and order; scandalous reports of the king's immoral behavior, particularly rumors of his homosexuality; the spread of heresy and witchcraft; and, of course, the Protestant succession.[60] For many Catholics, the Estates General offered Henri III one last chance to redeem his leadership by agreeing to sponsor sweeping reforms, beginning with his acceptance of a measure passed early on by the assembly barring Navarre from the throne. Many loyalist Catholics otherwise opposed to the League supported Navarre's exclusion because they no longer thought it possible to convert him. Even Renaud de Beaune, archbishop of Bourges and a longtime confidant of the king, called upon Henri III to ratify the resolution barring Navarre, given the peril royal inaction could pose to the Church and *estat*.[61]

The assembly's call for the king to take the initiative in handling the dynastic crisis took an unexpected turn, however. Henri III had accepted Leaguer resolutions, among them the exclusion of Navarre, as a way to regain credibility among Catholics. Yet even with these concessions, deputies at the Estates General still looked to the Guises as the champions of Catholicism. Fearing he might lose control of the assembly—and then his kingdom—Henri III took the desperate step of ordering the Guise brothers murdered on Christmas Eve, 1588.[62] Rather than bringing him security, the murder of the Guises proved to be an unmitigated disaster for Henri III. What little credit he still had among many Catholics disappeared as a result of the Guise assassinations. Even his most faithful supporters expressed revulsion at the bloody deed.[63] Some League writers went so far as to declare a preference for the heretical Béarnais over the tyrannical Valois. Moreover, Henri III suffered immediate excommunication for his violation of the Cardinal de Lorraine's clerical dignity—a ban which only the pope could remove.[64]

The tragedy of Blois sparked a general revolt against Henri III which in a few weeks saw many of France's major cities support the Catholic League. Guise's younger brother, the Duc de Mayenne, quickly assumed leadership of the movement and had the Parlement of Paris declare him *lieutenant général de la couronne*.[65] The ranks of the League swelled after the Estates General of Blois disbanded in late January 1589, leaving Henri III little choice but to withdraw to Tours, one of the few provincial cities remaining in royalist control. The king's fortunes only began to improve in April, when he concluded an alliance with Navarre in which he repudiated the exclusionary measure adopted at the Estates General.[66] Leaguer Catholics saw this as further confirmation of Henri III's secret atheism, and called upon all true Catholics to resist the *vilain hérode,* a near anagram for Henri de Valois, and his heretical accomplices.

Amazingly, Henri III managed to regain enough initiative over the next several months for Philip II of Spain seriously to contemplate overt military support for the League. This renewed initiative became especially apparent in July when the two Henris lay siege to Paris, rightly supposing that its fall would soon doom the League rebellion. But unforeseen circumstances again intervened to destroy these plans. On the early morning of August 1, a young Jacobin friar named Jacques Clément arrived at the royalist camp in St. Cloud insisting that he had a vital message to relay to the king. Royal guards brought him to Henri III, who unsuspectingly asked Clément to step aside with him to confer privately. In a flash, the friar seized a knife he had hidden in the sleeve of his cassock and plunged it into the king's chest. At first, royal physicians considered the wound only superficial, but their diagnosis proved mistaken when Henri III began to hemorrhage uncontrollably later that evening. Early the next morning he expired. Rather than inaugurating the Second Coming as Clément had hoped, his blow ushered the Bourbons to power amidst a storm of controversy and violence which only began to abate four years later when Henri IV finally agreed to convert to Catholicism.

3

To Convert a King

THE STRUGGLE OVER the Protestant succession altered the course and eventual settlement of the French Wars of Religion. It forced Catholics and Huguenots alike to recast many of the divisive issues raised during the wars so that their resolution came to depend on the conscience of one man, Henri IV. Discord had exploded since 1559 over such questions as the role of religion in civil society, the nature of dissent and sedition, and how best to achieve the ideals of piety and justice thought necessary for a well-ordered Christian polity. The issue of the king's religion acted as a prism through which were refracted many of the cherished aims and interests of educated elites in late sixteenth-century France, affording them—and us—new perspectives on these crucial concerns. In confronting the question of Navarre's faith, educated elites began to grapple with the difficult task of rebuilding a society shattered by a generation of strife. In the process, they laid the foundations for a new order we now call Bourbon absolutism.

Debates over the Heir's Faith (1584–1589)

The fascination that Catholic and Huguenot writers shared with Henri de Navarre's personality stemmed from their deep concern about the attributes of ideal kingship. As public respect for Henri III sank in the 1580s, contemporaries labored to formulate and then realize a monarchical ethic that limited abuses of power by an evil-minded king, yet safeguarded the full authority of the benevolent sovereign they all hoped would one day govern them. The idealization of monarchy helped to legitimize protest movements against Valois rule and the Protestant Henri IV. In these dreams of perfect government under an ideal king, each of the three major factions—Huguenot, loyalist Catholic, and Leaguer—generated its own competing myth of Henri IV which helped to define their positions and guide their behavior in the clash over France's future.

Contemporaries usually reduced the question of ideal kingship to three general topics of discussion. Considerations of the king's piety and devotional practices outlined his spiritual obligations; philosophical investigations dealt with his ethical behavior as well as the science of government; and discussions of courtly etiquette and savoir-faire spelled out the prince's need to conform to a social code of civility known as *honnêteté*.[1] The Palace Academy founded by Henri III in the 1580s, in which discourses about ideal monarchy dominated the agenda, represented an attempt by the embattled king to take the lead in public debates that often used him as a foil.[2] Needless to say, it failed to restore his credibility as king. His successor, Henri IV, faced much the same situation until he converted to Catholicism. How closely images of Navarre's character approximated or fell short of ideal kingship in the end depended on the assumptions of each writer and the polemical strategy adopted to sway readers.

The relationship between writers and the reading public remains obscure during the early modern period. Prefaces and *avis au lecteur* from the late sixteenth century show a more sophisticated understanding of how to manipulate public opinion.[3] The insatiable demand for reading materials of all kinds—pious manuals, scholarly treatises, poetry, and broadsides—suggests that the literate public wanted not only to learn, but also to be influenced. Indeed, the mirror of princes genre had evolved during these years to encompass not only the king's edification, but also his subjects' schooling in obedience. Beginning with Étienne de la Boétie in the 1550s, political thinkers started to emphasize the subject's responsibility for good government as much as the king's. Besides providing the *honnête homme* with general discussions about good government, political writers offered to guide readers through the problems normally encountered in the areas of counsel, delegation of authority, compensation, and courtly behavior. In this way, inquiry into the nature of monarchy became closely allied with questions about what constituted dutiful *service du roi*. After all, the cult of monarchy was also the cult of all those involved in the vast enterprise of winning glory for God and the realm.[4]

What God intended for France naturally varied with each party, though all agreed that a king's religion and moral character influenced, if it did not determine, the probity of his subjects. From the start, French Calvinists realized that the movement's future depended on Navarre's unswerving commitment to the Reformed faith—a commitment Huguenot assemblies had him periodically reaffirm during the 1580s. Agrippa d'Aubigné's bitter denunciation of Henri IV's apostasy in the late 1590s echoed the concerns of many Huguenots a decade earlier who feared the seductiveness of a conversion.[5] They remained silent, however, and took refuge in the hope—indeed the myth—of Henri de Navarre as a man who preferred death to betrayal of lifelong friends and convictions. Yet with the passage of time, Protestant anxiety rose by degrees as the temptation to convert became increasingly alluring. This anxiety can be measured in the changing polemical strategies that Protestant writers used to deal with the possibility of the king's conversion.

One of the earliest and most thoroughgoing Protestant attacks on the idea of Navarre's conversion appeared in a pamphlet published in 1585 entitled *Double d'une lettre envoiée à un certain personnage*. Often attributed to Duplessis Mornay, it was most likely the work of his close associate, Vincent Ferrier, a well-known Protestant minister.[6] The pamphlet relates a heated debate that purportedly took place in July 1584 between Duplessis Mornay and the Sieur de Roquelaure, one of a small but growing number of Catholics, many originally from Alençon's party, whose support of Henri lent substance to the claim that his cause transcended confessional affiliation. For Ferrier, however, the presence of these Catholics near the Protestant prince threatened to undermine Henri's allegiance to the Reformed faith.[7]

The *Double d'une lettre* revealed how the conversion question intersected with other issues raised during the Wars of Religion. One of the first and most enduring of these links equated Henri's salvation with that of France. For Duplessis Mornay, the Huguenot struggle for acceptance, along with France's recovery from civil war, depended on Henri's salvation as a Calvinist. Roquelaure, however, urged Navarre to convert because of the Catholics' grim determination to prevent a heretical succession. Only in this way could Henri spare France the agony of another civil war. France's survival thus lay in the balance regardless of how Henri chose to resolve the conversion question.

Echoing the crown's own case for Henri's abjuration, Roquelaure argued that Navarre could safeguard his eventual authority as king only by upholding the monarchy's sacred traditions. From a *politique* perspective—Ferrier used this loaded term when relating Roquelaure's discourse—Roquelaure urged Henri to go through with a public conversion to satisfy Catholics, even if his conscience bade him otherwise. This blatant distortion of Catholic arguments for Navarre's conversion was of course intentional because it left the moral high ground to Duplessis Mornay, who wasted no time in attacking the lamentable gap between external appearance and inner conviction approved by Roquelaure as good policy. Better to trust in God than in this wily bastard son of Machiavelli, Duplessis Mornay warned. Even if Navarre sincerely converted, he could never escape Catholic suspicions of hypocrisy.[8] A conversion therefore gave the papists an added excuse for sedition, as well as alienating Henri's Protestant allies at home and abroad. This implicit threat of Huguenot resistance haunted Henri over the next thirteen years until he finally settled the matter—at least for his lifetime—in the Edict of Nantes. Although such threats no doubt delayed Navarre's conversion, they did so at the price of poisoning his relations with the *réformés,* to the extent that in the mid–1590s he thought them no less rebellious than the Leaguers.

Curiously enough, the polemical boundaries between Huguenots and Leaguers, so well defined on most issues, virtually disappeared on the question of the king's conversion, because each thought it impossible for Navarre to join religious conviction with a change to Catholicism. This common ground was rather narrow, to be sure, since Leaguers refused to recognize Henri's claim to the throne because of his faith, whereas Huguenots refused to concede that faith had any bearing on the legitimacy of his claim. Their rhetorical strategies against a possible conversion nevertheless shared a common moral vocabulary about the dangers of hypocrisy that proved unsettling to Navarre's Catholic supporters, particularly after Henri III's assassination in August 1589. Both Huguenots and Leaguers believed the temptation to convert to be even greater following the regicide, and therefore focused increased attention on refuting loyalist Catholic efforts to persuade Henri to convert.

Loyalist Catholic views on Navarre's conversion did not remain fixed but rather developed as circumstances changed during the 1580s and early 1590s. Disagreements which occasionally arose centered not so much on the desirability of a conversion as on the crucial combination of reasons for Henri to return to the Church. The various strategies that loyalists adopted carried with them different implications which affected the meaning of Navarre's conversion. Insistence that Henri convert because the king commanded it, for example, could mean his conversion arose from compulsion, not divine grace. Arguments like the fictional Roquelaure's, which encouraged Henri to accommodate Catholic sentiment by going through with a public conversion even if he remained a Protestant at heart, left him open to accusations of hypocrisy. Another consideration concerned whether the proposed conversion would enhance or detract from Navarre's status as a Christian prince. The conversion of Henri IV thus involved a wide range of issues; as the debate unfolded however, attention came to focus mainly on the relationship between the king's conscience and royal *dignitas*.

Most loyalist discussions of Navarre's conversion stressed the vital association between Catholicism and the monarchy—a view shared by Leaguers as well.[9] Any attempt by Navarre to change the crown's traditional Catholic character, which dated back to Clovis, would weaken the monarchy's hold on French society through religion. Navarre's conversion, however, would strengthen this control by transforming religion into an instrument of order, not disorder.[10] Championing the more humane approach of *douceur*, loyalists emphasized the crucial importance of pious instruction and moral example in bringing about Navarre's reconciliation with the Catholic Church. They believed that Henri possessed those qualities, such as truthfulness, equanimity, and courage, that made his conversion inevitable. Yet if Navarre failed to confirm their high opinion of him, one loyalist Catholic warned in early 1587, they would have little choice but to oppose his candidacy for the throne.[11]

Huguenot and Leaguer views of Navarre's character, while opposing, possessed a static quality, unlike those of the loyalists, which depended not so much on who Henri was as on who he might become. This openness to future change on the part of loyalists had enormous significance as the controversy wore on, though they warned Henri that declarations of good intent were not enough, for "in such a weighty affair it's much better to speak by actions than words, which are cheap." [12] The act of conversion, not the possibility of it that Navarre dangled before Catholics, was ultimately essential for both his political and religious salvation.

The possibility of Navarre's conversion assumed mythic proportions for all parties. They frequently referred to the judgment of posterity, pointing out to Henri the certain obloquy that awaited him should he prefer worldly gain to true religion. Whether Henri one day received eternal renown or scorn thus depended on which way he aligned his confessional allegiances. An individual's legacy to posterity counted heavily, given the age's veneration of personal *gloire*. *Gloire* was a precarious quality that could be assessed only after death, for only then could one's life be properly judged and immortalized. Each of the factions naturally interpreted Henri's capacity to achieve grandeur differently. For loyalist Catholics, it could only be secured by a Catholic conversion, whereas Huguenots believed his reputation required him to remain faithful to Protestantism. For Leaguers, Navarre was beyond salvation and its secular equivalent, *gloire*. Contemporaries thus identified the conversion question as a crucial episode in Henri's life that had eternal significance for God and future generations.

Just as people gazed toward heaven and the future, so they turned their attention to the past during this period. For many Catholics, Navarre's heresy ran counter not only to Scripture and French tradition, but also to the beliefs of his royal ancestors. Family beliefs, like lands and offices, devolved on an individual as a trust to be handed down to heirs intact. A family's *gloire* was thus derivative, not fixed; it grew or diminished according to the abilities of its current trustee. Much of an individual's personal worth therefore depended on how well he either preserved or improved this ongoing heritage. This economy of *gloire* across time carried onerous responsibilities for Henri de Navarre, because upon him fell the rich legacy of the French monarchy. Huguenots believed that Henri had to enrich this legacy by returning it to the apostolic purity of the Reformed faith. As Leaguers saw it, Navarre had to be disinherited lest he sully this priceless heritage. And last, loyalist Catholics thought Henri endangered this thousand-year-old tradition by his refusal to embrace the faith of his royal ancestors. All three parties thus saw the historical destiny of France bound up in the conscience of Henri de Navarre. [13]

The succession of the Protestant Henri de Navarre forced French Catholics to reconcile their commitment to the monarchy with their spiritual allegiance to the Church. Leaguers chose from the start the path of resistance, whereas loyalist Catholics reserved it as an option during their campaign for Navarre's return to the Church. Navarre ignored loyalist pleas in the 1580s, however, because they focused too narrowly on the conversion's political and dynastic implications. He thought few French Catholics were ready to accept merely the outward show of a conversion given the manifest dangers of hypocrisy. Only the shock of the regicide in August 1589 compelled loyalist Catholics to turn away from the obvious secular reasons for Henri's conversion and confront the crucial question of his sincerity. When they did this, they challenged him to become what they wanted him to be: Catholic king of France.

Reactions to the Regicide

The violent death of Henri III on August 2, 1589, changed the entire complexion of the conversion debate and the course of the Wars of Religion. The dynastic distortions that touched his memory sprang directly from the complicated struggle over Henri IV's religion. When examined closely, the conscious manipulation and, at times, denial of royal ceremonial to the last Valois king can tell us much about contemporary notions of dynastic legitimacy, personalized kingship, and the symbolic punishment inflicted on past rulers. Heralding the first Bourbon as the answer to France's woes, Navarre's supporters worked hard to present his accession as a complete break with the past. Such selective *oubliance* was no doubt intended to ease the tensions that arose in the precarious coalition of Catholics and Protestants formed after the regicide. Public confidence required positive images of the new king's personality. One reason that this campaign worked so well was that Henri IV's publicists found a convenient contrast in the public memory of Henri III.

It mattered little that the last Valois's reputation was essentially the creation of League propaganda; so much the better, in fact, since loyalist writers, while perpetuating the dark myth about Henri III, could still in good conscience accuse the ultra-Catholics of antiroyalism.[14] A fundamental ambivalence colored the relationship between Navarre's supporters and the memory of Henri III after 1589. Only the dowager Queen Louise consistently urged a rehabilitation of her husband's memory long after most in France thought it best forgotten. To be sure, the constitutional implications of Leaguer political discourse demanded and received total condemnation by loyalists after 1589; the ritualistic assassination of Henri III in word and then deed required more selective treatment, however. The poison pens of Leaguer publicists established in graphic fashion all the imaginable *topoi* of evil kingship which Bourbon supporters could use both to distract attention from Navarre's Calvinist faith and then, after 1593, to promote the new cult of personalized kingship devoted to the converted Henri IV. Everything the last Valois was, the first Bourbon most definitely was not.

Contemporary fascination with the body royal can be seen in the contrast often drawn between these two rulers' sexual desires and proclivities. According to League writers, the dynastic crisis could be traced to Henri III's inability to sire an heir, which in turn found its cause in his reputed homosexuality.[15] For them, royal tyranny sprang from the king's unnatural lusts and sexual deviance. Along with sterility came powerful desires which the king and his *mignons* reputedly satisfied by raping nuns and sodomizing young boys.[16] Now let us consider for a moment Henri IV, or the Vert Galant. A rapist and sodomizer he was not. His robust and decidedly heterosexual appetites, rather than scandalizing his subjects, offered them a reassuring picture of royal virility which required only a good marriage to be fruitful.[17] Navarre's womanizing was thoroughly *françois,* whereas Henri III's effeminacy betrayed his maternal ancestors' origins in the shadowy land of Machiavelli.[18] Images of Henri III therefore stood as a reminder of Valois sterility, which had impoverished the realm by sapping its vital strength; Henri IV's boundless sexual energy, by contrast, now made possible the kingdom's renewal, because through his royal potency the seeds of future greatness could literally be sown. The meticulous recording of Louis XIII's every gurgle, burp, and fart, as Lloyd Moote has recently shown, attested to this continuing preoccupation with the body royal in the next reign.[19]

League descriptions of Henri III's physical debility—the oozing sores, noxious smells, and soft ashen pallor that made him resemble some creature of the night—served as a metaphor for the kingdom's dreadful condition under his rule. Heresy, immorality, and witchcraft had spread like cancers throughout the realm because the forces of darkness held sway over the king. The offensive mounted against these scourges during Henri IV's reign began, as one panegyrist later noted, with the banishment of the "astrologues, simples bacheliers et philosophes" assembled at the Valois court.[20] As regards Valois fiscal exactions, Henri III was often called a leech, or *sangsue,* who sucked vital substance from the public body.[21] Outrageous rumors claiming that he had licked blood from the swords used to murder the Guises, along with long-standing charges of necromancy, added defilement to rank parasitism. This unnatural treatment of bodies contrasted markedly with later depictions of Henri IV's virile accomplishments on the battlefield and on the hunting grounds. His *vif natural,* which enabled him to survive war wounds and assassination attempts (at least until 1610), made Henri IV seem almost indestructable. As such, he personified a strong, expansionist France confident of its future; rather than taking from his subjects, Henri IV gave them the proverbial "chicken in every pot."[22] The splendid and symbolically rich ceremonial of France's first Bourbon king, as seen in his entries into cities, *lits de justice,* and ultimately his funeral, emphasized time and again the simple themes of physical potency and renewal thought so crucial to restoring confidence in the crown after a generation of civil war. Denying such ritual celebrations of royalty to the memory of Henri III therefore increased the éclat of his successor.

Any mention of the body during the sixteenth century almost invariably carried over to considerations of the soul. Public executions at the time, particularly for heresy or witchcraft, punished the victim's body to provide a public spectacle of good's inevitable triumph over evil. Such a connection was quite naturally made in the Leaguer press after Henri III's assassination at St. Cloud in August 1589. It was God, after all, who had moved Clément to strike a king whose crimes, notably the murder of the Cardinal de Guise, had led to his excommunication. When depicting the dead king's imaginary burial and hideous punishment in Hell, some League writers invented for their readers a fictitious Henri III who confessed his sins and described his bodily torments in minute detail. In *Les propos lamentables de Henry de Valois* (1589), the late king tearfully regrets that in his search to "become immortalized, I have been forgotten." Though gone, he was not forgotten by his enemies. Now naked in Hell, racked by endless thirst—itself a metaphor for yearning after grace—he implores the reader not to follow in his footsteps, which only lead to perdition.[23]

Like so many others, this pamphlet, with its vivid appeal to the senses, gave readers a feeling of what it was like to be in Hell, which was surely where they would go if they did not support the Holy League. Body and soul thus became conjoined in the polemic over the fate of the assassinated king as well as the conversion of Henri IV.

While League writers knew what to do with Henri III's memory and the bodily sufferings imputed to him, Navarre and his supporters seemed less sure. Initially at least, Henri IV attempted to use the disgust and shock aroused by the regicide to rally support for his claim to the thrown. Thus he trid to prepare Catholics to accept the new reality of a heretical king by focusing their attention on the League's alleged complicity in Henri III's cruel death rather than on his own religious state. Funeral orations for the late king made an explicit connection between sedition and the murder, between the heresy of armed resistance to the crown and the late king's personal religiosity.[24] This conspiratorial mentality enabled loyalist Catholics to satisfy their suspicions about the League's supposed antiroyalism, thus smoothing the way for them to accept Henri IV as king. Clément's death at the scene of his crime fueled the polemic over the regicide because it substituted public speculation for direct interrogation of the assassin. In *L'antimartyr de frère Jacques Clément* (1590), for example, Étienne Pasquier presented a detailed, yet undocumented, description of the events leading up to the regicide. He addressed such basic questions as who the assassin was, how he had arrived at his decision to kill the king, and where he had procured the knife.[25] He and other loyalist Catholic writers left little doubt that Clément was merely the instrument in a far-reaching plot conceived by Leaguer fanatics; indeed, Leaguer panegyrics tended to confirm these suspicions by likening his assassination of Henri III to Judith's slaying of the tyrant Holofernes.[26] Support of Navarre's right to the throne thus became the best way for loyalist Catholics to avenge the attack on Henri III.

Difference of various degrees usually exist between an event and its literary reconstruction. Writers at the time associated the dying Henri III's behavior with certain normative attributes of kingship, such as piety, serenity before death, and a selfless concern for public welfare. They similarly explained the comportment of his servants in terms of fidelity, duty, and sacrifice. These images in the end mattered more than what actually happened at St. Cloud. Most reports of the king's last hours paint a glowing portrait of heartrending sadness and exemplary piety intended to move those who might be leery of supporting Navarre's cause. Henri III apparently lingered long enough for a Mass to be celebrated, during which he received absolution from his confessor—a point which became a bone of contention in the years ahead. Yet even these scenes of Henri III's final agonies seemed but a prelude to Navarre's dramatic arrival at the king's bedside. At that moment, dismay became joy, tears gave way to renewed conviction as royal authority passed from the hands of an exhausted Henri III to the new Bourbon ruler.[27] Woodcuts portraying this crucial last encounter between the two kings present it almost as a coronation rite wherein the last Valois invested his successor with the symbols of royal authority, a sword and a crown.[28] The conversion question surfaced in several narratives describing the deathbed scene. According to Philippe d'Hurault, Sieur de Cheverny, who in 1590 became Keeper of the Seals, Henri III asked Navarre to promise that he would seek Catholic instruction as soon as possible—a request Navarre apparently agreed to fulfill.[29] Having served his purpose, Henri III quietly expired, his body became still and his memory but a token of a time that many close to the new king would in the future wish to forget.

Although published accounts of the regicide helped Henri IV win public approval from Catholics, not all went so smoothly as they seemed to indicate. Before Navarre arrived at Henri III's side from Meudon on the evening of August 1, Catholic *grands* had had several hours during which to confer, though they left no trace of what they discussed. D'Aubigné, who arrived later that evening with Navarre, accused François d'O, Antragues, and Châteauvieux—all influential members of the king's council—of plotting to resist Navarre should the king die. D'Aubigné and many other Huguenots, of course, had every reason to try to poison Henri's relations with the loyalist Catholics.[30] Maximilien de Béthune, Duc de Sully, a principal minister later in the reign, described the atmosphere at the time of the regicide as one of reconciliation rather than remorse. He nonetheless expressed concern lest Henri III's imminent death lead to "great confusions due to the diversity of religion."[31] He advised Navarre to remain at St. Cloud through the night to consult with Catholics and prepare for the transition of authority. Sully's report of the courtesy and respect which Catholics accorded Navarre that night indicates that most had probably already resolved to support him.

Henri IV's efforts to associate his cause with the martyrdom of his predecessor greatly bolstered a claim to authority otherwise rendered suspect because of his stubborn allegiance to Calvinism. The Catholic death of Henri III, so celebrated in public literature, failed to be solemnized in the royal funeral ceremony of Renaissance France. Although mortuary masses in the weeks following the regicide honored Henri III's last moments on earth, his remains went unrevered.[32] This oversight derived in large part from the extraordinary circumstances of the time. First, the League controlled St. Denis, the traditional site for royal funerals, until July 1590; they had also moved the insignia customarily used in royal burials to Paris, where they remained until the city's recapture in March 1594.[33] Divisions in the Parlement of Paris, which ritually represented the king's justice, prevented its unitary expression in a cortege; the split in the law court also made it impossible for Henri IV to hold a *lit de justice* to confirm his new authority. It was unadvisable, given the war, for Henri IV to withdraw from public affairs while lengthy funeral preparations were made. And, finally, Henri IV's confessional deviance could not be reconciled with the burial ceremony's Catholic character.

The canonical irregularity of the deathbed absolution that Henri III had received made a royal burial in the hallowed ground of St. Denis unlikely as well. Yet this issue, too, provided an opportunity to promote the new king's cause. The diplomatic missions Navarre's supporters undertook to Rome over the next four years, beginning with the one headed by the Duc de Luxembourg in August 1589, all had as their ostensible purpose a confirmation by the pope of Henri III's last-minute absolution. How committed they were to settling the matter is questionable, however; the fact that it remained unresolved gave them an excuse to keep channels open with the papacy on more substantive issues, such as Navarre's conversion.[34] Neither Sixtus V nor any of his successors agreed to sanction Henri III's absolution; as far as they were concerned, the last Valois had died an excommunicant.[35] The long negotiations after 1593 that finally resulted in Henri IV's absolution by Clement VIII made no mention whatsoever of his predecessor's uncertain status.[36] Only the dowager Queen Louise continued to press, until her death in 1601, for a resolution of the affair, though her efforts proved unavailing. Although panegyrists at the queen's funeral extolled her steadfastness and piety, they could not help regretting that she had not had a nobler cause to champion.[37] A decade had apparently done little to soften the memory of France's last Valois king.

Thus, it was Henri III's death, not his life, which became the focus of loyalist propaganda efforts after 1589. This distinction was crucial because it stressed the discontinuities inherent in the succession; it was almost as if royal authority, while still preternatural, had to be cleansed of the unsavory blemishes that had tarnished it while in the hands of Catherine de Medici's sons. This break with the past began early on when Henri IV moved quickly to confirm and continue Catholic acceptance of his rule in the Declaration of St. Cloud, which he delivered to Catholic noblemen in the royal army on August 4. Henri IV framed the Declaration around the late king's death by inviting Catholics to share his sorrow and vent their anger against the League. The proclamation was not unlike a funeral oration in its edifying references to Henri III's courage and piety, though—significantly—Henri IV omitted the customary formula "que Dieu absolve" each time he mentioned his predecessor's name. Although other funeral orations at the time condemned the heinous nature of the regicide, they seem almost perverse in their recounting of Henri III's many faults. Jean Bechet, a court cleric, asked God not to judge the late king too severely, after which he proceeded to pray that greater divine favor be extended to the present king, Henri IV.[38] The implication, of course, was that Henri III's miserable life and death should serve as an object lesson to the living, including Navarre. Achille de Harlay, a *premier président* in the loyalist Parlement sitting in Tours, remarked after the regicide on the successful transformation of "the memory of this deplorable event into a singular desire to serve and obey the new king." [39]

Henri IV used the Declaration to raise Catholic hopes that he might soon change confessions. Recognizing that many feared the rule of a Protestant prince, Henri IV promised "by his faith and word as king" to maintain the Catholic Church in France "without changing it one bit, be it in matters of policy or practice, or concerning clerical persons or property." [40] He even reconfirmed the restrictions that recent edicts of pacification had placed on the exercise of the Reformed religion, pledging to fill royal offices vacated by Huguenots with "Catholics, so long as they are competent and remain loyal to the crown"—a definite improvement on the late king's policies. The most important portion of the Declaration dealt with Henri IV's desire to seek religious instruction from a national church council within the next six months. The promises Henri IV made in the Declaration of St. Cloud in effect replaced the coronation oath every new king customarily swore to his subjects upon coming to the throne. Often referred to as his *serment* (his actual coronation took place in February 1594), the Declaration represented a personal commitment by the new king to maintain the Catholic character of the crown and country.

Henri IV's willingness to set a timetable for religious instruction was a significant concession to the late king's disconsolate supporters. Without it, many more might have deserted him than actually did. One historian has estimated that more than one-third of the Catholics in the royal army forsook the Protestant king after the regicide, despite efforts by Catholic *grands,* such as Angoulême and Bellegrade, to rally the troops.[41] On the night of August 3, in fact, Biron, one of Henri III's most powerful commanders, contemplated withdrawing his forces until gold and assurances offered him by the Sieur de Sancy, a Huguenot, finally dissuaded him.[42] Huguenot lieutenants, such as La Trémouille and Châtillon, also abandoned Henri IV in disgust over the concessions he had made to papists in the Declaration. These desertions eventually forced Henri IV to lift the siege of Paris in mid-August, just as it appeared close to success.

The Protestant king tried to stem the disintegration of the royal army in a speech he delivered to noble captains on the evening of August 4. In it, he reiterated his promise to maintain Catholicism and honor the wishes of his predecessor, even though some of "the nobility in this army . . . circulate a rumor that they cannot serve me unless I profess Catholicism." He preferred to die rather than forsake God and his promise to consider a conversion in due time, adding that he stood a better chance of success with just "one hundred faithful Frenchmen" at his side than with "two hundred of these fainthearted sorts." In the end, he told them that he believed God always protected "gens de bien," and that those who deserted him in his hour of need demonstrated to all the world their lack of virtue and honor.[43] Allegiance to the Protestant Henri IV thus became for the *bon françois* the pinnacle of moral probity, desertion its nadir.

The Declaration of St. Cloud offered loyalist Catholics a way to justify their support of the Protestant king. Seizing this opportunity on the evening of August 4, many Catholic noblemen at St. Cloud swore a *serment réciproque* which harked back to the earlier feudal ties that had once bound the king to his vassals.[44] Catholic calls for vengeance against the perpetrators of the regicide also became tinged with an air of medieval nostalgia. As a result, the desire to avenge the martyred Henri III became one of the emotional touchstones of Henri IV's relationship with loyalist Catholics until his conversion in 1593. The revival of chivalry among members of the aristocracy during the late sixteenth century, both in deed and in literature, often lent the early years of Henri IV's reign all the earmarks of a medieval romance. At a deeper level, it reflected the close personal ties of *amitié* which Henri IV cultivated with Catholic noblemen, ties that enabled him to consolidate his rule during those uncertain months following Henri III's assassination.[45]

Besides emphasizing a symbolic break with recent royalty and thus a new beginning for France, the deliberate decision by loyalists not to rehabilitate Henri III's public reputation afforded the new king crucial time during which to settle the conversion question. The unusual circumstances surrounding the regicide and Henri IV's Declaration of St. Cloud helped to dispel Catholic fears of a heretical king. Although many deserted Henri IV, many more recognized him as king of Catholic France. Their acceptance of him proceeded in distinct stages, beginning with perceptions of Henri III's demise and ending with the Catholic nobility's oath of allegiance on the evening of August 4. This oath clearly implied that Catholic loyalty to Navarre was contingent on his eventual conversion to Catholicism. The regicide and the Declaration of St. Cloud thus inaugurated the complex and, at times, equivocal relationship that existed between the Protestant Henri IV and his Catholic supporters over the next four years.

Debates over Henri IV's Faith (1589–1593)

The struggle after 1589 over the king's religion rested not only on different ideas about a subject's duty and devotion, but also on the manipulation of images of Henri IV's character. League writers wasted little time, therefore, before disclosing the "hidden" intentions behind Navarre's supposed openness to a conversion. A fabricated dialogue, which appeared in 1590, between Navarre and a Protestant pastor named Antoine Mermet tried to demonstrate the inveteracy of Henri's heresy. Its author shrewdly played on loyalist perceptions of Henri as a man of his word to underscore the unshakable faith of the Béarnais in the Reformed religion. Since the regicide, Navarre had devised all kinds of subtle policies—or *artifices*—to further his objective of making France a Calvinist country. The outstanding example cited here was naturally the Declaration of St. Cloud.[46]

It was not always necessary for Leaguers to invent such revelations of Henri IV's aims. Incriminating statements often arose from the king's need to appease his Protestant allies. These same allies, such as Elizabeth I and the city council of Bern in Switzerland, in turn published such statements in order to bind Navarre more tightly to the Reformed cause.[47] All of this the League trumpeted as evidence of Navarre's unwillingness to convert. A letter from Catholics in Béarn described the cruel treatment they had received from Navarre, and ended with a plea to fellow Catholics not to put their trust in the wily heretic.[48] Simply because Navarre was a prince of the blood, Catholics should not conclude that he was an *homme de parole;* after all, the Béarnais had made similar promises to seek instruction after Alençon's death in 1584, none of which he ever kept.[49] For League writers, loyalist support of Henri IV rested on false assumptions about Navarre's character and his alleged attraction to Catholicism.

Many of these same fears affected Protestant responses to the conversion question after 1589 in ways which further soured Henri IV's relations with the Reformed movement. Some Huguenots felt especially uneasy because of Henri IV's apparent willingness to set a timetable for religious instruction. In late 1589, for example, Jean de Sponde, a prominent Huguenot advisor to Navarre who likewise became a Catholic in 1593, published a tract which presented Henri IV with strong political reasons not to convert. Sponde avoided the pious platitudes that Duplessis Mornay and Ferrier had voiced five years earlier and instead painted a gloomy picture of the disasters that awaited the king should he sacrifice his good name and soul for worldly gain. Rather than ending the wars, a Catholic conversion would only perpetuate them because Catholics would demand that the king prove his sincerity by waging war against the Huguenots. French Calvinists would then be forced to elect another protector to defend their communities and faith. These dire predictions, which almost came true after 1593 (and indeed did after 1610), probably gave Henri IV reason enough to hesitate before embarking on the perilous road to conversion. In the end, Sponde added to Duplessis Mornay's righteous opposition the spectre of armed resistance against Henri IV should he decide to embrace Catholicism.[50]

In the years ahead, other Protestant pleas against a Catholic conversion returned time and again to these themes of betrayal and disaster. One remonstrance delivered privately before the king in 1592— a time when Navarre began openly to consider the merits of abjuration—upbraided him for losing sight of the true faith. This shrill attack derided the king's clever handling of the conversion question, suggesting that perhaps Henri believed in neither confession. This veiled charge of atheism stole a page from Leaguer polemics about Navarre's lack of faith. Again, like ultra-Catholics, Huguenots offered a moral critique of Henri IV's wavering which justified opposition should the king's spiritual evolution go against their perceived interests.[51]

This menacing tone found no place in François de la Noue's eloquent analysis of the conversion question in 1591, one year before his death. A fearless Huguenot captain committed to his faith, La Noue addressed what no Huguenot had thus far dared to discuss openly: the possibility of Henri IV's eventual return to the Catholic Church. He warned his fellow Protestants not to resist the king should he one day convert, lest they bring upon themselves the war they so dreaded. Intimidation—be it by Huguenots or Catholics—corrupted Henri IV's relationship with God because it injected secular concerns into what was at heart a delicate question of conscience.

Without public calm, La Noue seriously doubted that Henri IV would ever have an opportunity to read Scripture, confer with saintly men of the cloth, and meditate on God's will. Only under these circumstances could the Holy Spirit move the king to see the light—a light La Noue purposely refrained from characterizing as either Calvinist or Catholic. In short, the road to Henri IV's conversion began once all his subjects returned to obedience. La Noue held out hope that the two faiths could one day be reconciled given their common belief in Christ and the Apostles' Creed, though such a settlement could never be made a precondition for the king's decision one way or the other. Again, as for Catholics, Henri IV's sincerity was the key issue. Yet whereas Duplessis Mornay and Sponde—like the

Leaguers—assumed that it was impossible for Navarre to join religious conviction with a conversion, La Noue purposely left the matter of religious truth open. Citing the principle of liberty of conscience, La Noue argued that the Huguenots had no right, let alone the power, to prevent Henri IV from becoming a Catholic should his conscience so dictate. Although not widely shared at the time, this admission of impotence went to the very core of the Huguenot dilemma of reconciling royalism with religious dissent.[52]

Some loyalist Catholics began to pick up on the rhetoric of liberty of conscience used by La Noue, though unlike him, they never abandoned the ideal of religious uniformity. Henri IV's royal *dignitas* constituted a temporary exception to this otherwise firm rule because the king's conversion had to be sincere if it stood any chance of ending the wars. Forcing the king to become a hypocritical Catholic certainly menaced the Church and France more than his present errors, some argued.[53] Although considerations of Henri IV's conscience and royal dignity demanded the utmost privacy, the ceremonies to be used in his conversion needed to exalt, not abase the majesty of the crown. This again argued against a precipitous conversion. The observance of royal ritual at the king's conversion would have to demonstrate Henri IV's sincerity as a Catholic as well as reaffirm his authority as king. Finally, a sincere conversion by Henri IV reduced the risk of a relapse into heresy by severing the ties that bound the king to the Huguenot party. In reconsidering the question of sincerity after 1589, loyalists began to reevaluate the nature and practice of French kingship. A crucial change took place after 1589, at least in print, in the ideas loyalist Catholics had earlier had about the subject's duty to uphold the timeless values of the monarchy and Christian society. Faced with the problem of unverifiable sincerity, they began after the regicide to ask whether a subject could demand anything of the king. Surely this was not duty but impertinence. Instead, the subject had first to fulfill his own *devoir* of obedience before he sought to enlighten Henri IV about his responsibilities as king. Increasingly, loyalist Catholics came to believe that the civil heresy of armed revolt by the League far outweighed the purported religious heresy of Henri IV.[54]

Concern for Henri IV's royal dignity was therefore critical in coaxing Catholic acceptance of his rule after a conversion. For this reason, loyalist Catholics rejected any overt meddling by outsiders in the special dialogue between Henri IV and God because this only tainted the king's eventual return to the Catholic Church. Discussion of the religious reasons for Henri IV to convert was permissible, however, because this helped to make the prospective convert more receptive to the Holy Spirit. Given Henri IV's unwillingness to convoke the national council promised at St. Cloud, these apologia of Catholic orthodoxy also kept the hope of his conversion alive as the war dragged on. Emphasizing the evangelical character of loyalist efforts to convert the king helped to defend the devotional integrity of Catholics who sided with him.[55] In fact, several writers framed their case for supporting the conversion as a catechetical exercise to aid the king in settling specific doctrinal questions. Even without any overt references to rank political considerations, the emphasis loyalist writers sometimes placed on civil peace and God's omnipotence clearly construed the king's liberty of conscience to mean a willingness to submit to forces greater than he. These writers often used the language of conversion to admonish fellow Frenchmen of both confessions to abjure all seditious activities and embrace royal service.[56] Just as God's mercy was still available to Henri IV, so were the king's enemies still capable of political salvation.

In many ways, Henri IV's catechism served as a guidebook of what constituted his kingly *devoir* and that of his subjects. Loyalist Catholics consistently asserted that Huguenots and Leaguers alike undermined the religious bases of political obligation by their rebellions. As a result, they often took an opportunity in Henri IV's catechism to define the responsible exercise of absolute authority by the king and the subject's corresponding moral commitment to uphold it. One work examining Protestant charges of Catholic idolatry, for instance, assured the king that the veneration of saints was the religious equivalent of honoring one's social superiors.[57] Both types of behavior sought the intercession of higher powers, one social and the other supernatural. The author fully expected Henri IV to appreciate the significance of this relationship. The Catholic argument for apostolic succession found in many pleas to Henri IV to convert admirably illustrates this conjunction between controversialist argument and political theory in the debates about the king's heresy. The Protestant claim that the abuses encrusting the Catholic Church signified a break from the pristine practices of the primitive Church failed to consider certain proofs of the Church's continuity through time, loyalist Catholics argued. For them, the institution of apostolic succession, that unbroken chain linking today's prelates with Christ's Apostles, more than confirmed the historical identity between the present and the primitive Church. Catholic apologists often corroborated this assertion by drawing an analogy between it and France's enduring identity through royal succession since the time of Pharamond—an argument that dovetailed nicely with Henri IV's own worries about Leaguer objections to his right to the throne.[58]

This theme of continuity through time often set the stage for loyalist Catholic attacks on Protestant ideas about the nature of legitimate authority. Whence do Calvinist ministers derive their authority to interpret Scripture and the teachings of the Fathers, they queried. Certainly not through apostolic succession, which besides forming an organic link with the past, also represented the visible conferral of pastoral office and the authority that came with it. Without this sanction, loyalists argued, the biblical interpretations forwarded by Calvinist ministers were no more than the personal opinions of fallible men to be rejected by the believer seeking divine truth. The legitimacy that clergymen derived from ordination, they continued, resembled that which Henri IV received by virtue of Salic Law.[59] The lesson for Henri IV, and other Huguenots as well, was that authority was legitimate insofar as its assumption conformed to traditional practices and procedures. In loyalist opinion, both the Catholic Church and the monarchy had a vested interest in maintaining this procedural definition of legitimate authority; the Church in order to combat the Protestants' more individualistic approach to the question of interpretative authority, the French monarchy in order to refute the elective theories of kingship advanced by the League after 1589. Thus, for loyalist Catholics, Henri IV's claim by the Salic Law complemented the Church's laws of episcopal succession and ordination. Moreover, his awaited return to the Church satisfied the equally pressing Law of Catholicity, thereby fulfilling all the conditions for his undisputed title to the crown.

Another lesson in the king's catechism taught that the abuses in the Church, while of serious concern, were not sufficient grounds for leaving it. The heresy of the Protestants was not that they sought reform, but that they sought it outside the Church, thus rending the sacred tissue of Christian unity. The inevitable result, in loyalist Catholics' opinion, was dissension and revolt. Pointing to sectarian divisions within the Reformed movement, loyalist Catholics rejected as specious the Protestant claim that it restored the unity of Christ's teachings. The misguided political principles of the Leaguers made them guilty of such fractious behavior as well. For loyalist Catholics, the enduring order born from unity, from the oneness implied in the formula *un roi, une loi, une foi,* could only be regained by Henri IV's and the dissidents' return to the universal Church.[60] Loyalist writers nevertheless readily admitted the need for Church reform in their pleas to the king to convert. Abuses were inevitable given the general tendency of all things—laws, institutions, and people—to degenerate over time, they argued. Renewal hinged on a return to the Church's basic principles of unity and legitimate authority. Without them, this decadence only accelerated and risked becoming irreversible. Catholics in late sixteenth-century France believed that the abuses in the Church and society at large had their roots in corrupted human nature. Personal sin created the conditions in which heresy flourished because it made individuals more prideful and, thus, more apt to flout the Church and king. Henri IV's Catholic supporters made it clear that heresy could only be extirpated from the Church and France once every individual had expelled sin from his or her heart. As in all affairs, the king had to lead the way for his subjects by a sincere conversion to Catholicism.[61]

Loyalist Catholics, and eventually many Leaguers as well, thus came to see Protestantism more as a symptom than a cause of the evils that assailed France. In this way, loyalist Catholics related Henri IV's confessional choice not only to Leaguer radicalism, but also to what they considered to be the origins and nature of Protestantism. Their policy of *douceur* toward the errant Henri IV recast Catholic strategies to undo the Reformation, at least in France, by predicating them on a self-examination by Catholics of their own relationship with God and commitment to the monarchy. A new evangelical fervor slowly replaced the force of arms as the war against Calvinism eventually became in the early seventeenth century one of political isolation, designed to recapture the machinery of local government through a well-organized and well-financed propaganda campaign to make Catholicism more attractive. Henri IV's conversion in 1593 resulted from this broader reorientation of Catholic activism at the end of the sixteenth century.

Loyalist Catholics tried in these ways to create an impression of the king that rendered him more favorably disposed to Catholic objections to his professed faith, while still maintaining in principle the respectful obedience due him as king. In effect, they attacked Protestant theology but not the king's right to believe in it. The king's catechism also distinguished its message from the League's by emphasizing the compatibility between Catholicism and obedience to a monarch who fully intended to be shown his errors. This important reinterpretation of the subject's duty furnished loyalist Catholics with a way to reconcile their commitment to the monarchy with their equally strong allegiance to Catholicism. Catholic allegiance to Henri IV demanded active participation in the conversion process through prayer, gentle admonition, and pious example.[62] Although couched in terms of controversialist argument and royal service, these open appeals to Henri IV to convert generated over time subtle pressures on him that attested to the growing impatience of his Catholic supporters for a settlement of the crisis. The constant agitation by loyalist Catholics after 1589—in print and in plots—reminded Henri IV that he could never take their support for granted. Just as Henri IV could not be forced to believe against his conscience, so Catholics could not be constrained to obey forever a heretical king. Loyalist Catholics considered the king's conversion essential for the establishment of civil harmony and the lasting moral order upon which the future glory of France and the Catholic Church depended. In the end, they obeyed Henri IV in order to convert him to this vision of religious and political renewal, to what Frances Yates has called "the grand enterprise of the Gallic Hercules."[63]

4

Piety and Politics

THE ISSUE OF Henri IV's faith sparked such bitter divisions among French Catholic elites because it brought into question their social status, political rights, and personal faith. The ensuing struggle to find a way to reconcile loyalty to the throne with the dictates of religion forced members of the nobility, the clergy, and royal officialdom to define where they stood in the ruling establishment and why. Debates over the polity—both civil and spiritual—made it imperative for Catholic elites to become involved in the contest over the king's conversion. Political action thus became allied with a thorough reevaluation of the country's social makeup and its relationship with royal authority.

Much of the debate naturally revolved around religion. Catholics on both sides often appealed to a deep sense of sacred community, by which they meant not merely membership in the institutional Church, but membership in the mystical body of all believers, or *corpus fidelium*. The Leaguers considered membership in God's Church synonymous with adherence to the Sainte Union, outside which there was neither political nor religious salvation. For the Leaguers, this "small number of true Catholics who keep faith with our Savior" represented the regenerated part of the Catholic Church, a lone bastion of religious purity in a world where the forces of evil ran rampant.[1] Individual and public salvation became linked through combined political action against Navarre, not passive acceptance of him as counseled by those *mauvais catholiques,* the loyalists. Loyalist Catholics often took the League to task for this scandalous identification of itself with the true Church, claiming that Leaguer priests frequently withheld the sacraments from those with whom they differed politically.[2] These mutual recriminations formed part of a larger campaign by all sides to win public support by presenting themselves as the true community of God's elect.

This lively search for a religious sanction for partisan action was closely allied with an intense debate over what it meant to be a *bon françois catholique*. Civic identity and obligations as well as the historical traditions which nourished them retained a strong religious component during this period. Leaguers and loyalist Catholics, for example, both acknowledged the sacred nature of French kingship and God's providential relationship with the French people throughout history.[3] This image of the perfect Frenchman faithful to the Church and loyal to the monarchy of course broke down as a result of Henri IV's accession in 1589. In the course of this debate, Frenchmen from all walks of life slowly redefined and then reaffirmed what they thought to be the traditional order of a society shattered by decades of domestic strife. They did so in ways that worked not only to strengthen, but to change the social order and their individual commitments to the monarchy once Henri IV redeemed it by his conversion in 1593. The conversion crisis as well as the dynamism of early Bourbon absolutism sprang from the fact that the issue of Henri IV's faith involved both the search for personal salvation and the search for civic identity, the two faces of what contemporaries called the *bon françois catholique*.

The Catholic Nobility

The bitter conflict over Henri IV's faith at the end of the sixteenth century created a crisis of allegiance for members of the Catholic nobility unique in the history of early modern France. Although noble fortunes perhaps suffered less during the Wars of Religion than was previously suspected, such relative financial security hardly made Henri IV's heresy any less frightening to the second estate.[4] The Protestant succession affected Catholic noblemen deeply because many of their privileges and rights derived from their relationship with the *roi très chrétien*. Though often overlooked, religious considerations also played a role in shaping aristocratic allegiance, especially as revealed during the nobility's active involvement in the Catholic devotional revival that swept through France early in the next century. The struggle over Henri IV's faith thus became of paramount concern for Catholic nobles as they searched for a way to remain loyal to throne and altar.

Political observers generally agreed that victory for the loyalists who supported Henri IV or the Leaguers who opposed him depended on which of the two gained the most support from the Catholic nobility. The French nobility provided a huge pool of trained officers and cavalry companies that were militarily indispensable in the fluctuating fortunes of civil war. The lure of titles, offices, and money which leaders on both sides dangled before the nobility meant little, however, if these rewards in any way compromised the nobleman's acute sense of honor. Material advantage sealed rather than initiated such pacts; *amitié* had first to be exchanged, then lucre. The campaign to win the hearts and arms of the Catholic nobility unfolded publicly in print and informally through letters as each side strove to convince men of the sword that their duty lay in upholding the true cause. The struggle over aristocratic support during the French Wars of Religion transformed the Renaissance debate over the nature of nobility from a scholarly exercise in rhetoric into an unabashed attempt to mold public opinion.[5] Writers alternately poured scorn, or heaped praise, on the nobility as the occasion demanded. They hoped to win the nobles' allegiance, if not by appealing to their sense of honor, then by shaming them.

The response of Catholic noblemen to the polemic over Henri IV's faith raises interesting questions about the impact of the printed word on the *mentalité* of the noblemen in the early modern period. Few men of the sword had ever considered it a mark of distinction to disdain literature and the arts; what they scorned was not knowledge, but pedantry. As patrons and collectors, noblemen had from the start helped to shape the French Renaissance, using their tastes and wealth first to acquire, then to display artifacts generated by the new culture to enhance their prestige. Some noblemen even tried their hand at poetry, prose, and technical manuals, often to critical acclaim.[6] Noblemen not only helped to create Renaissance culture; they also hungered after news, to judge from their correspondence during the 1580s and 1590s. Published accounts of military engagements and campaigns, the closest thing to newspapers at the time, mixed reports of the noblemen's courage with details about weapons and strategy that seemed especially suited to an aristocratic audience. Such information not only helped noblemen to justify siding with one of the parties, but also gave those who remained uncommitted an opportunity to gauge their neutrality as the struggle progressed. Withdrawal from public affairs was, after all, as much a political act as involvement. No less important than this deep interest in culture and politics was the Catholic nobility's growing willingness to sponsor religious reform and charitable works. All these activities shaped the nobleman's sense of identity and provided ways to broadcast it to society at large.

A brief perusal of pamphlets published during the Wars of Religion reveals that a remarkable number were addressed specifically to readers from the nobility. Prefaces and accompanying verse often extolled individual *grands,* whereas treatises and essays examined the issues of the day in light of what it meant to be aristocratic.[7] Noblemen, at least during the early wars, responded eagerly to the call to defend the true cause, be it Calvinist or Catholic. Provincial governors drew strength from this flood of noblemen into the political arena, organizing them in ways that increased their regional power.[8] Attempts by the Valois to discipline the *grands* and their armed followers often resulted in concessions that gave the *grands* even greater control over local military affairs and revenue sources. Henri III tried to reassert royal authority in the provinces by raising favorites, such as Épernon, Joyeuse, and François d'O, to *duché-pairies* and governorships, but to no avail. These new potentates often became as unruly as the older established lines, and provoked great public resentment against a king whose death many Catholics pointed to as a judgment of God.[9]

Clientele groups, particularly Catholic ones, proved to be highly unstable creations which the *grands* sometimes found difficult to manage. Some followers from the nobility drifted into other camps or struck out on their own; others, known as *casaniers,* preferred simply to stay home. It seemed that many middling noblemen suffered as a result of the capricious behavior and ambitions of *grands,* from whom they had hoped to gain money, lands, and privileges.[10] By the late 1580s, pamphleteers on both sides had to work hard to rally the noblemen's enthusiasm for the true cause; even *grands* such as the Duc de Nevers took to print in an effort to revive their precarious leadership. The struggle after 1589 over the noblemen's allegiance helped in the end to redefine the nobility's place in French society and its relationship not only with the *grands,* but with the new Bourbon regime.[11]

The loyalist case for the noblemen's support of the Protestant Henri IV naturally emphasized the nobility's traditional association with the crown. Supporters of Navarre contended that the nobility's exalted place in French society had originated and remained rooted in its service to the king. The privileges and rights that formed the essence of the nobility were the just reward for the noblemen's previous defense of the French throne. Moreover, the nobility only existed because of the king's right to elevate worthy persons above the common lot; without a king, the nobility as a concept—let alone a social order—simply could not exist. Loyalist writers found it easy to argue that noblemen who supported the League broke their oath to the crown, particularly after the Cardinal de Bourbon's death on May 7, 1590. No excuse, not even religion, could absolve the nobleman of his duty to France's "légitime et naturel" king—a duty which Henri IV generously recompensed, loyalists added.[12] Noblemen should realize that the demise of the monarchy entailed their own destruction, for noble status, although a birthright, attained its highest expression in service to the king.[13]

Such arguments that the nobility existed, however gloriously, only as a function of monarchy probably unnerved many noblemen who prized their independence from royal authority. It also paid scant regard to ideas about the mystique of the nobleman's *sang*—a favorite topic in aristocratic circles at the time.[14] A more effective way to enlist aristocratic support for Henri IV was to portray the League's defiance of him as a veiled attack against the nobility. For loyalists, the League manifested those dreadful contagions of avarice and ambition endemic in an unredeemed humanity. Loyalists either disregarded noblemen who were League adherents or scorned them as a perverted minority of an otherwise virtuous aristocracy, a "basse partie" seduced by Spanish doubloons and the Lorrainers' supposed desire to usurp the throne.[15] League apologists often had to wage an uphill battle to controvert this damaging portrayal. Urban radicals, such as the Seize in Paris, made it even more difficult for Mayenne and other League *grands* to win more aristocratic support in the fight against Navarre.

Whereas loyalists vilified the League as a social threat from below, Leaguers often attacked the noblemen who opposed them for their affiliation with the court, a place where they believed immorality and disbelief reigned supreme. They echoed the tirades of the 1580s against Henri III's *mignons,* lampooning Navarre's aristocratic supporters as "traitors to God, totally devoid of all virtue."[16] The reign of the heretical Béarnais seemed to many Catholics but a repeat of the vicious rule of his predecessor, the *vilain hérode.* Leaguers championed a radically different image of the ideal aristocrat, for whom the question of religion formed a *point de noblesse* that made resistance praiseworthy, not shameful. As Jehan de Caumont bluntly put it in 1585, "heresy and nobility are incompatible."[17] According to Michel du Rit, another well-known League publicist, the first mark of a true nobleman was the integrity of his faith in God, which in turn shaped his loyalty to caste and kingdom. A nobleman's personal honor consisted in how well he maintained his fidelity to God, without which his pursuit of glory became nothing more than conceit.[18]

For Leaguers, the bedrock of social order lay in service to God; loyalty to the king depended on how well he fulfilled the official duties entrusted to him by God. As they saw it, Henri de Navarre broke this trust by refusing to abjure heresy. Catholic noblemen therefore had to oppose him because the obligations each assumed as a Christian at baptism superseded all other promises, including the one to serve the king. Past crusades against the infidels in the East and the heretics at home attested to the nobility's historical role as *milites christiani.* The aims of the Holy League coincided with those of the Church and France, the noted Leaguer publicist Matthieu de Launoy concluded in an attempt to reassure wavering noblemen that piety and justice lay with the party of God, not Calvin.[19]

The connection that Leaguers made between personal piety and public duty appealed strongly to the nobility's desire to reclaim more political autonomy. Rather than dissolving the nobility's historical bonds to the throne, Navarre's heresy prompted Leaguers to urge men of the sword to redefine loyalty to the king within the prior framework of unalterable divine law. From this perspective, Navarre's heresy released them from their otherwise firm duty to serve the crown because his evil beliefs undermined the moral bases of French society. In fact, Leaguers thought the nobility's duty now demanded that it save the monarchy from the unfit pretender, thus making opposition to Henri IV the highest expression of the nobleman's loyalty to the crown. In their struggle to win the support of the Catholic nobility, writers on both sides laid claim to the idealized Frenchman who was loyal to both throne and altar.

How noblemen responded to this debate over their place in French society is difficult to measure. Although recent investigators have described in detail the clientele networks that made men of the sword a political force in the provinces and at court, they have either left unexplained or construed as cynical the ways in which noblemen justified their often fractious behavior.[20] The rewards and favors which *grands* exchanged with lesser nobles, and then with other social groups through clientage, cannot be considered apart from the ideas and values that gave the bonds of *amitié* meaning to them. This linkage was especially apparent during the struggle over Henri IV's religion. Aristocrats saw leadership not just as a matter of money and preferments, but also as a function of moral credibility. Loyalist *grands,* such as the Duc de Nevers, tried after 1589 to balance concerns about conscience and reputation with service to the Protestant king; the Tiers Parti conspiracy, which arose after 1590 among those of Navarre's Catholic supporters who threatened to join the opposition should the king remain a Calvinist, revealed that many loyalists were deeply ambivalent about Henri IV until his conversion in 1593.[21] Leaguer *grands,* by contrast, resisted in the name of the traditional monarchy; they found repugnant, however, the idea that urban notables could also share in the ennobling character of opposition to Henri IV. Writers on both sides therefore had good reason to question the depth of the aristocrats allegiance to their respective causes. Catholic noblemen eventually recognized Henri IV not primarily as their king, but as one of their own. Biron's execution in 1603 for plotting against the crown, along with prohibitions against dueling, in time helped to shatter that illusion.[22] In the end, however much jurists argued that the king commanded and subjects obeyed, noblemen held fast to the conviction that loyalty even to an absolute monarch preserved rather than compromised aristocratic honor and independence.

The Catholic Clergy

French clergymen also found the integrity of their persons and offices wrapped up in the question of whether to support the Protestant Henri IV. The dispute over the royal succession cut across the ranks of the first estate much as it had the Catholic nobility. Prelates bitterly castigated their rivals in the other party, while further down the ecclesiastical hierarchy, preachers battled one another in pulpits across France.[23] The regular clergy also became caught up in the conflict, with the newer orders, such as the Jesuits and the mendicants, generally siding with the League, whereas the older congregations, such as the Benedictines, usually opted for the loyalist cause.[24] Concentrating on the images of the popular League preacher and the *politique* prelate sheds little light on why the conversion question created such a painful dilemma for the entire French clergy, because these stereotypes often existed more vividly in polemical literature than in political reality.

The war of words over Henri IV's faith showed that contemporaries thought it necessary for religious justification to precede political commitment. Indeed, in the late sixteenth century, politics often seemed to be but a branch of theology when openly discussed. As interpreters of God's will, clergymen stood ready to provide the guidance and authority many believed necessary to vindicate the otherwise partisan struggle. The search for moral legitimacy frequently involved discussions dating back to the 1570s over Church reform and acceptance of the Tridentine decrees. This growing activism throughout the French church, though at times discouraged by the crown, represented an attempt by its members to reassert their traditional leadership over lay society after the inroads made by Calvinism.

Loyalist clergymen had made it clear from the start that Henri IV could not take their support for granted. In September 1589, Adam de Hurtelou, bishop of Mende, invoked the memory of Henri III when he begged Navarre to emulate the late king's piety by converting to Catholicism.[25] In a later letter apprising Henri IV of his efforts to fortify strategic towns in his diocese, Hurtelou closed with the promise to continue his loyal service and "mes dévotes prières" for the king's conversion.[26] Another bishop, Jacques Maury, questioned Henri IV's promise to protect the Catholic Church by pointing to the situation in Bayonne—a place where the Huguenots had apparently made some gains.[27] In late August 1589, Arnauld Sorbin, bishop of Nevers, assured the king that his recent meeting with Leaguers in no way jeopardized his service to the crown. Any reservations he had about Henri IV stemmed from his fear that heretics might soon claim access to Church property in his see.[28] As the deadline for the king's promised Catholic instruction approached in early 1590, Antoine Prévost de Sansac, archbishop of Bordeaux, chided Henri IV for not opening his "mind to the inspiration of the Holy Spirit." All good Frenchmen prayed daily for the king to convert, the prelate went on, though "God only inspires those who receive him without hesitation." Should these loyal servants despair about the king's willingness to convert, he warned, their concern for his welfare could come to an end.[29] Gallican prelates endorsed Henri IV because they believed him ready to entrust to them the direction of his conscience.

Early hopes for the king's conversion raised by the Declaration of St. Cloud were dashed by the spring of 1590, however. As a result, loyalist clergymen had to redefine past notions about clerical office and duty to justify continued support of a heretical king. For Claude d'Angennes de Rambouillet, bishop of Le Mans and a key adviser to Henri IV, clerical involvement in trying to end the war, although necessary, could go no further than pious example, prayer, and the Word of God. "These alone are a bishop's weapons," he wrote.[30] A godly peace required clergymen to abstain from any activity that ran counter to the principles of Christian charity and humility. In d'Angennes's opinion, the necessary separation between *sacerdotium* and *justicium* became blurred when clerics carried arms or meted out corporal punishment, thus intruding upon the authority that God gave lay judges over Christian society. Clergymen who violated the boundary between the spiritual and temporal spheres denigrated the dignity of the holy office entrusted to them by Christ.[31] The clergy's mission to save souls hinged on the believer's voluntary submission to the will of God and the doctrines of the Church; coercion, in contrast, only compounded the evils of error and heresy. D'Angennes's rejection of physical force in spiritual matters hardly meant freedom of conscience, however. On the contrary, it reflected the loyalist clergy's deep faith in the efficacy of Catholic instruction and the wondrous workings of divine grace. League preachers showed how little regard they had for their vocation and God's infinite mercy by their impious advocacy of violent remedies adopted from a corrupted world. The way to attain Christ's kingdom began by focusing not on the things of this world, but on those of heaven, loyalist clergymen often observed. In their opinion, clerics fulfilled the pastoral obligations of their office by pursuing the king's conversion along the path of gentle admonition and pious example, not armed rebellion.[32] Although the clergy had to refuse to abet tyranny or irreligion, it also had to forswear opposition to the prince lest such resistance provoke the wrath of God. It was better to follow Augustine's advice to flee or endure misfortune, not violently combat it, until such time as God changed the situation. In the end, gentle admonition and pious example offered the clergy a way to reconcile the need to respect temporal authority and to resist evil, to remain both *vrai catholique* and *bon françois*.[33]

Loyalist clergymen employed a well-worn rhetoric of suffering to interpret earthly misfortunes, such as the accession of a heretical king, as God's righteous punishment of the chosen for their sins. Catholic obedience to the errant prince in effect transfered the causes of such calamities to the subject's own peccant nature. True believers had to realize that their suffering was but God's way of communicating His love to them, for God only punished His children to make them more godly. Patient endurance and complete trust in God's mercy, later earmarks of Christian stoicism, sanctified Catholic obedience to the Protestant Henri IV because collective sin and its consequences could be expiated only through public prayers and processions, through collective penance and good works.[34] And no greater work existed for loyalist clergymen than the conversion of Henri IV. Thus, the moral messages loyalist clergymen advanced in support of Henri IV internalized the causes of the conflict in such a manner that the king's conversion hinged on the moral regeneration of his Catholic subjects. A Christian peace in society required all believers to be first at peace in their hearts.

The arguments loyalist clergymen used in support of Henri IV were put to the test in 1591 when Pope Gregory XIV excommunicated the king anew along with his Catholic followers. Sensitive to charges that they fomented schism and aided the spread of heresy, loyalist clergymen tried in September 1591, at the Assembly of Clergy in Chartres, to strike a middle way between their spiritual allegiance to Rome and their loyalty to Henri IV. Their task was not made any easier by Gallican judges, such as Antoine Séguier and Achille de Harlay, who claimed the right to adjudicate such affairs affecting the king's domain, or by Huguenots who construed the prelates' efforts to reconcile allegiance to Rome with support of the king as ambivalent and therefore untrustworthy.[35] After lengthy deliberations, the Assembly rejected the pope's bulls as contrary to the liberties of the Gallican church. The prelates argued that the crown's immunity to papal censure also extended to its royal officers. In this way, the Assembly tried to safeguard not only the questionable authority of the king, but also the leadership which loyalists at court provided during the conversion crisis.[36] The Assembly refused, however, to blame the pope for his actions, unlike the Parlement of Tours which had earlier in August declared the pontiff an enemy of the crown.[37] The prelates instead shifted responsibility for the bulls to the "ennemis de cest Estat," that is, the Leaguers and Spain, who they believed had prejudiced the Holy Father against Henri IV and his Catholic supporters. They tried to assure the pope that their nullification of the bulls in no way detracted from the honor and reverence all French Catholics owed him as the Vicar of Christ. Addressing the Catholics of France, the prelates urged "the weakest" among them to return to "their duty towards the king and the bishops by giving up their scruples of conscience."[38] In their eyes, disobedience to the king constituted infidelity to God's pastors—a crime, they pointed out, not far removed from heresy.

These reinterpretations of the Church's punitive powers further illustrate the loyalist Catholic tendency to regard moral questions in terms of individual conscience, which in turn informed the larger institutional and legal matrix of relationships governing society. Loyalist clergymen hardly abdicated their sacerdotal duty to chastise the sinful; they instead reaffirmed that true moral reform in France could only begin with the sinner's awareness of personal iniquity.[39] Catholic confessional practice in the late sixteenth century had slowly come to appreciate the psychological importance of Luther's emphasis on justification by faith, though of course not faith alone. In fact, the later Jansenist controversy over the nature of sacramental penance can be traced back to these disputes over the inner workings of religious belief and renewal during the Wars of Religion.[40]

Henri IV's clerical supporters worked hard to demonstrate the compatibility between their commitment to the Protestant king and their sacerdotal vocation. Only through the spiritual attributes of priestly office, they argued, could clergymen resist the king's heresy. This active yet pacific involvement in the king's conversion enabled loyalist clergymen to satisy both their sacred duty to combat evil and their civil obligation to respect monarchical authority. Moreover, any French Catholic could participate in the king's conversion if he followed the loyalist clergy's example of gentle admonition and prayer. The laity had but to repent for its sins in order to become an instrument of righteousness. After all, France's common misery stemmed from its people's common depravity, particularly the mortal sin of rebellion against divine authority as represented by the king on earth. The conversion of Henri IV therefore hinged on the collective reconversion of all Catholics to the eternal verities in the Gospels as interpreted by the clerical *fidèles au roy*.

Apologists for Henri IV's clerical supporters frequently contrasted this portrait of the ideal priest with another of League preachers, who they saw as false prophets leading the people to perdition by inciting them to rebel against God and the king. Critics of the League usually minimized the actual extent of episcopal involvement in it, preferring instead to view the League as a faction controlled by demagogic preachers who flagrantly disregarded their bishops' authority. Although overstated, there was some truth in the charge that preachers in Paris and other League cities wielded inordinate influence as policy-makers and military leaders. Some Leaguer prelates, in fact, found their authority compromised by influential clerics from the lower rungs of the Church hierarchy. In March 1591, for example, Jean de l'Aubespine, bishop of Orléans, complained to the legate-cardinal of Piacenza that his diocese was infested with rowdy preachers who contravened his injunctions forbidding unauthorized sermons. The city fathers also shared his alarm.[41] The city's governor, La Châtre, reiterated the bishop's request that the legate restore discipline because these unregulated sermons prejudiced his position as well.[42] Historians should not thereby assume, as many League preachers did, that all Leaguer prelates were actually secret *politiques*, however. What they need to do is to reassess the nature of episcopal opposition to the Protestant Henri IV.

The debate over clerical identity that often exploded in direct exchanges between prelates from both sides offers one way to begin such a reassessment. In February 1590, for example, the Cardinals de Vendôme and de Lenoncourt invited a number of Leaguer prelates to Tours for Henri IV's instruction. Although the meeting never took place, its mere suggestion elicited spirited responses from Leaguer clergymen who received the cardinals' invitation.[43] Arnauld Hennequin, the bishop of Rennes and a member of the Conseil de l'Union, angrily denounced the cardinals' insinuation that a refusal to attend the forthcoming assembly meant that he had no concern for the public good. He needed no lessons in civic duty from the prelates in Tours, offering his long years of service to the crown as a member of two Estates General and innumerable stints in the Breton provincial estates as proof of his devotion to the public weal.[44] He considered it his duty as a Frenchmen to accept recent edicts by the Parlement of Paris inaugurating the imprisoned Cardinal de Bourbon's reign as Charles X.[45] Hennequin also questioned whether Navarre truly sought spiritual enlightenment or merely pretended to do so to divide the Catholics. Under the circumstances, he thought it best to follow the pope's lead by resisting the heretical Béarnais. Another Leaguer prelate, François de Bouliers, bishop of Fréjus, rejoiced with the cardinals at the prospect of Navarre's speedy return to Mother Church, yet expressed concern lest it not "arise from the heart."[46] By no means did loyalist Catholics have a monopoly on interest in indwelling faith. Pierre d'Épinac, the archbishop of Lyons and another member of the Conseil de l'Union, swore before God that his only intention throughout the conflict had been to defend the traditional character of the throne as a *bon françois catholique*—a title that loyalist Catholics brazenly arrogated to themselves. He parried loyalist Catholic criticisms of the League's radicalism by presenting it as a bulwark of traditional French society. Ruled by a Catholic king who suffered cruelly at the hands of his enemies, the League existed solely to uphold the laws and institutions of the realm, Épinac insisted. Joined with him in this "Saincte Intention" to fight heresy were most prelates and nobles, nearly every Parlement, and "all the major cities of the realm."[47] Épinac's exaggerations aside, he made it clear that he believed all good Catholics had to resist Navarre's depredations against the Church until God moved him to see the light.

The papacy's near consistent support of Leaguer resistance furnished ample grounds for denouncing Henri IV's clerical allies as schismatics and abettors of heresy.[48] And loyalist clergymen did not take these charges lightly, as evidenced in the 1591 Assembly of Chartres. In 1589, Jean Boucher asserted that excommunicated clergymen could not exercise their priestly duties—a position Gregory XIV affirmed in 1591 when he banished Navarre's Catholic supporters from the Church.[49] Claims by the loyalist Assembly of Chartres that the pope had been misinformed undermined the pontiff's sacred obligation to combat the Church's enemies, another Leaguer wrote. Rather than converting heretics, those renegade pastors sought only to hoodwink the Catholics. "By what right do they think these words of the Apostle belong solely to them?" the author pointedly asked, adding that the pope intended by his bull merely to instruct Navarre's Catholic supporters "with all kindness to abandon the party of an obstinate heretic whose relapse earned him excommunication." [50]

Less conciliatory Leaguers often considered Henri IV's clerical allies to be frocked courtiers who trafficked in God's Word. They saw the royal court as a source of the moral iniquity and corruption that plagued French society; many believed that clergymen who resided there refused to denounce evil or even actively encouraged it lest they lose favor with the crown. The mundane pursuits that clergymen had long indulged in at Valois court now represented a form of clerical culture many Leaguers regarded as impious. For them, the court cleric was "a gilded hypocrite, devout only in appearance" who served only to satisfy the perverse pleasures of courtiers and the king.[51] Serious efforts to ameliorate this damning portrayal of court life had to wait until the next century and the rather prudish reigns of Louis XIII and Louis XIV.[52]

In the world of print, where these political nuances were often ignored in order to maximize the social and moral nature of the conflict, many writers construed these divisions among the French clergy as part of the ongoing rivalry between the episcopacy and the lower clergy. For loyalist Catholics, Henri IV's clerical supporters always represented the most healthy *(saine)* segment of the Gallican church, namely the prelacy. In contrast, they characterized Leaguer clergymen as lowly preachers and monks sponsored by foreign powers. They stigmatized the Jesuits in particular, regarding them as Spanish agents, promoters of the Inquisition, and regicidal maniacs bent on destroying the French monarchy. The highly visible role that preachers played in the urban League helped to substantiate charges that they disobeyed their superiors and manipulated the credulous populace. This does not mean, however, that the League lacked sympathizers in the French episcopacy. For their part, the Leaguers portrayed the king's ecclesiastical supporters as the embodiment of every imaginable clerical abuse. As they saw it, these *politique* priests put their loyalty to the monarchy before their allegiance to God. As a result, the apostolic mission of the Church necessarily devolved to those clergymen, whether prelates or preachers, who remained true to the Holy Father in Rome.

Two markedly different interpretations of the relationship between church and monarchy governed these divisions among French Catholics. Loyalists saw a creative partnership between throne and altar, one that endowed each with sacred, yet autonomous, missions in the establishment of God's kingdom on earth. The sanctity of the temporal sword—a basic tenet of Gallicanism—gave loyalist Catholics a foil with which to defend the religious integrity of civil society. Although jeopardized by Henri IV's heresy, this religious integrity could in the end only be maintained if the king's conversion originated in the collective conscience of the community and the soul of the sinner. In this way, the conversion of Henri IV represented for loyalist Catholics the ultimate vindication of civil society's sacred character. In contrast, the League perceived a more antagonistic relationship between church and monarchy, one in which the Church oversaw the crown's adherence to the divine purposes for which it had been created. For Leaguers, the religious integrity of civil society could be reestablished only after the court was purged of all vice and returned to its sacred mission of advancing the faith. The first step along this road to renewal was for Henri IV to be replaced by a more suitable Catholic king. In this way, the controversy over Henri IV's susceptibility to conversion formed part of a larger effort to redefine the peculiar identity of French Catholicism, so battered after years of domestic strife and the challenges of Protestant and Tridentine reform. Although this new identity took discernible shape only during the Catholic devotional revival of the seventeenth century, the search for it began at the height of the struggle over the conversion of Henri IV.

The Catholic Judges

No study has yet explained why so many members of the magistracy, long the most vocal proponents of monarchical authority, decided in the late 1580s to come out so vehemently against Henri III and Henri IV. The discontent in the royal courts that exploded in 1589 into open division arose from a variety of factors: the bankruptcy of the crown's policies toward heresy, particularly its controversial use of judicial offices as bargaining chips with the Huguenots (the famous *chambres mi-parties*); encroachments by the Conseil du Roi in areas previously reserved to the sovereign courts; the judges' own anti-court sentiments and moral repugnance at Henri III's excesses; the Parlements' self-styled role as champions of the Gallican church and the laws of the realm; and the repeated violation of these laws by the king's ministers.[53] Already in 1563, judges in the Parlement of Rouen had justified their opposition to a royal *lit de justice* on the grounds of conscience—a maneuver that became typical during the years ahead.[54] As in the cases of the Catholic nobility and clergy, questions of conscience became inextricably bound up in the magistrates' conception of their office and official responsibilities, as well as the special problems they faced in the governing structure.

Parlementaire sentiment for the League grew at a time when only Huguenots and Catholic *mécontents* seriously questioned the League's royalist character. Criticism from such groups probably enhanced the League's credibility as a viable alternative for disaffected French Catholics prior to 1589, especially for judges who valiantly worked to uphold the monarchy and the church. When this image of the League broke down at the Estates General of Blois, the judges had to try to recast their political allegiances yet maintain corporate unity. The Guise assassinations so polarized public opinion that this task became impossible, however. The League rebellion in early 1589 against Henri III eventually provoked a split in the courts, with many judges declaring for the League while others stood by the king. In a desperate effort to bolster his authority, Henri III transfered the Parlements, Chambres de Comptes, and Cours des Aides from areas infected with sedition to those still under his control in March 1589. This move forced judges who still wavered either to follow the king into "exile" or to remain at their posts.

Most judges chose to remain at their posts in cities taken over by the League, not because they harbored deep sympathy for Catholic militancy, but because they believed such steadfastness better enabled them to stand above the partisan struggle and act as a restraint on League radicalism.[55] As a result, the reconstituted Parlements loyal to Henri III at first attracted only a handful of judges, and those often by default. Achille de Harlay, for example, joined the king in Tours in July 1589 only after he had been forcibly ousted from the Parlement of Paris. The Parlement of Tours garnered only eleven members from the Parisian court as of April 1589, whereas the Parlement of Caen, transfered from Rouen, saw only ten judges initially respond to the king's call. An even more abysmal situation existed in Carcassonne, where the reconstituted Parlement of Toulouse at first attracted only one councillor.[56]

In the end, only the Parlement of Bordeaux remained relatively intact, yet in many ways it was the exception that proved the rule. Henri IV's Declaration of St. Cloud only temporarily allayed the unease of the Bordelais judges about a heretical succession. In fact, their recognition of Henri IV came mainly as a result of the threat by the provincial governor Matignon to send troops into the court to force their compliance. A set of instructions composed in January 1590 for the Parlement's emissaries to the royal court made it clear that continued recognition of Henri IV as king depended on positive signs of his willingness to go through with the conversion. The envoys' report to the king revealed the calculated ambiguity of the royal court's acknowledgment of Henri IV as a king whose legitimacy had yet to be fully established. A majority of the judges had apparently advised the law court to defer recognition until after the king's conversion, though eventually the magistrates decided to support Henri IV's claim to the throne.[57] The Parlement of Bordeaux let it be understood that although it remained committed to the traditional forms of French monarchical government, the burden of restoring them to their original purity rested on Henri IV. Matignon had initially construed the Parlement's reluctance to acknowledge Henri IV as part of a plot to join the widening rebellion.[58] In another light, however, the judges' reservations stemmed from their fear of the violent unrest that could follow a heretical succession. Some magistrates worried that acceptance of a Protestant king violated the oath they had made to Henri III at the Estates General of Blois to fight heresy.[59] The judges thus hoped to maintain pressure on Henri IV to fulfill his promise to seek Catholic instruction while justifying to the public their decision to obey him. It was a stance that gave Henri IV very little room within which to maneuver.

Although membership in the loyalist courts grew at a varied pace over the next few years, loyalists managed to achieve only rough parity with the Leaguer courts by the time of Henri IV's conversion in July 1593. In the meantime, loyalist Parlements vied with their

Leaguer rivals for the title of *cour souveraine* and the aura of legitimacy that came with it. Mayenne, for example, received an enormous political boost in late 1589 when the Parlement of Paris renewed his position as "lieutenant général de la couronne et de l'estat de France" while the Leaguer king, Charles X, remained imprisoned. The Parlement later established the duke as regent during the interregnum it declared following the Cardinal de Bourbon's untimely death in May 1590.[60] The Parlement of Tours solemnly nullified these decrees, thus eliciting its own condemnation from Paris, as the campaign for *parlementaire* authority quickly degenerated into a volley of mutual recrimination that lasted until the end of the war.

This fratricidal struggle sometimes went beyond accusations of treason and injustice hurled back and forth between the judges. Loyalist *parlementaires* who fled Toulouse saw their colleagues who remained behind authorize the confiscation of their property in the city; in response, loyalist judges initiated proceedings to disbar Leaguer magistrates who failed to rejoin the reconstituted court.[61] After his conversion, Henri IV often had to countermand these proscriptions for the sake of peace, much to the chagrin of loyalist judges. Reprisals from outside the Parlements also menaced judges as the perception of the impartial magistrate disintegrated under the pressure of partisan politics. The celebrated executions of Brisson, Larcher, and Tardiff by the Seize in the autumn of 1591 exposed the vulnerability of judges who tried to work for Catholic reconciliation.[62] Although the executions only made most judges in Paris more sympathetic to Henri IV, they still thought it necessary for him to convert before they recognized him as king. On the other side, the Parlement of Tours sometimes acted more royally than the king, much to his displeasure, as, for example, in the court's harsh attacks on Gregory XIV in August 1591. Only in March 1593, after the Leaguer Estates General in Paris had moved to elect a Catholic king, did members from the rival Parlements finally begin to meet in secret negotiations to work out an end to the conflict. After much handwringing and discussion, the Parlement of Paris mustered the courage to come out openly in favor of the king's conversion in its famous resolution on the Salic Law passed on June 28, 1593. In it, the *parlementaires* denounced the Estates General's electoral scheme as contrary to the Salic Law, yet at the same time carefully stipulated that any king of

France had to be Catholic to be considered legitimate. Thus, the judges in Paris withheld full recognition from Henri IV until his conversion had become an established fact. Little wonder, then, that Henri IV rejected any suggestion of inviting the Parisian judges to St. Denis; as far as he was concerned, they still remained guilty of sedition.[63]

Although divided during the conversion crisis, many royal judges shared certain assumptions about the independence of judicial office. André Maillard, a presidial judge in Burgundy, closely examined these common beliefs in 1585 in his supplication to Navarre to convert. Anxious to defend the integrity of judicial office, Maillard presented his case for the conversion as prompted by three distinct considerations: "the devotion I have for my religion, the natural love of my country, and the service I owe to princes of the blood."[64] Guillaume du Vair, who chose to remain in Leaguer Paris, essentially reiterated these points in his treatise *De la constance,* published at the end of the wars.[65] Speaking for other judges, Maillard regarded this congeries of allegiances as inseparable, for no one could stand without the others. Moreover, royal service extended beyond obedience to the prince to the eternal principles of piety and justice that the crown was also dutybound to uphold. As guardians of the law, royal judges considered its maintenance a collaborative effort between themselves and the prince.[66] Service to the prince therefore obliged them to make sure that he respected divine and customary law, even should he think differently. Recent attempts to enhance the crown's legislative prerogatives often showed this to be the case, Maillard pointed out.[67] In his opinion, a magistrate's honor and dignity required him to fulfill this special role of guardian of the king's law.

These precepts led Maillard to construe a judge's obedience to the crown as a right to act and think differently from the king if necessary to preserve the law. The moral obligations that came with judicial office differed little from the rationale Henri IV used to delay his conversion. Both the king and his judges saw loyalty as a matter of conscience that defined their personal and public identities. Like the Catholic nobility and the clergy, many Catholic magistrates considered it their sworn duty to oppose the prince should he flagrantly disregard the moral obligations imposed on them by public office and their personal sense of honor. The key difference for them again lay in whether or not Henri IV truly contemplated a conversion to Catholicism.

The Catholic Estates of France

The debates in the 1580s and 1590s over what it meant to be *bon françois catholique* not only affected the play of allegiances during the war, but also helped prepare the way for many of the important political changes that later occurred in the seventeenth century. New notions about who rightfully composed the Catholic estates of the realm took shape during these years, which foreshadowed the absolutist regime later established by Henri IV and his successors. Early modern society envisioned itself as comprised of corporate groups *(corps)* which collectively made up the estates of the realm.[68] After the Reformation, a further distinction was added to the traditional orders of the clergy, the nobility, and the third estate: these were all also Catholic estates. The addition of this religious criterion, first evident at the Estates General of Orléans in 1560, became a subject of controversy later during the conversion crisis as Catholics on both sides competed for the title of *estats catholiques*. At stake was the claim to represent the kingdom and to decide its political fate. In July 1589, the head of the League, Mayenne, issued a call for all *bons françois catholiques* to begin the long process of selecting deputies to attend an Estates General for the purpose of ending the succession crisis.[69] Although it was originally scheduled to meet in January 1590, the convocation of the Estates General by the League suffered from seemingly interminable delays over the next three years as its location shifted with the fortunes of war and political intrigues within the League. When it finally met in Paris in early 1593, it extended the previous exclusion of Huguenots to all Catholics who had opted to support the Protestant king from Navarre.[70]

From the outset, loyalist Catholics had vigorously contested the League's attempt to monopolize the distinction of *estats catholiques du royaume,* though they purposely eschewed the temptation to organize their own Estates General. For them, the Catholic estates of the realm became manifested in a new milieu and different institutional setting, that of the royal court. This new meaning of estates emerged clearly in loyalist Catholic accounts of the days that followed Henri III's assassination. Memorialists presented the oaths sworn by loyalist *grands* to Henri IV as collective acts made on behalf of the Catholic estates of the realm; these same estates also empowered envoys to go before the pope to explain why he should work for the king's conversion, not his permanent exclusion as advocated by some in the League.[71] Sympathetic observers also referred to Catholics who gathered at St. Denis in July 1593 to witness the king's return to the Church as representatives of the Catholic estates of France.[72] This loyalist conception of the Catholic estates still adhered to the confessional distinction used by the League. Loyalists also added a political requirement, albeit of a different sort. Assured of their religious integrity, loyalist Catholics included fidelity to the king as the litmus by which to determine membership in the Catholic estates. Moreover, they renounced the potentially unmanageable Estates General, choosing instead to view the estates as a reflection of the hierarchy at court. Inclusion in the Catholic estates of France required both social prestige and high visibility at the center of royal power. In a treatise written in early 1593, Pomponne de Bellièvre, a close adviser to Henri IV, impugned the legitimacy of the Leaguer Estates General by reference to these new criteria. His repeated use of the verb *de cognoistre* (to know) clearly pointed to the new mechanism, recognition at court, used to determine who belonged to the Catholic estates of the realm.[73]

These debates reflected a growing disenchantment among important segments of the Catholic establishment with the traditional representative institutions of the Renaissance monarchy and the concomitant search for new forms of collective involvement by the elites in the task of government. Every faction, convinced that it alone embodied the true spirit of France, had endeavored since 1560 to make the Estates General and its provincial equivalents serve its own partisan purposes—a process which finally culminated in the Leaguer Estates General of 1593.[74] Since 1560, the monarchy, too, had encouraged this factionalism in the Estates General by countenancing the adoption of exclusionary principles which tended to harden party lines, not promote greater unity. By the time of the Estates General of Blois in 1576, confessional orthodoxy had become a prerequisite for inclusion in the assembly; twelve years later, again at Blois, every delegate had to swear an oath of allegiance to the Holy League to have his credentials confirmed. The Chancellor Michel de l'Hôpital had recognized this dangerous trend early on, though few had heeded his warning that the Estates General, once looked upon as an integral part of the country's governing apparatus, risked destruction by this insidious *esprit de parti*.[75]

Long regarded as a bulwark against disorder, the Estates General had come to be seen in the early 1590s first by loyalist Catholics and then by others, particularly moderate Leaguers in the Parlements, such as Michel Marillac and Jean Lemaître, as a source of the country's ills, not their solution.[76] As this perception grew, the *estats catholiques* that had remained loyal to Henri IV began to lose faith in the traditional institutional organization of the three orders of society. They opted instead to identify the estates with the hierarchical power structure surrounding the throne at court, not the chambers specially adorned to give the orders symbolic expression. For them, one's standing at court, construed in terms of his fidelity to the monarchy, rather than the clumsy and potentially disloyal selection process that mobilized communities and *corps* across the land, determined membership in the *estats catholique*. Although the monarchy later experimented with different forms of elite participation, as in the Assembly of Clergy and the Assembly of Notables, it never allowed any to become a truncated version of the Estates General.[77] Service at court and in the king's councils, long the primary avenue of individual or familial involvement by the elites in government, gradually assumed a representative character in French society at large; loyalty to the crown served as the political requirement, whereas the ethos of politesse acted as a social determinant for inclusion in the *estats catholiques du royaume*. The belief that political and social advancement at court also meant admission to a privileged commonwealth representative of the realm underlay much of the Catholic elite's commitment to the absolutist regime erected by Henri IV and his successors in the seventeenth century. The brief revival of the Estates General in 1614–1615, again as a result of partisan pressures exerted by the disgruntled Prince de Condé, only confirmed this tendency to redefine the meaning of estates.[78] This crucial redefinition of the estates of the realm, so important for the later political culture of the Ancien Regime, proved to be one of the most enduring consequences of the struggle over the conversion of Henri IV.

5

The Fight for the King's Faith

FROM THE OUTSET, Henri IV believed it paramount for the League to acknowledge his legitimacy as king before he would contemplate a conversion. However unrealistic, this attempt to separate his question of conscience from politics allowed him to keep his options open—and all sides guessing—as events unfolded after August 1589. The various factions saw the situation differently, however. Loyalist Catholics feared that exchanging the king's conversion for League recognition could destroy belief in Navarre's sincerity, thus tainting it as a possible resolution to the conflict. It would also justify past Leaguer resistance to the crown—an interpretation that was not lost on League leaders. Yet the politics of the king's conversion went far beyond a simple quid pro quo between abjuration and recognition, though that issue proved to be the principal stumbling block. As will become clear, Henri IV's willingness to consider a conversion changed with events. Catholics, too, rarely let the religious nicety of a voluntary conversion stand in the way of seizing whatever opportunities they thought could possibly hinder or induce Henri IV's reconciliation with the Church. In the end, however much Catholics on both sides tried to don the mantle of moral superiority, they found that they could not escape the cruel uncertainties of the last religious war. And the greatest uncertainty remained not knowing what Henri IV's eventual decision might be. Knowledge of the evolving political and military situation after 1589 is therefore essential to understanding why the king's conversion eventually took the form it did in the summer of 1593.

Phoenix from the Ashes (August 1589–March 1590)

For loyalist jurists, the idea that *la mort saisit de vif* meant that Henri IV became king the instant his predecessor expired. Yet what is a king without a kingdom? royal panegyrists later asked.[1] Belief in God's solicitude for the struggling Navarre received strong confirmation during the weeks following the regicide. Henri IV performed his first "miracle," as one contemporary wryly put it, by obtaining the allegiance of many leading Catholic *grands* in the royal army. Although the Declaration of St. Cloud temporarily averted mass defection in the ranks, the alliance could still break down because no one knew whether Catholic loyalty to Navarre could survive a major military setback. With this in mind, some powerful Catholic noblemen, such as Épernon and Vitry, chose to leave court rather than serve a Protestant king. In October 1589, a conspiracy to provoke a mutiny in the loyalist garrison stationed in Tours, although a miserable failure, warned Henri IV that he could not take Catholic support for granted.[2]

Even more worrisome were Huguenot grumblings about the concessions Henri IV had made, however tentatively, to Catholics in the Declaration of St. Cloud. These anxieties surfaced later that autumn at the synod of Calvinist churches which met in St. Jean d'Angely to discuss whether another protector should be elected given the king's apparent openness to a conversion. Although Henri IV angrily accused the assembly of courting sedition, he assured them that he had allied with the Catholics only out of necessity, not out of any personal attraction to Catholicism.[3] Even so, the closer Henri IV drew to Catholics over the next several years, the more Huguenots quite naturally questioned his capacity to lead the Reformed movement.

To be successful, Henri IV's efforts to balance the competing demands of his coalition partners, and thus maintain maneuverability on the conversion question, required military victories. His prospects certainly seemed bleak during the weeks following the regicide as Mayenne rapidly prepared to carry the war to the Béarnais. In early August, Mayenne decided to test the depth of Catholic support for Henri IV by calling upon other League leaders to assemble their troops and march straight to Paris. This move compelled Henri IV to lift the siege of Paris and disperse his forces throughout the provinces. He hoped thereby to avoid an early and possibly disastrous engagement with Mayenne's superior forces. Political considerations also motivated this redeployment. Many officers from the nobility returned to their home provinces, ostensibly to attend to personal affairs long neglected during the summer siege. In reality, they withdrew to the sidelines to see whether Henri IV would be overwhelmed by the gathering armies of the League.[4]

All eyes turned to Normandy in early September 1589 as Mayenne chased Henri IV toward the sea. Mayenne's frequent boasts that he would bring the Béarnais back to Paris in chains could not hide the distressing fact that several League commanders, notably Mercoeur and Nemours, proved unwilling to place their forces at Mayenne's disposal. The decisive engagement finally commenced on September 21 at the battle of Arques when, after a series of brilliant cavalry charges, Henri IV routed Mayenne's superior forces, constraining the League leader to beat a hasty and humiliating retreat to Paris. Henri IV won the battle despite the last-minute defection of the Catholic Swiss pikemen in his service who abandoned the army not so much out of religious scruple as to protest arrears in payment. The king nevertheless had the ringleaders summarily executed before the entire army, letting the deserters serve as an example to others who might contemplate betrayal.[5]

Having established his credibility by force of arms, Henri IV spent the next month securing control of Normandy, the richest province in the realm. By the end of October, with only Le Havre, Avranches, and Rouen remaining in enemy hands, wavering supporters began to rejoin Navarre, while English reinforcements and funds arrived along with the congratulations of Elizabeth I.[6] With Mayenne's army in disarray, Henri IV turned his attention again to Paris, capturing several key *faubourgs* in early November. The situation had apparently come full circle since those uncertain days in August as Henri IV again maneuvered toward the capital. Although Henri IV never lost the military initiative after Arques, it remained to be seen whether he could end the conflict without going through with a conversion. Indeed, his initial openness to confessional change, so pronounced in August, waned noticeably after these startling military successes.[7]

Henri IV's victory at Arques proved to be a turning point for the League as well. The Duc de Mayenne never recovered from the debacle; provincial leaders who had earlier ignored his call for Catholic solidarity became even less inclined to follow him after his defeat. Provincial separatism and personal jealousy, which had long promoted this baneful disunity among the Leaguers, became rampant in the months ahead. As a result, Mayenne became increasingly dependent on Spain and the papacy for the funds and arms necessary to strengthen his tottering leadership of the League. It was not long before he found it nearly impossible to forgo League support without exposing his weaknesses.[8] Mayenne's isolation within the League meant that he could no longer pretend to speak on its behalf should loyalists propose serious negotiations. In fact, Henri IV's attempts after Arques to force Mayenne to the bargaining table only pushed the duke further into the arms of Spain and those in the League who were committed to prosecuting the war at all costs.

One reason that the possibility of compromise appeared so dim until 1593 was that both sides saw the outcome of the war in apocalyptic terms of total victory or utter defeat. The great significance which all parties gave to matters of conscience also frustrated any hope of a negotiated settlement. It is therefore all the more remarkable that informal talks actually took place intermittently between Henri IV and League leaders from August 1589 to July 1593. Henri IV's overtures to Mayenne in early August 1589 set the pattern for the years ahead as each side pursued its own private agenda instead of working for a compromise. Henri IV used the talks not to reach a settlement, but to gain time and improve morale in the royal army.[9] After Arques, he discovered that just as Mayenne had not wished to negotiate from a position of strength, so he would not from one of weakness. Leaders on both sides regarded negotiations as part of their respective war efforts, not as steps toward a peaceful resolution of differences.

Serious discussions also failed to take place because Huguenots close to the king, such as Duplessis Mornay, insisted that they be involved in any talks, though they only sought to undermine the discussions through leaks or misinformation. Henri IV bowed to these pressures, despite his halfhearted complaints to Catholics, because such subterfuges provided him with a discreet way to delay the conversion. On one occasion in late 1589, for example, Duplessis Mornay divulged to a known Spanish informant details of secret talks he had recently had with Villeroy, whom he then blamed for the leak when confronted by the king.[10] Leaguers, too, often acted at cross-purposes. Mayenne's vacillations frequently led loyalist to accuse his advisers Villeroy and Jeannin of duplicity, when in fact they merely suffered the consequences of the duke's compromised position. The Spanish ambassador, Bernardino de Mendoza, had spies who kept him informed of Mayenne's every move, thus enabling Spain to check any desire on the duke's part to treat with Navarre. Tracing the tangled skein of informal discussions, secret meetings, and conferences which took place among Catholics over the next few years reveals how accident and misunderstanding, duplicity and intrigue, all contributed to undermining the possibility of arranging a truce which would enable Henri IV to begin his long-awaited instruction in the Catholic faith.

The fact that negotiations always failed did not mean that they were without significance. As League radicalism and Spanish intervention increased over the next four years, many moderate Leaguers began to reassess Henri IV's receptivity to Catholic instruction and willingness to convert. This gradual readjustment in attitude kept lines of communication open between them and loyalist Catholics who grew impatient with the king's dogged refusal to abjure Protestantism. The mere fact that Catholics on both sides talked so much about peace made the awful spectre of loyalist Catholic defection a distinct possibility for Henri IV. This fear constantly haunted him and in the end finally convinced him in 1593 to go through with the conversion. The evolution of peace talks among Catholics therefore merits close attention.

The peace proposals which Navarre and loyalists sent to Mayenne shortly after the battle of Arques illustrate the kinds of problems that arose during negotiations over the next three years. They also showed early signs of loyalist Catholic independence from the Protestant king. The first set of terms sent after Arques came expressly from Navarre, who offered peace but no mention of his conversion. The second message, this time from the loyalist Catholics, asked the duke to make a formal request *(semondre)* to Henri IV to convert. Its only proviso, which turned out to be the chief stumbling block later, was that Mayenne first agree to recognize Henri IV's right to the throne. Should this enterprise prove successful, the loyalist Catholics assured Mayenne it would bring him "très grand honneur." [11]

Loyalist attempts to collaborate with Mayenne on the king's conversion split the duke's advisers. Political considerations and tactical strategy more than religious objections and ideology underlay their disagreement. Those opposed to the offer, such as Philippe Desportes and François Péricard, urged Mayenne not to open direct relations with the loyalists until he had first consulted the pope, his foreign allies and, most important, the Catholic estates of the realm. If he proceeded alone, they argued, he would only become further isolated. Although Leaguers across France recognized him as *chef du parti,* they had never intended for him to dispose "of such important matters without first consulting them." [12] After Arques, prudence dictated that the duke recoup his authority over the League before attempting to lead it to a peace conference. Mayenne agreed with this cautious assessment, and in early October sent a rather terse reply to the loyalist camp stating that peace could be achieved only when the safety of Catholicism had been assured by Navarre's conversion.

Villeroy and Jeannin took a more favorable view of the loyalist offer. They argued that it was more dangerous for Mayenne to ignore the possibility of Navarre's converting without League involvement than to face the ire of Philip II and hardliners in the movement. Jeannin believed that many Leaguers, particularly among the nobility, considered the question of Henri IV's faith negotiable, though care had to be taken not to conclude an accord unless it explicitly committed Navarre to a conversion.[13] Villeroy agreed and, in a separate memorandum, further elaborated on the manner in which Mayenne should take up the loyalist proposal. Like those in the duke's council who rejected the offer, Villeroy appreciated the dangers Mayenne would risk should he rush into negotiations unprepared to insure Navarre's conversion. Papal approval of the king's conversion had to be secured, for example, before Catholics could accept Navarre as "worthy of holding the scepter." [14] Villeroy also offered advice on how to deal with the expected objections of Spain. All in all, Villeroy hoped Mayenne could create a climate of opinion at home and abroad receptive to a conversion sponsored by the League. He even went into the political advantages Mayenne would accrue should Navarre still refuse to accept such reasonable conditions. Chief among these was the possible defection of loyalist Catholics.

Villeroy and Jeannin obviously thought Mayenne had everything to gain if he acted boldly and forced Navarre to declare his intentions. Yet they failed to appreciate the many pitfalls Mayenne faced after Arques as well as Henri IV's own fear of preconditions that might compromise his authority as king. In many ways, it was politically safer for Mayenne and Navarre to wage war than to seek a lasting peace. In the end, the advocates of a negotiated conversion were too fine in their calculations of what was required for a successful settlement. All spoke of the need for papal involvement, Spanish neutrality, a restoration of Mayenne's authority over the League, calm among the Huguenots, and, finally, Henri IV's willingness to gamble on the conversion. The success of these complicated attempts to make the king's conversion the vehicle of an overall settlement depended on a conjunction of circumstances beyond anyone's power to control.

Papal cooperation was perhaps the most critical variable in plans for a political resolution to the conversion crisis. Not only Leaguers, but also loyalist Catholics devoted much attention to winning papal support, beginning with the Duc de Luxembourg's mission to Rome in August 1589. At first, Sixtus V reaffirmed his commitment to the League by refusing Luxembourg's request to validate the episcopal absolution bestowed upon the late king.[15] Sixtus V believed that papal interests would be best served if France remained united under a native Catholic king; he therefore welcomed the proclamation of the aged Cardinal de Bourbon as king as the best temporary expedient. He understandably feared the success of Philip II's scheme to place his daughter the Infanta on the French throne almost as much as he feared a Huguenot victory under Henri de Navarre. The pope soon realized that his initial inclination to support the candidacy of the Duc de Lorraine or any other Guise pretender only perpetuated the instability in France. News of Henri IV's overwhelming victory at Arques more than Luxembourg's entreaties finally convinced the pope, who only four years earlier had issued the provocative bull *Brutem Fulmen,* that some sort of accommodation had to be reached with the Protestant king.

Thus began one of the most intriguing phases of Franco-papal relations during the late sixteenth century. Less than two months after Henri IV's accession, Sixtus V, reversing years of bitter opposition, seemed ready to accept Navarre's readmission to the Church. Resistance in the Roman Curia and pressures from Spain failed to deflect Sixtus V from this new conciliatory course.[16] After his death on

September 7, 1590, however, papal opposition to Navarre's conversion reached great heights under Gregory XIV (September 1590–October 1591), and only gradually subsided under Clement VIII (January 1592–October 1596) after Henri IV's conversion had become an established fact. Sixtus V's short-lived attempt to persuade Navarre to convert, though ultimately unsuccessful, nevertheless boosted the confidence of loyalists that they, not the Leaguers, embodied the true spirit of the Church militant.

Sixtus V's shift in policy seemed doomed from the outset, however. He certainly blundered in late September 1589 when he chose as legate to France the Cardinal Caetani—a man destined to become one of Henri IV's most implacable foes. Caetani's initial instructions from the pope directed him to proceed at once to Paris in an effort to reconcile the warring factions. Caetani's orders called for talks not only with League leaders and the Spanish ambassador, but also with Henri IV and prominent loyalist Catholics. Sixtus V hoped the legate could persuade Navarre to recognize the rights of his uncle, who most expected to live only a short while. In the meantime, Henri could prepare for the imminent succession by converting with papal assistance and a guarantee of papal absolution. Sixtus V made a major concession when he invalidated Navarre's 1572 conversion to Catholicism—a move which, contrary to the League's position, meant that Henri IV was no longer a relapsed heretic, but rather a misbeliever capable of instruction.[17]

Like Villeroy and Jeannin, Sixtus V approached the question of a negotiated conversion cautiously, warning Navarre that his Catholic supporters backed him only in the hope that he might soon convert. To lend substance to this caveat, the pope exhorted Montmorency, the *politique* governor of Languedoc, to assist the legate in the upcoming talks. Vatican sources reveal that Sixtus V considered it essential to commit Catholics in Henri IV's coalition to the papal plan, naming as possible collaborators a number of powerful *grands* who later became involved in the Tiers Parti conspiracy.[18] The pope apparently interpreted Luxembourg's mission to Rome as a sign of loyalist Catholic willingness to push Navarre toward the conversion if the Holy Father agreed to cooperate with them. Sixtus V again blundered, however, because Catholic pressure on Henri IV to convert subsided sharply after Arques; instead, as Caetani warned in January, all signs pointed to the imminent victory of the Béarnais over

the League. Sixtus V's miscalculations soon made his conciliatory policy one of vacillation and outright contradiction. In the end, the
pope needed the loyalist Catholics more than they thought they
needed him.

Sixtus V's inability to prevent Caetani from pursuing a bellicose
policy toward Navarre underscored the pope's growing isolation in
Rome. Although Henri IV allowed the legate passage through terri-
tories he controlled, Caetani refused to meet either with him or with
loyalist Catholics. Instead, he dealt exclusively with the Leaguers,
who sent escorts to protect him as he slowly wended his way to Paris
where he arrived on January 5, 1590.[19] Three weeks later, Caetani
outlined his objections to meeting with Navarre, stating that it was
unseemly for him to seek out a relapsed heretic who gave no indica-
tion of being well disposed to the Catholic Church. The legate no
doubt knew that since Arques, Henri IV had made it a point to attend
Calvinist services each week, thus advertising his confessional ties
with the Huguenots.[20] Caetani also declined to confer with any turn-
coat Catholics who abetted the Béarnais. The legate's intransigence
led many, including the pope, to accuse him of being a Spanish agent.
Although he did have close ties with Mendoza while in Paris, Caetani
took this inflexible stance because of the League's distressing state
after Arques. He continually cited the dangers that Catholicism
would face should the League collapse, urging the pope to send more
subsidies to Mayenne and to work for increased military assistance
from Spain. In Caetani's opinion, opening negotiations with Navarre
on the conversion question would only court disaster as long as the
League remained weak.[21]

Although some loyalist Catholics initially hoped the legate might
sponsor a negotiated settlement, they soon found that they had no
alternative but to reaffirm their commitment to Henri IV. Powerful
Catholic *grands,* such as the Duc de Nevers, who had up to this point
remained neutral, opted to back Navarre because of the legate's meddling in France's internal affairs.[22] Some went even further, warning
Caetani that he risked fomenting a schism between France and
Rome.[23] Caetani's partisanship paid dividends for the League, however, as he worked to restore the movement's solidarity. He was quite
adept at using the Parlement of Paris and Sorbonne to lend an official
cast to his policies.[24] At the same time, he delivered sermons through-

out the city in which he attacked Navarre's supposed openness to a conversion. The legate also convinced League prelates to boycott the assembly of clergy that met in Tours in February to discuss the king's Catholic instruction.[25] To forestall separate accords with the wily heretic, Caetani threatened to excommunicate anyone who came into contact with Navarre or his agents. In this he anticipated the policies of the irascible Gregory XIV by over a year.

By early March, the League's dark days seemed almost over due to the legate's energetic leadership. This was not to be, however, as a new crisis erupted which was to undo the legate's work. Hoping to capitalize on the League's renewed sense of mission, Mayenne again decided to enter battle, this time on March 14 near the little town of Ivry. There the duke suffered another defeat every bit as disastrous as the one at Arques; indeed, after Ivry, little stood between Henri IV and Leaguer Paris as the city quickly prepared for the anticipated siege. Humiliated once again, Mayenne prudently retired to Soissons, not Paris, where League preachers reviled him daily. Mayenne's prestige sank so low that his rival, the Duc de Nemours, assumed command of the Leaguer capital and soon became the darling of the Seize. Meanwhile, Mayenne tried to cope with desertions and the dismal prospect that Spanish intervention—and his dependence on it—was now inevitable if he wished to survive politically.[26]

After Ivry, a new round of secret talks began between the two sides, though these soon became deadlocked on the familiar problem of arranging League recognition before a royal conversion.[27] Henri IV's military successes, though not possible without Catholic support, tended only to move him further away from a conversion now that a military resolution appeared within sight. This explains why the siege of Paris, which lasted from April through August 1590, marked a crucial turning point in the struggle over the king's faith. With less pressure on him to convert and the League's armies in disarray, Henri IV felt confident that he could force Paris to surrender a few weeks after his victory at Ivry. Many loyalist Catholics shared his ebullience. Three days after Ivry, François d'Orléans reported to Nevers that "the inhabitants of Paris are in such desperate straits that I believe they will be starved into submission within fifteen days."[28] The unexpectedly stout resistance of the city permanently destroyed these hopes, however. Moreover, the siege so embittered the combatants that a negotiated settlement appeared unlikely. After the siege of Paris, France seemed destined for perpetual civil war unless Henri IV decided that his only alternative was to go through with a conversion.

The Siege of Paris (April–August 1590)

The siege of Paris was as much a struggle for people's minds as a struggle for the city's walls. Along with the cannonades came a barrage of pamphlets from both sides exploring the issues of peace and resistance. Henri IV and his advisers thought a siege could only lend force to those in Paris who favored reconciliation. Henri's failure to capture the city that summer can in fact be traced back to this initial miscalculation. As the siege wore on, more extremist elements in the Paris League, particularly the preachers, emerged as the dominant force in city politics and remained so until the autumn of 1591.[29] In their sermons, the preachers used apocalyptic imagery to liken the struggle to one against the Antichrist and his minions; they equated any talk of surrender with treason to God and therefore considered it punishable by death. In Leaguer accounts of the siege, the people of Paris became the "vrais Macabees" led by pious clerics who brandished swords and carried "a crucifix and image of the Virgin Mary as their banners."[30] This litany of Christian resistance against evil received doctrinal confirmation on May 7 when the Sorbonne determined that, even in the event of Charles X's death (he in fact died that day), Henri de Navarre could never be received as king of France. It was heretical even to discuss the possibility of his accession should he convert because "there would be the obvious danger of falsehood and perfidy, so ruinous to Catholicism if he covers these up with an empty absolution."[31] In other words, not even the pope, who at the time pursued a conciliatory policy toward Henri IV, could absolve the Béarnais of his crimes against God.

In many ways, this hardheaded attitude toward Navarre was meant to prepare the Leaguers for the possible surrender of Paris, but not an end to the war. Several months later, the Parlement of Paris made it a civil crime to talk of peace with the heretic, while special tribunals throughout the city ferreted out *simulez catholiques* still in their midst.[32] The city fathers empowered Nemours to requisition vital foodstuffs from notorious hoarders whom he punished severely for *politique* conspiracy. During the desperate days of August, when the urban poor reportedly resorted to cannibalism, Caetani ordered the precious objects used in divine service—chalices, plates, and reliquaries—to be melted down and used to bribe loyalist sentries to let food pass through the lines to the starving city. Even Estoile, who hardly sympathized with the rebels, marveled at the city's stubborn resistance.[33]

Contemporaries and historians have long pondered why Henri IV chose not to exploit the overwhelming military advantage he held during the early weeks of the siege. The reason lies in his changing relations with his Catholic allies. Their initial enthusiasm to take the war to the Leaguers soon gave way to growing concern about the possible dangers of a violent resolution. From the start, they advised Henri IV not to storm the city lest this action undermine the image of him as a benevolent monarch in search of true religion. Navarre apparently agreed. By August, some loyalists feared that an armed victory over Paris might actually reduce the likelihood of the king's conversion.[34] As a result, Henri IV and his Catholic allies, though motivated by different reasons, gradually limited the siege's objectives to a lenient peace with the Parisians predicated on the League's eventual recognition of the king. This reluctance to bring the city to its knees gave the Parisians just the opportunity they needed to mount their defense against the Béarnais.[35]

Henri IV's enticing offers of clemency and peace were not without effect, however. Despite the threat of execution, some in Paris began in July to call openly for negotiations with the Béarnais. It was hardly coincidental that the *Journée de pain ou de paix,* perhaps the most serious popular challenge to League rule in Paris before its fall in March 1594, occurred on August 2, only two days after Henri IV permitted women and children to leave the city.[36] Henri IV's gesture, though certainly magnanimous, in effect made the siege unwinnable for him despite the brief tumult. To appease the rioters, who had demanded peace if city authorities could not give them bread, League leaders agreed to send Albert de Gondi, bishop of Paris, and Pierre d'Épinac, archbishop of Lyons, to discuss the possibility of a truce with Navarre.[37]

Initial hopes of a peace settlement soon gave way to disappointment because the prelates—acting on explicit instructions from Mayenne—set the king's conversion as a precondition for League recognition.[38] Navarre, in contrast, insisted on an unconditional surrender without any mention of his conversion. Despite the obvious dangers of continued war, this apparent willingness to talk again clashed with each side's sense of honor and conscience. Because further discussions appeared useless, Henri IV angrily dismissed the prelates on August 5, instructing them to tell the rebels in Paris either to surrender or to prepare to be pillaged.[39] Dispatches intercepted from the Spanish ambassador suggested that the peace talks had all along been merely a ploy to gain time while a Spanish relief force under the Duke of Parma marched to the city's rescue.[40] Navarre's blustering only stiffened the city's resolve to hold out until Parma arrived a few weeks later, forcing the king once again to abandon the siege and, with it, virtually all hope of compelling the League to recognize him.[41]

Henri IV's failure to capture Paris in 1590 resulted as much from the king's refusal to consider a conversion as from the Leaguers' stout resistance. The stalemate created by Spanish intervention eventually forced loyalist Catholics to reassess their relationship with the Protestant king. In fact, some had already begun to have second thoughts about the desirability of a victory by force of arms because it would only lessen the chances of the king's conversion. Even Henri IV did not fully endorse a military resolution, because he much preferred the voluntary submission of his subjects to a forced obedience.[42] After the siege of Paris, therefore, the outcome of the conversion crisis came to be decided more in the antechambers of the royal court than on the field of battle.

The Rise of the Tiers Parti
(September 1590–November 1591)

No one needed to remind Henri IV that the good fortune he had enjoyed during the first year of his reign was largely due to loyalist Catholic support. His future success hinged on averting the nightmarish possibility of Catholic defection, though to retain the loyalty of Catholics he risked poisoning his relations with the Huguenots. Henri IV's ambivalence toward a conversion thus stemmed in part from the inevitable tensions at play in this uneasy confessional coalition. After the siege of Paris, some loyalist Catholics, chafing at the king's indecision, began to consider options other than undying support of Navarre's claims. The most dangerous of these became known as the Tiers Parti conspiracy.

Jealousy and reluctant cooperation had characterized relations between loyalist Catholics and Huguenots from the start. Some loyalist pamphleteers, such as Théophile Fréderic in his *Le pacifique* (1590), tried to gloss over the conflicting objectives of these two groups by emphasizing the theme of vengeance and minimizing religious differences.[43] Several accounts of the king's victories at Arques and Ivry described how Huguenots and loyalist Catholics joined together in prayer before taking to the field against the League and Spain, those "blasphémateurs, Mahomestes ennemis de Jesus Christ."[44] Other pamphlets, however, showed each group trying to claim separate credit for the king's successes.[45] Less publicized sources confirm that Huguenots and loyalist Catholics constantly vied with each other to influence the direction of the king's confessional allegiances. Though some Huguenots objected to Henri IV's ties with the Catholics, others, such as Duplessis Mornay, recognized early on that the king had to maintain the Catholic complexion of the court, if only to forestall the possible defection of Catholics.[46]

Until his conversion in 1593, Henri IV tried as best he could to follow Duplessis Mornay's advice to "win over the Catholics but not lose the Huguenots."[47] Yet friction continually arose over questions of military strategy, negotiations with the League and the papacy, appointments to royal offices, and the conversion. Household lists for the years 1589–1593 clearly reflected Catholic dominance at court, but Henri IV frequently relied on a shadow cabinet of longtime Huguenot associates, such as Sully, Duplessis Mornay, François de la Noue, and Jean de Serres, to help determine policy.[48] Some loyalist Catholics bitterly complained that this inner circle undermined their efforts to serve the king honorably. Nevertheless, in the area of royal appointments, the Huguenot gains remained limited because Henri IV was afraid to contravene existing royal legislation, which reserved all offices to Catholics. Navarre's efforts to balance these competing interests, though politically necessary to preserve the coalition, led to a debilitating dualism in the royal government because neither group thought that it held the place it deserved at court. Henri's conversion in 1593 would end these tensions by shunting aside the Huguenots.

After the siege of Paris, Henri IV found it necessary to make additional concessions to loyalist Catholics to retain their allegiance. As a result, the tenuous confessional balance at court slowly began to shift in their favor, particularly after Cheverny's appointment as Keeper of the Seal in September 1590. Until that time, the seal had been variously held by the cardinal de Vendôme, Beaulieu Ruzé, Biron, and François d'O, all of whom, except Beaulieu Ruzé, had resented the Huguenot presence close to the king. This shifting of power had caused a great deal of confusion and jealousy among Henri IV's councillors as official decrees began to reflect the factionalism at court. The post of Keeper of the Seal was important in royal decision-making because the seal rendered acts by the king's council official. The situation became so bad that Henri IV assumed the post himself from December 1589 to July 1590. Henri IV apparently counted on Cheverny's reputation of impartiality and his past experience as Keeper of the Seal under Henri III to impart some semblance of order to the disorganized proceedings at court and in the royal council.[49]

Confusion at court also arose from the fact that the composition of the king's council varied considerably as Navarre traveled about the country. In some ways, political and military necessity had forced a temporary return to the peripatetic *curia regis* once characteristic of Capetian France. At the front, aristocratic officers from both faiths tended to dominate the royal entourage, whereas at Tours and other loyalist cities, the presence and influence of the clergy and Catholic judges correspondingly increased. The king's continuous movement therefore disrupted the smooth operation of the royal government. To remedy this state of affairs, Cheverny set about reorganizing the king's council by regulating its hours and makeup. In time, his efforts helped Henri IV rise above the competing cliques at court and thus enjoy the greater freedom of action that came with royal aloofness.

Drawing on his past experience, Cheverny reshaped the court in ways which enhanced its Catholic character. The relative independence that Henri IV gave him in these matters perhaps reflected the king's budding awareness that Catholicism better expressed the attributes and authority of French kingship than did Calvinism. The aura of royal majesty and aloofness, so essential to the king's political independence, could not easily be cultivated while he was riding a horse or through the relations of *amitié* he had long had with Huguenots. From late 1590 onward, Catholic clergymen began to enjoy a more visible presence at the court of the Protestant king, particularly after Henri IV accepted Cheverny's plan to reconstitute the royal chapel under Renaud de Beaune, archbishop of Bourges. In fact, while Henri IV remained a Protestant, royal governance of the Gallican church essentially fell to Beaune, who as *grand aumônier du roi* supervised ecclesiastical appointments and the distribution of benefices under crown control.[50] The royal chapel also celebrated Mass daily for Catholics at court, offering special prayers for the king's safety and conversion. Clerical influence through the royal chapel thus gave Catholics greater control over both court protocol and Church affairs. The familiar rhythm of Catholic ceremony traditionally observed at court remained intact; indeed, Cheverny clearly intended his reforms to "show not only that the king bore no animosity toward Catholicism, but also was most disposed toward it."[51] Although the League construed these changes as moves to institutionalize the religious disparity between king and realm, loyalist Catholics considered them temporary, if unavoidable measures to be endured until such time as God—and circumstances—persuaded Henri IV to reconsider the merits of a conversion.

The Catholic complexion of Henri IV's court after 1590 found further expression in official entries into towns loyal to his cause. The religious ceremonies used during an entry not only excluded Huguenots, but also broadcast the orthodoxy of the court to the public. The royal entry into Chartres in April 1591, after a three-month siege, provides a fine example of how Catholicism began to color Henri IV's public actions. On April 18, the bishop of Chartres, Nicolas de Thou, called together his canon clergy to organize the city's formal surrender to the king. He then sent two clerics to brief the king and the Chancellor, François d'O, on the "ceremonies which will be held."[52] At eleven o'clock the next morning, the chancellor arrived at the cathedral with a considerable number of Catholic noblemen "to perform the necessary devotions there." At three o'clock, the city's clergy assembled on the steps of the cathedral to receive Henri IV. In the name of the city, de Thou swore everlasting fidelity to the king and begged him to take the cathedral and Catholicism under his special protection. De Thou then invited the king to go into the cathedral "with the Catholic nobility" to celebrate a *Te Deum* and "other ceremonies ordinarily observed during royal entries."[53] After hymns of thanksgiving, the bishop blessed the courtly congregation, which included the Protestant Henri IV. Such ceremonial displays of Catholic affection occurred whenever Henri IV again had to play the role of Catholic king.

Loyalist Catholic ascendancy at court after 1590 was often cited as proof of Henri IV's willingness to convert, though public shows of pious intent meant little without concrete moves to begin instruction. The failure of the siege of Paris made it seem all the more imperative to loyalists for France to have a Catholic king. As their frustrations mounted, their relations with Navarre became strained. These circumstances encouraged some to explore alternative ways of settling the dynastic crisis, the most serious of which became known as the Tiers Parti conspiracy.

Catholic frustration with Henri IV's procrastination drew strength from the jealousies simmering in the new royal family.[54] The most serious challenge came from the king's cousin, the Cardinal de Vendôme. Rumors surfaced in late 1589 that Vendôme aspired to the throne should Charles de Bourbon die in prison.[55] The fact that Vendôme had never taken clerical vows meant that he could still marry and possibly provide Catholic heirs. This was important, if only because Henri IV's estranged relationship with his wife, Marguerite de Valois, added the problem of divorce to that of conversion. Vendôme's undeclared candidacy throws a different light on the cardinal's efforts to win Catholic support for Henri IV during the months following the regicide. Vendôme had based his case for Henri IV primarily on the need for the king to convert, and only secondarily on the Salic law. The cardinal may have hoped that loyalist impatience with the king's delays would eventually be transformed into support for him.[56]

Few Catholics mentioned in their correspondence to what extent they became involved in Vendôme's machinations; the cardinal left little evidence of his plot because of the obvious danger of discovery. Our knowledge of the conspiracy instead comes largely from the cardinal's critics—a group that included mainly Huguenots and a handful of Catholic jurists. They generally agreed that sympathy for the Tiers Parti was strongest among loyalist prelates and officials from the previous regime. De Thou and Sully both suspected that Jean Touchard, abbot of Bellozane, and Jacques Davy Duperron, later bishop-elect of Evreux, were the "personnes malintentionées" behind the plot, though the latter played a double game.[57] According to Sully,

Nevers and Biron subverted the siege of Paris by allowing food sup-
plies to reach the starving city.[58] Longueville, Épernon, d'O, La
Guiche, and Châteauvieux, all former servants of Henri III, also figured prominently among "les malins catholiques."[59] Suspicion of
involvement should not, however, be equated with active participation in the Tiers Parti; after all, those making the accusations probably reasoned that the more wary Henri IV became of loyalist Catholics, the less likely he would be to convert to Catholicism.

Vendôme's conspiracy encountered problems from the start.
Secrecy proved impossible to maintain because Henri IV had reliable
informants, such as Duperron, close to the cardinal. This made loyalist Catholics understandably reluctant to become openly involved
in a Tiers Parti. Loyalists also feared that disobedience could force
Henri IV to fake a conversion—an outcome many thought worse
than no conversion at all. Vendôme's rash attempt in March 1591 to
enlist the support of Gregory XIV exposed the limits of loyalist resistance. Whatever sympathy the cardinal had enjoyed among disgruntled Catholics quickly evaporated after his debacle in Rome became
known.[60] Nevers led the way in late June 1591 when he prudently
reaffirmed his undying support for Henri IV. Other Catholic *grands*
and prelates whom the king suspected of involvement soon followed
suit as Vendôme's cause, not Henri IV's, suffered loyalist defection.[61]

The half-hearted commitment to a military resolution which many
loyalist Catholics showed after Ivry reflected the other side of their
dilemma: to force the League to accept Henri IV before he recanted
only reduced, in their opinion, the likelihood of his conversion. As a
result, Tiers Parti activity often meant little more than a desire to
pursue a negotiated settlement with the papacy and moderate Leaguers. Nevers's frequent contacts with Villeroy, for example, hardly
constituted perfidy, as his critics charged, because he regularly
informed the king of his dealings. As he explained it, he hoped to
secure a truce only so that the king could begin his Catholic instruction—a laudable enough goal given Henri IV's public statements.[62]
For Nevers and other impatient loyalists, the League had to be put on
the defensive just enough to become open to negotiations, yet kept
strong enough to make Henri IV actively consider his conversion. Although the League's theories of elective kingship and legitimate resistance demanded utter condemnation, the Catholic character of the

crown had to follow destruction of the rebellion as a political force. Tiers Parti Catholics wrestled with this paradox until the day of the king's conversion.

Henri IV could do little to combat the Tiers Parti as long as its sympathizers decided not to act on their vague threat to abandon him to both his enemies and his heresy. The force of the Tiers Parti lay in the potential, rather than the actual, realization of uniting Catholics behind a resolution which excluded Henri IV. Rather than attempting to replace Navarre with a Catholic Bourbon, loyalists such as Nevers and François d'O tried to push him toward conversion. However much Henri IV wished to avoid the road to St. Denis, he found himself ineluctably drawn to it whenever loyalist talks with the League indicated a possible rapprochement.

One reason that Vendôme's plot failed so miserably in 1591 was that it came on the heels of Gregory XIV's bulls, issued in March, which excommunicated Henri IV and all his Catholic supporters, including the cardinal.[63] The pope had apparently interpreted rumors of a Tiers Parti as evidence of the imminent disintegration of Henri IV's coalition. Many Leaguers, particularly in Paris, had called for the bulls as the last push necessary to bring about a split in the loyalist camp; Villeroy, however, had warned Mayenne that the bulls only risked strengthening Henri IV's ties with loyalist Catholics—a prediction that came true later that summer. In fact, the pope's provocative action emboldened Henri IV to move even further away from conversion when he issued a new comprehensive policy statement on July 6 known as the Edict of Mantes.

Two separate declarations made up the Edict of Mantes. In the first, Henri IV hoped to relieve Catholic anxieties about his conversion by restating his desire to seek Catholic instruction once he had "le loisir" to do so. Unlike the earlier Declaration of St. Cloud, however, this new pledge omitted any timetable for his instruction.[64] The second, more controversial part of the Edict of Mantes made these gestures by the king seem empty. It revoked the 1588 Edict of Union and replaced it with earlier pacification measures which granted concessions to the Huguenots. Officeholding was among the new privileges Henri IV gave Protestants in the Edict of Mantes, and one which represented a clear challenge to Catholics at court. Moreover, it lent credence to Leaguer charges that heretics had invaded the royal government.[65] Although Vendôme fulminated against these new laws, the Edict of Mantes cleared the king's council with scarcely any opposition. The unwillingness of loyalist Catholics to stand by the ambitious cardinal during the summer of 1591 hardly meant that they had abandoned all hope of a negotiated settlement. Although Gregory XIV's bulls had brought loyalist Catholics closer to the king, there nevertheless remained the poignant question of future relations with the papacy. Loyalist prelates took the lead here in late August when they denounced the Parlement's sharp attacks on the pope. Their campaign later that fall to soften the judges' stand allowed Vendôme to mend some fences with loyalist Catholics who believed that the Parlement's actions opened the door to a possible schism with Rome.[66]

Loyalist pressure on Navarre to move forward with a conversion gained momentum among prelates that autumn at the Assembly of Clergy which met in Chartres. The assembly tried to keep alive the possibility of Catholic reconciliation mediated by the papacy because the prelates considered this the key to winning Henri IV back to the Church. Gregory XIV's death in October raised further hope of such an outcome. The prelates criticized recent papal policy but not the late pope, arguing that he had been an unwitting dupe of slanderous Spanish tongues.[67] In early November, the assembly renewed requests for another mission to be sent to Rome to tell the new pope, Innocent XI, of Henri IV's long-standing intention to begin Catholic instruction as soon as possible. The assembly also suggested that, as a sign of his goodwill, the king should set aside one day each week for catechism, particularly because he seemed to have ample time "to go pay his respects to Madame de Soissons," one of his current mistresses.[68] Such sarcasm reflected the mounting frustration felt by loyalists at Navarre's continuing indecision; arguments that too many obstacles still stood in the way of his conversion no longer held the weight they once did. Henri IV prudently accepted the idea of a new initiative in Rome as a way to placate these impatient clerics. He still had much to fear should that coterie of discontented Catholic noblemen and prelates who made up the Tiers Parti decide to carry their grievances into open opposition. Navarre continued to hold out for a military resolution, and expressed great hope that the siege of Rouen, which had begun in November, could be the decisive turning point. He was soon disappointed, however, as Parma again entered France with a formidable relief force.[69] As a result, Henri IV's relations with loyalist Catholics seemed even more uncertain by the beginning of 1592.

The Search for Catholic Unity
(December 1591–October 1592)

Henri IV's troubles in keeping his coalition together paled before the growing factionalism that rent the League in 1591. As usual, the storm was centered in Paris, where confrontations between moderate urban notables and the Seize threatened to break out into armed violence. Mayenne prudently kept his distance from the fray, waiting for the right moment to intervene and perhaps recoup his lost authority over the city. That moment came on November 15, when several leaders of the Seize, in a bid to rid the city of dangerous *simulez catholiques*, seized the *parlementaires* Barnabé Brisson and Claude Larcher, as well as an officer in the Châtelet, Jean Tardif, for *politique* conspiracy. After a mock trial, they had the prisoners summarily executed the next day. This attack on the Parlement's dignity presaged an irrevocable split in the Paris League—one which Mayenne, after a few weeks of typical indecision, finally moved to control. He came to Paris—in force—and had those principally responsible for this outrage rounded up and then hanged at Montfaucon on December 4. In doing so, Mayenne proved he was still a force to be reckoned with, not only in the city, but also in the country at large. For all intents and purposes, the sway that the radical Seize held over Paris ended during those bloody days in late 1591. The Seize thereafter survived only on Mayenne's sufferance, to be periodically unleashed whenever the *ligueurs politiques* flouted his authority. Although the radicals' words still stung, the Seize never again posed the threat it once had to moderates in Paris over the next twenty-eight months—a period that encompassed nearly half the time the League controlled Paris.[70]

Shortly after the hangings on Montfaucon, Mayenne renewed hopes of a negotiated settlement when he again decided to test the waters of Catholic reconciliation. In December 1591, he opened indirect talks with Vendôme in an attempt to give new life to the Tiers Parti. This time, however, Vendôme exercised greater caution by deciding to inform Navarre directly of all topics discussed. These basically revolved around the worrisome problem of how to time

League recognition to coincide with the king's abjuration.[71] Whatever chance the negotiations had of success came to an end a few months later when Henri IV stipulated Duplessis Mornay's inclusion in them—a move which certainly meant the king was not ready to have any compromises made for him by his Catholic supporters.[72] Acting on explicit orders from the king, Duplessis Mornay demanded a complete surrender by the League before any discussion of the royal conscience could begin. This inflexible stance so discouraged Villeroy that he threatened to break off the talks, which was, of course, precisely what Henri IV wanted.[73]

Mayenne had a great deal to lose should the discussions come to an abrupt end. Whatever momentum he had gained in December had by now been nearly spent as the Spanish pressed him to convoke an Estates General to change the succession. In an effort to keep the talks alive, Mayenne notified Villeroy in late March of his readiness to recognize Henri IV the moment he converted, provided that Navarre agree to treat him honorably. But Mayenne again refused to make this stance public, partly because he feared Spanish retribution, but also because he believed that the initiative for the king's conversion still had to come from loyalist Catholics. The duke made a major concession, however, when he agreed to accept a conversion not sanctioned by the papacy. Should Henri IV still persist in his heresy, Mayenne thought that he would have no alternative but to back a Catholic Bourbon for the throne. Mayenne's apparent readiness to consider either a Tiers Parti resolution or the king's conversion under episcopal auspices grew as his influence over the League once again diminished.

Before revealing Mayenne's offers, Villeroy asked Henri IV not to allow Duplessis Mornay to attend any future discussions "à cause de sa religion." His request found some support among Henri IV's Catholic advisers, such as Louis Revol, who had already begun to withhold key documents from Duplessis Mornay. Henri IV succumbed to these pressures and ordered Duplessis Mornay not to attend the next pourparler at Noisy on April 2.[74] Unencumbered by the shrewd Huguenot, Villeroy and the bishop of Paris, Gondi, who had joined the loyalists several months before, quickly agreed that Henri IV had to set a timetable for his conversion before opening serious negotiations with the League. The League's submission to Navarre, they thought, could thereafter be more easily arranged to satisfy the king's dignity and honor. Villeroy and Gondi also believed that an initiative should be made to include the new pope, Clement VIII, in the king's instruction and conversion. The resolutions adopted at Noisy showed a genuine willingness among moderate Catholics to work around the major points of disagreement. Hopeful that this progress foreshadowed a breakthrough, the negotiators agreed to meet again at Grignon on April 10.

When Henri IV learned of these resolutions, he wasted no time in abandoning his brief experiment of allowing loyalist Catholics a free hand in talks with the League. He wisely chose not to break off the talks completely, but instead to return to his old policy of trying to control their agenda through Duplessis Mornay, who met with Villeroy on April 3. Despite objections by loyalist Catholics, Duplessis Mornay again renewed demands that League recognition precede the king's conversion, because it was Mayenne who had to provide guarantees, not the king. Henri IV's inflexibility on this matter all but insured the failure of the upcoming interviews at Grignon because it put loyalist Catholics in the unenviable position of having to pursue objectives directly at odds with the wishes of their king. The fact that the talks continued at all after this sudden setback must be attributed to the tenacity of the negotiators. On April 10, Bellièvre and Villeroy tried to salvage the progress made at Noisy by calling for a temporary truce.[75] Yet even this lone resolution faced formidable obstacles, and not only from Huguenots, who had begun to doubt Henri IV's ability to resist Catholic pressures for his conversion. As in the past, Mayenne had second thoughts about dealing with Navarre whenever the talks appeared on the verge of a breakthrough. His growing coolness to the negotiations gelled a week later when he publicly announced that no settlement was possible until the king had converted.[76] This backpedaling by both Henri IV and Mayenne had significant consequences as moderate Catholics became more inclined after Grignon to act independently of their leaders. In fact, on April 29, Villeroy went so far as to offer truce conditions to loyalists without consulting Mayenne. When pressed by Villeroy, some loyalist *grands*, such as Longueville and Aumont, expressed a willingness to leave Navarre if the king still refused to go forward with his conversion should Mayenne accept the truce proposal. Loyalist Catholic impatience also became evident during the siege of Rouen when, according to Biron, rumors of a peace settlement sparked unrest among the troops.[77]

In his later memoirs, Villeroy justified his decision to go beyond the scope of his commission by claiming that he was motivated solely by a concern for France's welfare. Henri IV, however, had every reason to believe that Villeroy's gambit was merely another attempt to cause discord among his Catholic supporters. As he saw it, Villeroy hoped to lure them into discussions which the king disapproved of and which Mayenne considered unbinding. Certainly Villeroy's refusal to give written responses to amendments suggested by loyalists confirmed these suspicions of duplicity.[78] Henri IV still thought it too risky to dampen loyalist Catholic enthusiasm for Villeroy's truce proposal, however. In early May, Duplessis Mornay urged the king to allow the talks to continue, even if they made it necessary for him to set a date for his long-awaited catechism. Later that month, in fact, Duplessis Mornay began to prepare Huguenots for such an eventuality. He asked a number of Huguenot ministers to come to court ready to participate in a conference for the king's instruction. Though it would hardly be the full national church council mentioned several years earlier, the idea of a conference still permitted the Huguenots to pursue reformation by disputation—an approach which had proved successful in the past. The visible growth of Catholic frustration in recent months had convinced Duplessis Mornay that the Huguenots had little recourse but to try to defeat the Catholics by force of argument. Although criticized by some in the Reformed community, Duplessis Mornay appreciated the risks involved in a strategy which aimed to prevent Navarre's defection by converting his Catholic supporters to Protestantism, however unrealistic this may have seemed.[79] Indeed, Catholics on both sides considered Huguenot participation in the king's catechism out of the question.

As informal talks continued that summer, loyalists pushed for another mission to Rome, this time led by Gondi and the Marquis de Pisani, to sound out Clement VIII about the feasibility of an all-Catholic conference to oversee the king's conversion. Revol even hoped to persuade the pope to nominate Henri IV as king in the Leaguer Estates General, scheduled to meet in autumn, once Navarre had begun Catholic instruction.[80] As the prospects for peace brightened that summer, it now became Mayenne who insisted on Duplessis

Mornay's continued involvement in the negotiations. The duke apparently counted on Duplessis Mornay's intransigence to prevent any further progress in the discussions. Both the Huguenot adviser and the League leader shared an aversion to talks which they believed only compromised their respective positions and causes. Leaguer and Huguenot opposition to Henri IV's conversion still drew strength from the fact that conciliatory Catholics on both sides had not yet found a way to guarantee the king's conversion without giving the sordid impression that it formed part of some crass political bargain.

The *Semonneux* Affair (October 1592–December 1592)

Although obstacles remained, many observers by late summer 1592 believed it would be only a matter of time before Navarre announced his decision to seek Catholic instruction. Rumors flew of Henri IV's readiness to go to Mass if the pope agreed to absolve him. League preachers did their best to quell this enthusiasm, especially in the Leaguer capital.[81] In Paris, hopes for the king's conversion ran highest among judges in the Parlement and officials in the city council. In late October 1592, fearful that Henri IV might convert without League involvement, they organized a bold attempt to force Mayenne to come to terms with Navarre. The *semonneux* affair, as it came to be called, also represented another challenge to hardliners in the Seize. On October 20, several judges and lesser robe officials from the city government met secretly in the Cordelier monastery in Paris to discuss ways to open channels to Navarre. Pierre Pithou and Matthieu Lavergne, two *avocats* in the Parlement, introduced a resolution which called upon Mayenne to make a formal request *(de semondre)* to Navarre to abjure his heresy and embrace Catholicism. In exchange, they offered to recognize Navarre's right to the throne. Should Navarre refuse to consider this reasonable appeal, they would have to make every effort to bring the loyalist Catholics into the upcoming Estates General, pushed back to December, for the purpose of electing a Catholic king.[82]

On the surface, at least, these proposals represented nothing new. The difference lay in the wording the *semonneux* chose for their resolution, which marked a significant departure from earlier formulations of the thorny problem of recognition and conversion. In it they acknowledged Navarre's royal majesty and pointedly declared that they were his subjects.[83] Even so, they emphasized that service to him still required his profession of Catholicism. The motion passed overwhelmingly, though a few expressed fear of possible retribution from the Spanish garrison stationed in the city. On October 30, the *semonneux* presented their resolution before an assembly of Paris *quartiers*, and thirteen out of sixteen districts approved the measure.[84] The *quartiers* also voted to invite loyalist Catholics to join them in electing a suitable Catholic king should Navarre still refuse to convert. Catholic reconciliation, which they believed essential for the country's welfare, would be achieved either with the king's conversion or without it.

Dismayed by the prospect of endless civil war, moderate Leaguers in Paris presented to both Mayenne and Henri IV what they thought to be an ideal opportunity to break the deadlock over conversion and recognition. Yet rather than seize on the *semonneux* summons as a way to recapture leadership over the movement and escape Spanish dependency, Mayenne pushed even harder for an Estates General because he still thought it necessary to consult the entire party before seeking a rapprochement with Navarre.[85] Henri IV hardly greeted the *semonneux* with open arms, either. Their promise to recognize him formally once he began his Catholic instruction seemed an empty gesture, given their caveat about seeking loyalist Catholic participation in the Esates General should he still refuse the summons. From his standpoint, the *semonneux* affair merely represented another sly attempt by the League to drive a wedge between him and his Catholic supporters. In his response to the *semonneux* in early November, Henri IV restated his belief that "a person's conscience is such a precious thing that it's best not to wait for the King to compromise his own by such vile arrangements."[86] Moreover, should he eventually decide not to embrace Catholicism, his subjects were not thereby released from their obligation to obey him as king. Some loyalist Catholics, such as Nevers and Longueville, expressed dismay that the League's most conciliatory gesture to date had received such a curt response from the king. As in the past, the closer Catholic reconciliation came to realization, the more willingly Navarre and Mayenne listened to the conversion's foes. In the end, the *semonneux* failed because they forced the two leaders to risk their delicate coalitions on talks which could lead to their mutual downfall.[87]

Nevertheless, the *semonneux* affair marked a great step forward in the evolution of Henri IV's conversion to Catholicism—not because it succeeded, but because it failed. Its failure in time encouraged moderates on both sides to strike out on their own, to conduct their leaders to a peace settlement whether or not they wanted to follow. By early 1593, only a few weeks before the Leaguer Estates General assembled in Paris, an emerging consensus could be detected among conciliatory Catholics in both camps. They agreed that the king's conversion was the key to lasting reconciliation; that League recognition of Navarre's royal dignity could be negotiated once the royal catechism began, then be sealed before the king's conversion was consummated; and, finally, that papal absolution, while highly desirable, was not altogether necessary for a valid conversion. Perhaps the most important development of all was the growing appeal of an all-Catholic conference to discuss ways to end the conflict. By the time the Estates General opened on January 17, 1593, Henri IV therefore had every reason to fear the emergence of a truly formidable Tiers Parti of Catholics committed to his immediate conversion or to his immediate ouster should he refuse to see the light.

6

The Move to Convert

AMONG THE FACTORS which pushed Henri IV toward St. Denis that winter was the feeling of war-weariness that visibly grew among the peasantry and townspeople of France. Although difficult to measure, this apparent exhaustion after years of fighting weighed heavily in both sides' calculations. There are indications starting in late 1592 that informal local truces arranged on the initiative of local commanders began to proliferate as the clientele networks and party organizations that had sustained the conflict finally began to disintegrate. One of Nevers's captains in Champagne, for example, cited lack of pay to the troops as the reason for the spate of unauthorized truces recently concluded between some of his officers and enemy towns.[1] Similar developments occurred in Brie, Burgundy, Dauphiné, and Languedoc. Such dire reports from the provinces warned leaders on both sides that the people of France no longer had the will to fight. By spring, the perception of war-weariness gave Mayenne and Navarre added incentives to break the deadlock on the conversion question. As a result, both sides began competing to decide what would constitute an everlasting peace. Some pushed for the election of a Catholic king, while others worked for a peace settlement based on the king's conversion.

Another catalyst for Henri IV's budding resolve to convert came when the Leaguer Estates General finally met in Paris on January 17 to discuss Catholic reconciliation.[2] The radical proposal to elect a Catholic king found a weak following among Leaguer deputies when Cardinal Pellevé, who headed the first estate, introduced it on April

2. Though shocking to loyalists, this proposal actually worked in their favor because it deepened existing divisions in the League. The Estates General of 1593 represented a threat to Henri IV altogether different from the one supposedly posed by theories of elective kingship. His deepest fear was that the assembly could precipitate the formation of a Tiers Parti of Catholics powerful enough to demand his conversion or abdication.

Such fears were not unfounded. Mayenne's patriotic call in December 1592 for all Catholics to join the Estates General elicited a warm response from loyalist Catholics, some of whom suggested that observers be sent to the assembly.[3] In an open letter dated January 5, Mayenne agreed to accept any observers sent by Catholics in the opposing camp. Downplaying the alleged domination of the League by Spain, Mayenne stressed that he and all other *bons françois catholiques* in the League shared loyalist concerns about the welfare of the crown and the Church.[4] Of course, he omitted the inflammatory suggestion made by some Parisian preachers that the Estates General, once assembled, move swiftly to elect a Catholic king. He instead confined most of his letter to platitudes about the need for peace and Catholic reunion.

The most provocative part of Mayenne's invitation was the brief portion he devoted to Henri IV's legitimacy and the feasibility of a conversion. Here he made a number of important concessions. He acknowledged Navarre's hereditary right to the throne, publicly stating that had Henri IV converted after the death of his uncle in May 1590, he would have found "the Catholics of the Holy Union ready to render him the same obedience and fidelity" that they had given to the Cardinal de Bourbon.[5] This option remained open provided that Navarre agree to undergo "a true and not feigned conversion." The duke's shift on the conversion question even offered Henri IV a way to resolve the crucial question of sincerity. The best proof of the king's sincerity, Mayenne asserted, lay in his willingness to accept as honorable and necessary all past League resistance. Until Navarre showed such signs of heartfelt faith, however, Mayenne would remain firmly opposed to the heretical succession. He then proposed that *bons françois catholiques* from both sides meet in a conference to discuss ways to end the wars.

In the past, Mayenne had continually frustrated conciliatory moves among Catholics by refusing to mention publicly the possibility of

Henri IV's conversion. Now, on the eve of the Estates General, Mayenne elevated to official policy the view that Navarre had but to convert to gain the affection of all his Catholic subjects. A week later, he informed loyalists that he intended to take up the *semonneux* proposal once the Estates General met. Mayenne perhaps hoped by so doing to capture the sympathy of moderate Catholics who still grumbled about the duke's past vacillations. He also thereby tried to set the Estates General's agenda before it met on January 17.

The Estates General of 1593 revealed how much the League had changed since the movement's heyday in 1588. The Catholic nobility, whose enthusiasm for the League had waned considerably since the regicide, seated only eighty-eight deputies and formed the smallest chamber at the Estates General. Most noblemen came from Brittany, Champagne, and Burgundy—all provincial strongholds of the Guise family.[6] The clergy and the third estate, in contrast, managed to seat deputies from nearly every district consulted, though their numbers approached only by half the size of other, less partisan Estates Generals during the sixteenth century. Royalist writers often drew such comparisons to prove the assembly's illegality, though they must not blind us to its significance in moving Henri IV to convert.[7] The fact that the Estates General met at all represented a stunning political achievement, given the years of growing disunity within the League. Moreover, the wide acceptance that the Estates General received across much of France meant that for many Catholics it was not a rump body. The Conseil de l'Union, headed by Mayenne, declared its readiness to defer to the Estates General because, according to Leaguers, the assembly held sovereignty during a succession crisis. It remained to be seen whether the Estates General, benefiting from this renewed sense of unity, would take the path of a negotiated settlement or continue along the one of armed resistance. Much depended on how loyalist Catholics responded to Mayenne's invitation to discuss with them their possible participation in the Estates General.

At the time, many loyalist Catholics expressed surprise at the large turnout for the Leaguer Estates General. Although they vigorously contested its supposed authority to change the succession, they accepted the assembly as the duly constituted representative of the League. This distinction helps explain why Mayenne's overture of January 5 elicited two very different responses from loyalist Catholics, one conciliatory on the questions of peace and Catholic reunion, the other a condemnation of the assembly's constitutional pretensions. This dual response also reflected their ongoing ambivalence toward Henri IV, thus intensifying his fears of a Tiers Parti. The decision both to praise and to blame the Leaguer assembly was made quickly after the arrival of Mayenne's public letter. On January 11, Cheverny called together leading loyalists at court, such as François d'O, Châteauvieux, and Revol, to discuss what reply, if any, should be made to Mayenne's offer. Working in close consultation with the king, they all agreed to "make a counter offer *(contresemence)*."[8] Silence on their part, they thought, would only boost Mayenne's efforts to appear a champion of peace and Catholic reunion. It would also risk turning "all of the kingdom . . . against us."[9] A failure to respond favorably to Mayenne's overture could push many otherwise moderate Leaguers to support the election of a Catholic pretender. The loyalists therefore urged Henri IV to allow them to take up Mayenne's offer of a conference to discuss peace and reconciliation. If the conference failed, they wanted the Leaguers to shoulder the blame.

Henri IV had little choice but to accept their request to meet with the Leaguers in a conference. The spectre of a Tiers Parti now seemed all too real, despite repeated assurances by loyalists that they would serve Navarre whether or not he decided to convert. Henri IV obviously thought it imprudent to obstruct a meeting whose general agenda concerned only the welfare of the realm and religion. If the talks should fail, he, too, wished the responsibility to lie with the League, not himself. Unable to forbid the talks, Henri IV entrusted their failure to his enemies. He therefore agreed to let loyalist Catholics proceed with their *contresemence*, provided that they also denounce the illegality of the Estates General. Cheverny and the others at Chartres welcomed this opportunity to allay the king's suspicions of a Catholic conference. Unable to decide on the tone of their response, they instead chose to speak in two voices, one gentle and the other stern. This left the distinct impression that Henri IV had to be placated with a condemnation of the Estates General before he would allow his Catholic allies to pursue what could prove, at least for him, a disastrous conference with the Leaguers.[10]

Some loyalist Catholics, sensitive to this rift, tried to harmonize these two conflicting approaches in draft proposals that they submitted for the king's declaration against the Estates. Sometime after the meeting of January 11 in Chartres, Bellièvre hastily composed a tract against the Estates that differed significantly from the text Henri IV adopted later that month. The appeal for Catholic unity that Bellièvre made to the "men of honor and valor in both parties" never found its way into the final version published on January 29, though his defense of the Salic Law did. Also dropped was Bellièvre's discussion of the "peace with dignity" that Mayenne had raised in his letter of January 5; in it, Bellièvre agreed with the duke that a durable peace required magnanimity, not harshness.[11] Although not mentioned in the king's attack on the Estates General, the notion of a dignified peace for the Leaguers continued to be discussed among moderate Catholics during the months ahead.

Another draft composed for the king's declaration, this one anonymous, moved even further away from the stern condemnation sought by Henri IV. After establishing the conventional argument that the Estates General existed only at the king's pleasure, the writer went on to consider its powers should the throne be vacant or in dispute. In either situation, the power to convoke the Estates, and thus establish its legitimacy, fell to the Catholic "princes du sang royal, pairs de France et officiers généraux du couronne." The similarity between this formula and the one used to describe loyalist missions to Rome was unmistakable and carried implications which Henri IV no doubt saw. This interpretation virtually invested leading loyalist Catholics, from princes of the blood to court officers, with constitutional powers to determine, first, what constituted a succession crisis and, second, to convoke an Estates General to name a king. If loyalist Catholic defection should occur, it seemed plausible that these arguments could be used to justify reunion with the Leaguer Estates.[12]

When it finally appeared, Henri IV's Declaration against the Estates did not even dignify these novel interpretations of the monarchy with a response; this did little, however, to allay his fears of a Tiers Parti. Henri IV confined his Declaration to the familiar polemic over his right to the throne and the subversive nature of the League. He made no reference to reconciliation beyond demanding the immediate and unconditional surrender of all Catholics who bore arms against him. The only mention of the conversion came in his restatement of the reasons that he had long used to defend his indecision. Although Henri did not know it at the time, this was to be the last occasion on which he publicly cited these excuses.[13] Henri IV's attitude toward the conversion began to change after January as new developments, particularly the rapid progress made in the peace talks, forced him to reconsider the possible merits of an abjuration.

Loyalist reaction to the harsh words that Henri IV leveled against the Estates General ranged from displeasure to the perfunctory applause of an audience left unimpressed.[14] Many feared that the Declaration of January 29 would jeopardize the conciliatory response that had been sent to the Estates on January 21. In their *contresemence,* loyalists had accepted Mayenne's offer to meet together in a conference, but had refused to disavow Henri IV, as had been requested. Such a meeting had to be viewed not as an act of separation from the Protestant king, but as testimony of his like-minded desire for peace. Yet while loyalists supported Henri IV as France's rightful king, they did not dwell on the proofs of his legitimacy. They extolled obedience as the best way to convert the king to Catholicism, yet without going into the matter deeply. They instead adopted the convenient fiction that the proposed conference, which they eagerly awaited, would meet only to discuss peace and Catholic reunion, as originally suggested by Mayenne. The *contresemence* ended with an admonition to the Leaguers to take up the challenge of peace.[15]

The loyalist *contresemence* created a sensation when it arrived by herald at the Estates General on January 23. Lines were quickly drawn as the assembly debated over the next month whether to pursue the idea of a Catholic conference. Some observers, underestimating the appeal of such a conference, thought it only a matter of days before radicals would ask the Estates General to elect a Catholic king.[16] Proponents of the conference generally found support in the second estate and among the more highly placed members of the clergy and magistracy, particularly judges from the Parlements. The opposition drew strength from the cardinal-legate de Piacenza; the Spanish ambassador De Feria; the head of the first estate, Cardinal Pellevé; lesser clerics; and, initially, the third estate. On February 25, after all excuses for further delay had been exhausted, the matter finally came before the three chambers for a vote. According to one deputy, support for a conciliatory response had grown not only among the clergy, but also among the third estate. In fact, the Breton delegation threatened to leave the assembly if the measure failed to pass.[17] The vote became a test of strength between the advocates of reconciliation and those of continued resistance. The final tally proved to be a resounding victory for the former, as each estate voted to go ahead with a Catholic conference.

Like the loyalist *contresemence,* the Estates' resolution purposely avoided the knotty issues of recognition and conversion. It instead limited the conference's objectives to the same general concerns about religion and the public welfare which Mayenne had cited in his *lettres patentes* to authorize the assembly. Presented in this way, a vote against a Catholic conference would deny the Estates General's stated mission. Although it refused to meet with Navarre or any other heretic, the assembly saw no reason not to "confer with Catholics in his service."[18] By accepting the measure, the Estates General thus officially abandoned the League's past policy of abiding by papal injunctions against contact with Catholics who supported Henri IV. Excluding Navarre's claims from the proposed agenda allowed the Estates General to sidestep the delicate question of loyalist Catholic relations with the Protestant king. Instead, the deputies presented the conference as a unique opportunity to bring dissident Catholics into the League. These concerns became the centerpiece of the letter which the assembly sent to Chartres on March 4 in favor of the meeting.[19]

Many loyalist Catholics at court considered the Estates General's letter of March 4 the decisive breakthrough needed to bring Catholics closer to a negotiated settlement. Potential problems of course remained, particularly the king's reaction now that a peace conference seemed imminent. Henri IV apparently found the Leaguers' letter provocative in its failure to take up the question of recognition and obedience. Ten days later, Revol hurriedly wrote to Nevers and the Cardinal de Vendôme, who had returned to Tours, and told them to come quickly to Chartres to persuade the king not to reject the Estates General's most positive overture to date.[20] While loyalists pressed Navarre for a favorable decision, Bellièvre and Épinac carried on an informal, yet frank, exchange of ideas and opinions about the prospects for peace. Neither expressed any illusions about the enormous difficulties the conference would face should it meet. Épinac underscored the need to do what befitted God's honor, advanced the Church, and preserved the realm. Although many Catholics agreed on these ultimate objectives, they still differed greatly on how to achieve them. Some wished to establish religion by the *estat,* Épinac explained, and others sought to base the *estat* on religion. Épinac saw no other way to resolve this quandary than by Henri IV's converting to Catholicism. Bellièvre basically agreed. The archbishop's discreet inquiry into the king's current attitude toward a conversion brought the laconic response from Revol in late March that "no one can promise anything with certainty." Though ostensibly not on the agenda of the proposed conference, the question of the king's conversion still dominated the less public, but no less crucial discussions between moderate Catholics as they searched for a way to end the war.[21]

The deadline of March 20 set by the League passed without official word from loyalists in Chartres. Finally, on April 2, there arrived in Paris a letter dated March 29, in which loyalists assured the assembly of a favorable response no later than April 15.[22] Leaguer opponents of the talks, still reeling from the vote of February 25 for moderation, denounced the perfidy of the *faulteurs d'hérétiques* when they introduced later that afternoon the famous resolution to elect a Catholic king. That measure made little progress because the three chambers voted to accept the loyalist request for a delay, though they did so with strong words should their hopes for a conference be dashed. As proof of their good intentions, the Estates General sent a letter on April 2 asking the loyalists to furnish information about the organization of the conference, the number of deputies to be chosen, their qualifications, and the scope of their commissions.[23] The assembly suggested that twelve persons of the highest character be chosen by each side and that the conference site be somewhere between Paris and St. Denis. All *gens de bien* in Paris hoped that the loyalists would seize the hand of friendship extended to them.

The loyalist delay had stemmed from Henri IV's unwillingness to approve a conference without further guarantees from the League.[24] On April 3, in an ominous show of solidarity, Vendôme, Cheverny, Montmorency, and a number of other *gentilhommes catholiques* in Chartres forced Navarre to cease stalling and authorize a favorable response to the Estates General.[25] Loyalists asked to meet with League representatives as soon as possible because Henri IV could still change his mind at any time. They agreed to send twelve deputies for the conference, which they suggested be held in Suresnes, a suburb west of Paris. Ten days later, the Leaguer Estates General agreed to meet the king's Catholic supporters at Suresnes on April 23. Perrot, a royal councillor, wrote that during the upcoming conference "we will finally be able to penetrate the designs of those who have it within their power to make peace."[26] This applied as much to Henri IV as it did to Leaguers when, after years of ineffectual negotiations, setbacks, and mutual mistrust, Catholics from both sides finally sat down together in late April 1593 to discuss peace, Catholic reunion, and, in time, the conversion of Henri IV.

Seeing the Light (January–April 1593)

As the proposal for a Catholic conference earned support after January, Henri IV slowly began to reconsider the possible merits of a conversion. Though pressed by Catholics, particularly after plans for the conference gained momentum in March, Henri IV refused to divulge his thoughts until May, when he announced his decision to begin Catholic instruction. Another reason that Henri IV remained tight-lipped about his changing attitude toward the conversion lay in his self-conception as king. He thought it beneath his dignity to parade before his subjects matters that touched the royal conscience. For him, as well as for many later theorists on monarchy, the royal conscience formed part of the *arcana imperii* of kingship which shielded the crown from a prying public. Henri IV's elusiveness also affected his behavior during these months as he constantly moved about the Île-de-France. Though ostensibly military maneuvers, these wanderings seemed motivated by Henri IV's desire to remain one step ahead of loyalist Catholics who badgered him about the conversion.

In his declaration of January 29 against the Estates General, Henri IV restated for the last time the hackneyed reasons why he had for so long delayed Catholic instruction. His arguments had lost much of their original force now that Catholics talked of a truce. Sully's memoirs reveal better than any other source Henri IV's change of heart about a conversion once it became clear that both sides intended to pursue the idea of a conference. Hindsight no doubt played a role in shaping Sully's recollections of these nocturnal conversations with the king, since his memoirs were written some twenty-five years later. Henri IV apparently summoned Sully to his bedchamber late on the night of February 15 to talk over possible "new plans regarding a conversion."[27] As Sully recalled, the king faced two dangerous alternatives. Should he decide not to convert, it would be only a matter of time before his Catholic allies deserted him.

Should he agree to convert, however, the Huguenots would probably elect another protector and prepare for war with the new Catholic king. This tragedy could perhaps be avoided by reissuing past edicts of pacification favorable to Huguenots. Sully was convinced that the two confessions could live in harmony if the monarchy stood above faction.

According to Sully, the best way to defuse a future Huguenot revolt would be for Henri IV to convert before the Catholics managed to come together and demand his conversion. Once the proposed conference began, he warned, the king would have little power to influence its outcome. If a conversion was necessary, then it had to occur before political forces coalesced to compel the king to convert. Little time remained to put off a decision, because it was equally imprudent to discourage loyalist hopes for a conference and a negotiated settlement. As Sully succinctly put it, "Your Majesty must make an absolute resolution *(absolue résolution)* without consulting anyone." [28] This "absolute resolution" laid the foundations of later Bourbon absolutism.

Sully's advice to Henri IV to convert freely lest he be forced to do so, naturally brought up the question of sincerity. Political considerations aside, he told the king to undertake a conversion only in good conscience. Good as well as bad Christians could be found in both confessional camps. According to Sully, salvation was not so much a question of theological subtleties as a matter of moral rectitude and adherence to a basic set of beliefs which both confessions essentially accepted. Sully's irenicist views of Christianity, by trivializing doctrinal disputes, probably helped Henri IV overcome whatever scruples may still have stood in the way of a Catholic conversion. For Sully, Henri IV could either be saved as a Protestant but lose his crown, or be saved as a Catholic and reunite the realm under his strong rule. At the end of these talks, Henri IV confided to Sully that he had at last resolved upon "a course of action by which I will easily achieve all I have fought for, without upsetting anyone." [29] By late February 1593, at least according to Sully, Henri IV seemed ready to begin his conversion, barring any sudden disruption of the upcoming Catholic conference.

The king's openness to conversion grew clearer over the next two months. In March, for example, there were reports that Henri IV had met informally with Huguenot ministers and Catholic prelates to discuss points of doctrine. He also apparently spent several long evenings in close consultation with Claude d'Angennes, the bishop of Le Mans, and Duperron, whom pundits later dubbed "Monsieur le Convertisseur."[30] By April, the king's desire for instruction had become widely known. Henri IV attended at least two of the public debates held in Mantes that month between Duperron and several prominent Protestant divines.[31] Palma Cayet later wrote that Duperron had so impressed Henri IV with his erudition and arguments that afterward the king remained doubtful only about three points: the invocation of saints, auricular confession, and papal primacy.[32] Rumors of a Tiers Parti continued to surface at court during March and April, no doubt contributing to the king's steady drift toward a conversion. Even De Thou, a staunch supporter of the king who scorned such intrigue, impatiently wrote to Bouillon on April 11 urging him to press the king to make a decision regarding his faith. Continued delay, he warned, risked provoking a mass defection by loyalist Catholics, who might "do something out of despair which they will later find impossible to amend by reason."[33] As for the royal conscience, De Thou thought that Henri IV violated his sacred duty to succor his people by not converting to Catholicism. He prayed for the king to begin Catholic instruction during the upcoming conference of Suresnes, scheduled to convene on April 23. His continued refusal, De Thou cautioned, threatened to destroy not only himself, but also the realm he had vowed to defend.

The Conference of Suresnes (April 23–May 17, 1593)

After many delays and much anxiety, the conference of Suresnes finally opened on April 23. Both sides had chosen representatives who had long advocated a negotiated settlement built around the king's conversion. The deputies sent by the Leaguer Estates General came from the moderate *semonneux* wing of the movement. Pierre d'Épinac led the delegation and was joined by two other clerics, François Péricard, the *mayenniste* bishop of Avranches, and Geoffroy de Billy, abbot of St. Vincent-de-Laon and later bishop of Laon in 1601.[34] The second estate sent two members: André de Brancas de Villars, admiral of France and League governor of Normandy, and

François d'Averton, comte de Belin and governor of Paris. Magistrates and former crown officers made up the rest of the delegation: Jeannin, Villeroy, Jacques Le Maître, Louis de Montigny, Nicolas Pradel, Étienne Bernard, and Honoré de Laurens.[35] Thus, men of the robe dominated the group, although a prelate served as its spokesman.

The loyalist Catholic delegation possessed a similar social profile and political temperament. The lone cleric in the group, Renaud de Beaune, headed a group that included two sword noblemen, François le Roi de Chavigny and Nicolas d'Angennes de Rambouillet—the remainder consisted of crown officers: Bellièvre, Revol, De Thou, Gaspard Schomberg (himself a convert to Catholicism), and Godefroi le Camus de Pontcarré.[36] These envoys, like their counterparts from the League, came from circles in Henri IV's coalition that had long fought for a negotiated settlement. This general like-mindedness made the participants, as well as sympathetic observers, optimistic that some kind of permanent solution to the crisis could be found at the conference. It became clear over the weeks ahead that whatever ideological differences still separated them, members from both delegations conformed to a common code of civility and courtesy that kept the talks alive. The initial bonhomie of the first meetings, which only broke down later after serious discussions began, also kept alive Henri IV's fears of a Tiers Parti. In the early meetings, both sides evidenced a strong desire to overcome whatever obstacles threatened to disrupt the conference. The League's objections to the inclusion of Rambouillet, whom it accused of complicity in the Guise assassinations, were quickly ironed out during the first few days, for example.[37] Both sides also agreed on April 30 to dispense with all titles and distinctions in an effort to avoid unnecessary quarrels over precedence and procedure. After an exchange of their commissions, some loyalist delegates expressed dismay that the League's negotiators had been empowered only to report information to the Estates General, not to conclude a general accord.[38] Beaune, however, quickly reassured other members in his delegation that the Leaguers, as *gens de bien,* negotiated in good faith. Notions of civility and courtesy such as these encouraged the compromises necessary to sustain the conference. By May 4, a truce—subject to renewal—was worked out for a period of ten days. This gave Paris and its environs their first taste of peace in nearly four years and raised hopes throughout France that an end to the strife was finally in sight.

Although the conference of Suresnes had ostensibly met to consider only peace and Catholic reunion, the talks soon turned after these preliminary meetings to the nagging problem of Henri IV's conversion. On May 5, Beaune and Épinac began the first in a series of learned debates on the conversion question, examining what it meant and entailed for Catholics to consider a conversion sincere. During the course of these debates, which lasted until June 13, Beaune and Épinac articulated the two contrasting visions of Catholic activism that had long confronted each other on the issue of Henri IV's faith. As in the past, the two differed little in their perception of the ideal outcome. Both prelates, for example, decried the miseries brought on by the war, citing in particular the ruination of the nobility, the impoverishment of the people, and the evil sacrileges committed daily. Both lamented the sorrowful lack of piety and morality in recent times, the only remedy for which lay in a sweeping change of men's characters and human institutions.

These broad areas of agreement served only to emphasize the points of disagreement between the prelates. In his opening harangue, delivered on May 5, Beaune asserted that civil peace and moral renewal required all subjects to recognize and obey the authority held by Henri IV. He then reiterated the standard argument of the king's readiness to convert were it not for the League's rebellion. Henri IV's separation from the Catholic Church, for example, stemmed more from unwitting error than an unshakeable belief in heresy. As a clear-headed *homme de parole,* Henri IV could not help seeing the infallible proofs of Catholic orthodoxy. For Beaune and other loyalist Catholics, to deny the possibility of Henri IV's conversion through persuasion and instruction denigrated the power of God's Word. The prelate from Bourges also noted that recent changes in the king's behavior indicated a growing attraction to Catholic ceremony and doctrine. He mentioned the king's recent attendance at a colloquy in Mantes between Duperron and several Protestant ministers, after which Henri IV apparently removed his hat as a Catholic procession bearing the Host passed by.[39] The king also seemed to derive spiritual comfort from sermons he had heard lately in the royal chapel. Recent diplomatic missions to Rome, moreover, attested to the king's readiness to seek an understanding with the pope. In Beaune's opinion, all signs pointed to the king's imminent conversion, provided that the Leaguers encourage rather than block its realization.

In response, Épinac cited the entire repertoire of established authorities—Scriptures, patristic texts, canon law, historical precedent, reason, and experience—to justify the League's rejection of a heretical king.[40] In his opinion, lasting peace required confessional unity as well as obedience to the crown; indeed, one without the other was not possible in Catholic France. The best way to combine them was for Navarre to convert, though Épinac considered this unlikely, given his low opinion of the heretic's supposed remorse. True conversion occurred only as "une oeuvre de Dieu," not at the penitent's convenience. Épinac mocked Henri IV's alleged reverence toward the Church when he alluded to Beaune's anecdote, remarking that if Navarre tipped his hat, it was probably to salute the fine ladies he saw in the street, not to honor the solemn procession. He also asked how Navarre could be moving toward the conversion while he still allowed Huguenots to occupy sensitive posts in his government. And, finally, he rejected the contention that Navarre's beliefs constituted only doctrinal error, not heresy. Thus, while Épinac still held out the possibility of Navarre's conversion, he considered it crucial to emphasize the enormity of Navarre's sins. Until loyalist Catholics could present more conclusive proof of Navarre's sincerity, he and other *françois catholiques* in the League had no choice but to oppose the heretic's pretensions. Chavigny reportedly rose to protest Épinac's defense of the rebellion, but Beaune cut him off and moved to adjourn the meeting given the lateness of the hour.

The next day the prelates resumed the debate and went on to consider the relationship between Navarre's private motives and his public acceptance as king. They examined, for example, the reasons why Henri IV had delayed his Catholic instruction for so long; what limits, if any, restrained papal power in France; and the prerogatives of the royal conscience. According to Laurens, the meeting of May 6 often degenerated into acrimonious dispute, not so much between Épinac and Beaune, as among the other delegates at the conference.[41] Despite these disturbances, neither side seriously considered breaking off the talks. On May 10, the two prelates tried through words sweetened with delicate courtesy to smooth over the rancor of the last session. Épinac voiced a readiness to accept Navarre as king once "he truly became a Catholic in a manner satisfactory to the Holy Father in Rome." [42] Beaune conceded the need for Henri IV to be sincere, and agreed that the pope should be invited to take part in the king's conversion. Furthermore, both sides shelved the question of League recognition of Navarre's right to the throne; it seemed that problem would take care of itself once Navarre embraced the faith. The delegates then voted to adjourn the conference for a week in order to report to their respective leaders the progress thus far attained.

The recess provided an opportunity for both sides to take stock of the prospects for peace, Catholic reunion, and the king's conversion. Although each had striven to remain courteous, neither had appeared willing to compromise any of the vital principles they believed at stake in the dispute. Beaune blamed the deadly sin of rebellion for the ills that afflicted France and the Church, while Épinac attributed these woes to the spread of heresy. Beaune argued that all good Catholics should join together to eradicate the civil heresy of armed sedition against the crown, while Épinac countered with the demand that Catholics direct their energies against the spiritual heresy of the Reformed religion. The speeches delivered by Beaune and Épinac made it seem only a matter of time before the conference broke down, as in the past, over these diametrically opposed views of the conflict. It is altogether misleading, however, to gauge the conference's impact on Henri IV solely in terms of these formal harangues. They conveyed only the public visage of the conference, not the less formal, but perhaps more decisive conversations that took place among the delegates during the nearly three weeks they spent together in Suresnes. With no Huguenot observer there to keep him informed, Henri IV had to rely on Catholic reports that tended to play down points of difference, and instead emphasize the *honnêteté* of the League negotiators.[43] These reports perhaps gave the impression of greater progress than had in fact been achieved, at least according to the formal speeches later redacted for publication. For Henri IV, the mere fact that Catholics from both sides had come together to discuss the possibility of peace in a civil, if inconclusive fashion, was reason enough not to delay the conversion any longer. It was not what he knew, but rather what he did not know, that made Henri fear the three-week conference.

These uncertainties explain why Revol and Schomberg found Henri IV at last ready to set a date to begin Catholic instruction when they arrived in Mantes on May 11. That they were not overly surprised by the king's decision suggests that he had perhaps already gone over the matter privately with some of his Catholic advisers.[44] During the next five days, they and the Cardinal de Vendôme discussed details of the announcement with the king, setting July 20 as the start of the royal catechism; they also discussed the possibility of a unilateral truce in an attempt to associate the theme of peace with the king's conversion.[45] The only precondition Henri IV attached to the announcement concerned the Huguenots. In an effort to allay Huguenot anxiety about their future, Henri IV commanded loyalist Catholic leaders in Mantes to promise to abide by the guarantees accorded the Reformed community in the 1591 Edict of Mantes. On May 16, they complied with this request by swearing to a formal "Promesse des Seigneurs du Conseil du Roy en faveur de ceulx de la Religion."[46] Some eighteen prominent Catholics, including Montmorency, Cheverny, and François d'Orléans, signed the oath, though the names of François d'O, Vendôme, and Longueville were conspicuously absent. The ambivalence that had for so long marred relations between Huguenots and Catholics at court, in the royal council, and in the field could not be easily erased by a single act, though Henri IV was to try again five years later in the more sweeping Edict of Nantes. Whatever its defects, the promise of May 16 apparently satisfied Henri IV enough that he did not delay the formal announcement he had planned for the next day when the conference was to reconvene in Suresnes.

The signal honor of making the announcement fell, not unexpectedly, to Renaud de Beaune. The declaration he delivered merits a close look because in it the loyalist Catholics revealed for the first time how they intended to conduct the king's conversion. Beaune made it clear in the beginning of his speech that Henri IV's desire to convert vindicated loyalist Catholic principles of respectful obedience and conversion through *douceur,* not force. He assured his listeners that Henri IV's request for Catholic instruction resulted from the fact that he was "already in his heart a Catholic."[47] The king would long since have converted had it not been for domestic rebellion and foreign intrigue. As evidence of the king's good intentions, Beaune mentioned that invitations were being sent to clergymen selected to assist in the royal catechism. He passed over the question of whether representatives from Rome or the Estates General would be asked to attend, though he did urge the Leaguers to reconsider their opposition to the king. The speech ended with a generous offer to grant a general truce for three months provided the Leaguers respect it. Obviously not prepared to comment on all this startling news, Épinac hurriedly asked for another adjournment so that he could confer with Mayenne, the legate, and the Estates General about this "sudden" turn of events. Although the conference of Suresnes continued to meet over the next few weeks, it no longer held centerstage after the announcement of May 17. All eyes turned instead to Henri IV to see if he truly intended to go through with his promised conversion to Catholicism.

The Preachers' Fury (May 17–July 25, 1593)

Preachers in Paris quickly mobilized against the proposed conversion, attacking Navarre in terms reminiscent of the arguments used to rally League opinion during the siege of 1590. Estoile reported that almost every day after May 17 the pulpits of Paris rang out with denunciations of the false peace promised by the Béarnais. On May 23, Christophe d'Aubray, the *curé* of Saint-André-des-Arts, told his parishoners, many of whom he knew "visited St. Denis everyday," that a godly peace with the heretic was impossible "regardless of any abjuration, which you can be sure will be nothing but sheer hypocrisy."[48] Boucher echoed this fear of dissimulation, claiming that Navarre still consulted Calvinist ministers and attended clandestine Calvinist services. League preachers offered evidence to prove that Navarre only intended to feign a conversion, in order to humiliate and then destroy the united Catholics. They continually warned their flocks that Roman Catholicism faced a far greater peril if Navarre went to Mass than if he remained a heretic.

Recognizing with alarm the growing attraction of many Parisians to the idea of the king's conversion, preachers in Paris concentrated their attack not so much on the possibility of conversion, as on its proposed forms. In a sermon on May 23, Boucher conceded that although Navarre could perhaps be readmitted to the Church as a penitent, his past crimes against God made it impossible for Catholics ever to accept him as *roi très chrétien*.[49] If Navarre truly felt contrite, he should retire to a monastery to pass the rest of his days in penitential atonement, Boucher recommended. Even League preachers now conceded that a conversion could restore Henri IV's dignity as a

Christian, though never as king. The dilemma they faced was to try to convince Catholics to distinguish, like them, between a true and a false conversion. The Parisians' willingness to do so gradually ebbed, however, as the date set for the king's conversion approached.

Boucher and his fellow preachers contended that the conversion proposed at St. Denis made a travesty of true Christian repentance; the announcement of May 17, they argued, merely confirmed the heretic's hypocrisy by its blasphemous anticipation of divine forgiveness. Others attacked the festive air which accompanied the plans at St. Denis as contrary to the somber demeanor expected of a true penitent. Some offered as proof of how little time Navarre actually devoted to spiritual pursuits the loyalist attack on the citadel of Dreux on July 5; others cited scurrilous stories about the Vert Galant's dalliances with young ladies. The preachers also questioned whether excommunicated Catholics had any right to receive the heretic back into the fold. Consumed by avarice and ambition, these false Catholics intended to use the elaborate ceremonies planned for Navarre's conversion to cover up the heretic's dissimulation. The mere suspicion of hypocrisy was enough for diehard Leaguers to remain committed to further resistance, despite its growing unpopularity.

These efforts by the preachers nevertheless failed to revive the movement's willingness to resist Navarre. Fewer and fewer Catholics considered the preachers' objections persuasive enough to justify the cruel consequences of further bloodshed. This dwindling enthusiasm often led to open acts of defiance against the preachers after May. Some boldly disrupted the sermons by mocking the *curés* in their pulpits, while Estoile, though not unbiased, reported that attendance in the more radical parishes of the city dropped sharply as the conversion date approached.[50] Even the legate-cardinal of Piacenza discovered that his voice, unlike that of Caetani in 1590, added little to the preachers' persuasiveness. The absence of papal involvement in the proposed conversion troubled him deeply because it could provoke a schism. Rumors that summer that Henri IV intended to make Renaud de Beaune patriarch of the Gallican church lent some substance to the legate's fears.

The legate's views, however, carried little weight with many in Paris and the Estates General, who scornfully regarded him as the private chaplain of the Spanish ambassador. This simmering mistrust finally exploded on June 16, when an angry mob hurled stones and epithets at the legate as he passed in his carriage. Shocked by this assault on his apostolic dignity, Piacenza fled for protection to Mayenne's residence in the hôtel de Nemours. Afterward, he ventured forth on the streets of Paris only with an armed escort. The attack on the legate and other incidents against the Seize reflected how little popular support the radicals now enjoyed in the city. Elsewhere they commanded even less respect.[51]

The steady decline of the preachers' appeal was due not only to the arms and arguments of loyalist Catholics, but also to the determined work of powerful groups around Mayenne and in the Parlements who had long challenged the Seize for control of the movement. Encouraged but still wary of what the king's conversion held in store, moderates in the League counseled prudence and further discussion with Navarre's Catholic supporters on such crucial issues as guarantees for the Church and political amnesty for them and their followers. As the conversion approached realization that summer, it became clear that even moderate Leaguers in the nobility and the Parlements, whom many considered the most likely to defect, found that they could not do so with the honor they thought essential for a sound peace. The Parlement of Paris's celebrated resolution in favor of the Salic Law on June 28 amply showed the limits of Leaguer accommodation. It stopped short of conceding recognition of Henri IV's right to the throne when it reaffirmed the need for the king to be Catholic to be considered legitimate.[52] The risks of continued warfare obviously could not overcome the judges' concern for honor and conviction. Though otherwise open to the negotiations, they considered the hand that Henri IV and his Catholic supporters extended to them after May 17 still more clenched than open. For them, it still remained to be seen whether the king's conversion would bring with it a lasting peace or condemn France to perpetual war.

7

The Conversion at St. Denis

The Calling of Witnesses (May–July 1593)

THE CONVERSION OF Henri IV was orchestrated after May 17 in a manner designed to capture public attention. Excited by the news, some Catholics began to celebrate the king's conversion even before it occurred. The next step after the announcement was to call together witnesses. On May 18, Henri IV sent letters to clergymen and magistrates selected to assist his return to the Catholic faith. The king later invited Catholic noblemen through more personal missives which spoke of his *amitié* toward them. These invitations bear a close look because they reveal the initial meaning that Henri IV and his Catholic advisers ascribed to the conversion.[1]

Although the invitations echoed long-standing loyalist arguments for the king's conversion, they had to begin to confront the problem of the king's sincerity, and thus his acceptability to a hostile public. In turn, these concerns had to be balanced with the new prerogatives of the royal conscience. Rather than going into details, Henri IV simply reassured each recipient of his readiness to do "everything expected of a Christian king."[2] There were limits, after all, to how abjectly the royal penitent could beg God's forgiveness. The king therefore left the defense of his sincerity to others who witnessed its existence firsthand.[3] Navarre's letters of invitation shifted attention away from personal motives to the conversion's public benefits. His desire for Catholic instruction arose, for example, from the need to succor his downtrodden people after years of civil war. He felt compassion, not vengeance, toward Leaguers whose misplaced concern for religion could now be forgiven. Henri IV presented his wish to convert as a lofty act of benevolent kingship which did not, as some Huguenots argued, compromise his royal authority. To peace and prosperity was added the hope of mending divisions in the Church.[4] Henri IV's concern for salvation thus became simultaneously an act of public redemption and a glorification of God's Church. In this way, God's grace to the errant prince presaged the divine forgiveness available to every subject who forswore violence and embraced the royal penitent as king. Those subjects included Huguenots as well as Leaguers.

The speed with which the king's council sent these circular letters attested to the meticulous planning that had gone into the announcement at Suresnes. To judge from the roster of those who later attended the ceremony at St. Denis, no fewer than sixty copies of these letters were issued on May 18. Even that figure hardly approaches the actual number the king sent, because some powerful nobles, such as Nevers and Épernon, as well as judicial delegations from south of the Loire, failed to attend. Some cited unstable local conditions or fears of schism because the papacy was not involved. Consideration must also be given to the common excuse that unsafe roads prohibited travel.[5]

Taken as a group, the notables invited by Henri IV hardly represented a broad cross-section of Catholic France. Still fearing a possible Tiers Parti, Henri IV underscored Catholic divisions by inviting only long-time supporters to St. Denis. Even the Paris *curés* whom he asked, such as René Benoist, Claude Morenne, Jean de Chavignac, and the dean of the collegial clergy of Notre Dame, Louis Séguier, though not directly affiliated with the loyalist coalition, had sufficiently demonstrated their hostility to the League—at great risk—to be included in the festivities. In fact, Benoist eventually became the king's personal confessor.[6] The letters of invitation clearly were sent only to those who had demonstrated fidelity and service to the monarch. Besides lending the conversion more éclat, the recipient's attendance signaled to the community at large his inclusion in that select company of "notables personnages et fidèles serviteurs" who made up the true Catholic estates of the realm.[7] The invitations defined in affective language the power enjoyed by proximity to the king, rather than by reference to God, aristocratic privilege, or the civic republicanism espoused by some urban Leaguers. Indeed, the king's special favor brought the recipient closer to God, reaffirmed the honor of the nobility, and upheld the public good. Loyalists thus planned Navarre's conversion as a courtly triumph of the royal conscience over its enemies, heresy and sedition. Inclusion required conformity to loyalist Catholic notions of obedient *douceur.* This applied not only to Leaguers, but also to Huguenots, who soon discovered that they had no role to play in the king's victory over "misbelief." In this way, the king's conversion merged the political nation with the true Church of God.[8]

Henri IV and his Catholic advisers reconfirmed rather than erased the existing lines of division in French society. The presence of Huguenots could of course be used to impugn the king's sincerity, while any attempt to include Leaguers devalued loyalist arguments in favor of Henri IV. Unwilling to strike out on the unknown path of pacification before he converted, Henri IV wisely put off the delicate problem of how to conciliate Huguenots and former Leaguers without undermining his own credibility as *roi très chrétien.* The decision to exclude supporters of the League was by no means absolute, however. Indeed, statements made by loyalist delegates at Suresnes after May 17 suggested that Leaguers could participate in the conversion if they recognized Henri IV as king.[9] At the close of the conference on June 23 in La Villette, Bellièvre struck a conciliatory chord when he wrote to Leaguers that "the aim toward which all good men strive is to live together in peace and dignity."[10] He considered a dignified peace to be any settlement which safeguarded Catholicism and upheld the honor of all Catholics who voluntarily submitted to Henri IV. He believed that such a settlement was possible if the Leaguers would accept the sincerity of the king's desire to embrace Catholicism. They had but to seize the opportunity before it slipped away.

This apparent openness is misleading, because loyalist Catholics made only a halfhearted effort to forge a wider sense of Catholic unity around the king's conversion once they set it in motion. Leaguers such as Épinac therefore remained circumspect lest they be duped by this "vain hope of conversion."[11] This distrustful attitude was unthinkable to loyalist Catholics who had staked their reputations and fortunes on the realization of the promise of St. Cloud four years earlier. To doubt the imminence of the king's conversion was tantamount to denying their own devotional integrity and political credibility. The certainty of the conversion's occurrence thus became a common refrain among loyalists during the early summer. On July 2, for example, Louis Birague ended a letter to Nevers with the prayerful injunction that God soon bless them with "the peace . . . desired by so many good men and our soon-to-be Catholic king, whose conversion everyone holds as a certainty." [12] Ten days later, Bellièvre implored the governor of Paris, the Comte de Belin, not to doubt the king's intentions because "the conversion is so near that you should consider it already accomplished." [13]

Loyalist Catholics thought that many moderate Leaguer noblemen and judges would be ready to defect if given the right opportunity. Some wags even joked that the resolution to elect a Catholic king, introduced back in April, had advanced the loyalist cause as much as the prospect of the king's conversion. [14] One observer remarked that Henri IV's decision to receive Catholic instruction had rendered "the people so disposed toward peace that it no longer seems possible for the League's leaders to control them." [15] Ten days before the conversion, however, Revol openly expressed fear that Paris might still withhold recognition from the king out of fear of the Spanish garrison stationed in the city. [16]

The loyalists' growing sense of righteousness frequently led them to send contradictory signals, however. In early June, for example, Henri IV authorized grain shipments to Paris as part of an effort to identify the conversion with prosperity. [17] Meanwhile, some of his Catholic advisers urged him to prosecute the war more vigorously by besieging the citadel of Dreux, which fell on July 5. By doing so they hoped to counter Leaguer claims that military necessity had constrained Henri IV to go through with the conversion. They also believed that a victory by the king would encourage disaffected Leaguers to abandon the doomed rebellion. [18] When Leaguer delegates at La Villette cried foul, Henri IV coldly retorted that "I do not respect anyone in the League enough to gauge my actions by their counsels." [19] Sensing triumph, loyalist Catholics paraded these contrary images of Henri IV as benevolent king and stern warrior in an attempt to demoralize the League and hasten its disintegration. In this calculation they were mistaken, however.

Leaguers failed to defect because they still refused to forsake their belief that heresy threatened the Church and the realm more than did resistance. Rather than abdicating their own sense of integrity—even in the face of inevitable defeat—Leaguers stood ready to measure the king's sincerity by his willingness to grant them a peace with honor.

All concerned knew only too well that a new era would begin for France the moment Henri IV stepped through the portals of the abbey church of St. Denis. The question that stirred their imaginations was whether that future would be one of new hope or of continued despair.

Why St. Denis?

Many reasons explain why Catholics involved in the king's conversion chose the royal abbey of St. Denis as the most appropriate setting for Henri IV's return to the Catholic Church. Named after the mythic Apostle of the Gauls, the abbey of St. Denis had served as a sacred repository for the collective memory and remains of French kings and queens since the days of the Merovingians. It was there, too, that past kings of France had gone to take into battle the *oriflamme,* the venerated lance draped in red and yellow silk said to have been bestowed on France by Jesus Christ during the Crusades. The monks of St. Denis had the special privilege of saying mortuary masses and prayers for this hallowed community of royal souls consigned to their care. In fact, some monks referred to their special mission when they contested the prominent role assumed by royal chaplains during the king's conversion. The chronicles which the monks compiled over the centuries also immortalized this rich royal legacy for future generations. Moreover, the abbey's treasures contained many sacred objects which reflected the anointed character of the French monarchy, objects such as the royal insignia used in the coronation ceremony at Rheims and the reliquaries and holy texts used in processions and liturgical services for royalty at St. Denis.[20]

Like other Catholic institutions in France, the royal abbey of St. Denis had been swept up in the struggles sparked by Henri IV's claim to the throne. Even before his accession in August 1589, some monks had opted to join the Holy League after the death of their abbot, the Cardinal de Guise, while others followed their new abbot, the Cardinal de Vendôme, into Henri IV's service. Each faction claimed that it alone fulfilled the sacred duties of the abbey. In fact, shortly before St. Denis fell to loyalist troops in June 1590, the League's lieutenant governor of Paris, the Duc d'Aumale, persuaded several sympathetic monks, including the grand prior, to transfer sacred objects found among the abbey's treasures to Paris for safekeeping. In the process, he hoped to transfer some of the abbey's prestige to his cause as well. The Leaguer monks of St. Denis who took refuge in Paris frequently displayed the cult objects of royalty in devotional processions organized by the Seize, while those who stayed behind in St. Denis closely guarded what remained of the abbey's *trésor*. Both sides tried to reclaim the abbey's historic mission of celebrating the glory and majesty of the French monarchy in an effort to broadcast their own royalist sentiments.[21]

The decision to stage Henri IV's conversion at St. Denis thus associated the king's experience with some of the most potent symbols of the Gallican cult of monarchy. St. Denis was above all the place of spiritual transition for royal souls. When Henri IV passed through the abbey portals, he—like his predecessors—left behind one life and entered a new and higher form of spiritual existence. Architecturally, in fact, the abbey church had been conceived by abbot Suger back in the twelfth century as a "sermon in stone."[22] The light which streamed through the rich stained-glass windows in the apse bathed Henri IV, when he eventually stood before the altar, in the brilliance of the Lord. The conversion at St. Denis thus reaffirmed Henri IV's destiny to inherit the heavenly kingdom of God as reflected in the crowns sculpted in the portal frieze—a commonplace about French kingship most recently reflected in Henri III's heraldic device of the three crowns, one celestial, the other two for France and Poland.[23] Henri IV's spiritual death and rebirth through conversion prepared him for his glorious entry into this special community of royal souls congregated at St. Denis. Surrounded by effigies of his predecessors, Henri IV paid filial homage to his Catholic ancestors, particularly Saint Louis, when he converted. Nicolas de Thou, bishop of Chartres, remarked on the rich devotional mystique which the choice of St. Denis lent the ceremony; in fact, he compared Henri IV's experience to that of Clovis, who had apparently been catechized there "by bishop St. Solimé before his baptism at Rheims by St. Rémi."[24] As another writer at the time put it, the abbey church of St. Denis stood as a temple of holy truth through the ages.[25]

The King's Catechism

Henri IV's formal Catholic instruction commenced on July 15 once the twenty or so clergymen he had invited assembled as scheduled in

Mantes. Although the king met briefly with them there, nothing is known of what they discussed. A handful of Protestant ministers also gathered in Mantes, still hopeful that they might play a role in the king's instruction; they had even prepared position papers on doctrinal questions, but to no avail, because the Catholic clergymen refused to let them participate.[26] The Huguenot divines remained in Mantes until July 23, two days before the king's conversion at St. Denis. As Huguenot hope dwindled during the dog days of summer, rumors began to circulate of a move to elect a new protector.[27] Excluded from the king's instruction and uncertain of their future, French Calvinists displayed the kind of nervous dread and resolve that had led them in the 1570s to take matters into their own hands.

Mantes apparently served as a staging ground for the clergy before they made their formal entry into St. Denis. There they began to talk over the texts of the king's abjuration and profession of faith; they also appointed a secretary to record their meetings. Over the next five days, their ranks swelled so that by July 20 some forty prelates and doctors of the Gallican church took part in the solemn entry at St. Denis to await the arrival of Henri IV.[28] The king's catechizers came almost exclusively from the upper rungs of the church hierarchy. Episcopal churches and abbeys loyal to Henri IV constituted the largest and most influential contingent, which included two archbishops, ten bishops, six cathedral deans, and seven abbots. Next came a diverse assortment of doctors of theology and canon law, among whom numbered four *curés* from Paris, three cathedral canons, two monks from St. Denis, and a Dominican friar. Although not in the group specifically designated to take part in the king's instruction, other clergymen, such as clerics in the royal chapel, also witnessed the conversion's proceedings. The clergy's numbers continued to grow after the entry into St. Denis, until some one hundred Catholic clergymen, including their entourages, stood in attendance at the king's conversion on July 25. This large turnout, which surpassed in size the first estate assembled by the League in Paris, surely helped to lend credence to the claim that Henri IV consulted the entire Gallican church when he converted to Catholicism.[29]

Upon entering St. Denis, the clergymen went straight to the abbey church, where they celebrated Mass and offered public prayers to God to bless the penitent king. They then repaired to the abbatial palace, currently occupied by the Cardinal de Vendôme, to prepare for the king's arrival. Over the next two days, the clergymen resumed work on drafting the king's abjuration and profession of faith. These two key documents required care because they had to offer compelling proof of Henri IV's total acceptance of Catholicism. Not all went smoothly, however, as Vendôme tried to introduce two proposals which, though quickly rejected by the assembly, threatened to disrupt the proceedings. In the first, he called upon the king to condemn the Huguenots in his profession of faith. If accepted, this measure could signal a return to the violent persecution of these important allies. The prelates managed to persuade Vendôme to withdraw the motion, arguing that it was unessential for the convert's salvation; they also perhaps secretly feared that such strong language could cause Henri IV to reconsider Catholic instruction.[30] The king's abjuration sufficiently denigrated the Reformed faith, they pointed out, because in it Henri IV had to demonstrate a thorough grasp of the reasons that he had forsaken Calvinism and embraced Catholicism.

Vendôme then questioned the conversion's validity without papal involvement—a concern shared by Catholics on both sides. A lively debate ensued among the assembled clergymen over how to justify to Rome a separate Gallican solution to the conversion crisis. In rejecting Vendôme's arguments, the clergy stopped well short of declaring the king's episcopal absolution a special prerogative of the Gallican church. Instead, they liberally interpreted the Tridentine decree which allowed episcopal absolution in cases normally reserved to the pope if the penitent faced the peril of imminent death. Anxious not to offend the pope or delay the king's conversion, the clergy underscored the provisional nature of absolution *ad cautelam,* which could be fulfilled, they conceded, only once the pope bestowed his own blessings on the royal convert. The clergymen at St. Denis thus tried to keep the ceremony's texts free of statements which might compromise Henri IV's future relations with both the Huguenots and Rome.[31]

Another matter which came before the assembly, this one more amicably resolved, was the delicate question of ecclesiastical jurisdiction over the king's conversion. Although abbot of St. Denis, Vendôme could not bestow absolution on the king because he had never been ordained. He therefore had little choice but to concede this privilege to Renaud de Beaune, who in addition to being archbishop of Bourges, was also *grand aumônier du roi* and head of the royal chapel. Philippe du Bec, bishop of Nantes and later archbishop of Rheims, received the honor of celebrating Mass at the king's conversion. Vendôme nevertheless asked for and received the right to precede Beaune and Du Bec during the solemn procession to the abbey church. In this way, he hoped to preserve the honor of the royal abbey, under whose jurisdiction the king's conversion still fell despite the temporary reduction in the abbot's role.

Henri IV arrived in St. Denis on the evening of July 22 with a huge retinue of noblemen and royal councillors. The clergy met the king at the town gate and then accompanied him to this lodgings in the Hôtel de Ville amidst the wild applause of joyful onlookers who lined the streets. During the reception, Henri IV announced a new extension of the ceasefire until the end of the month. He also gave strict orders that no scouting patrols or foraging parties be sent to the environs of Paris during the time of his conversion; any military activity would seem improper while the king was devoting himself to godly pursuits. Henri IV later added secret instructions, however, for his forces to be ready to move at a moment's notice.[32]

Henri IV then went to the abbatial palace, where the clergymen asked him how he wished to conduct his catechism. Although the king esteemed them all, he apparently thought it best to confer privately with four prelates—a request the assembly readily granted. Henri IV chose as his special interlocutors Beaune, Du Bec, Angennes, and Duperron, all longtime associates and advisers on affairs of church and state. The next morning, the king's formal instruction began when he met with the four prelates behind closed doors in talks which lasted until one o'clock in the afternoon. During the meeting, they went over drafts of the king's abjuration and profession of faith. They worked quickly because Henri IV had come to his instruction fairly well tutored as a result of the public disputations over doctrine held in Mantes earlier that spring.

The king's instruction at St. Denis diverged sharply from his promise in the Declaration of St. Cloud to link his conversion to an overall settlement of religious differences. This was not unexpected, of course, though it finally sealed the issue for the handful of Protestant ministers who still waited patiently in Mantes to be summoned by the king. Even more anomalous was Henri IV's decision to be instructed privately in his council, not publicly in a church. Although this move avoided the undignified spectacle of public reproof, it also contravened conventional expectations of a public catechism. These and other concessions to the royal conscience later made it possible for Leaguer diehards to argue that Henri IV had specified both the form and content of his reconciliation with the Church.

The king's catechizers tried to mask this discrepancy in the revivalist language and symbolism of Tridentine Catholicism. Surviving accounts of the king's instruction, compiled later for the pope's scrutiny, carefully presented the controversialist arguments used to persuade Henri IV to abjure his errors and embrace the faith. They covered Catholic teachings on the Eucharist, the veneration of saints, purgatory, auricular confession, and papal primacy in the Church.[33] No reference to the past political struggle can be found because the king's conversion presumably transcended worldly affairs. Henri IV's catechism therefore read like a primer in Catholic piety and controversialist argument intended to demonstrate the inevitability of the Church's triumph over heresy.

Much like earlier *récits de conversion,* the king's catechism at St. Denis used theological differences to elaborate on the threat that Protestantism posed to Christian society and to the individual.[34] One account of Henri IV's instruction, for example, attacked the Calvinist doctrine of predestination because it released the individual from all responsibility for his actions; what incentive did one have to be virtuous, it asked, if God had previously determined the fate of his soul? Another piece elaborated on the supposed affinity between Calvinism and atheism, charging that the Huguenot call for liberty of conscience merely masked a desire for moral license.[35] The king's catechizers also used the splintering of the "deformed Reform" as proof of its immorality. In their minds, Calvinism promoted moral disorder by surrendering to individual opinions, not visible authority, while the growing particularism evident in the Protestant movement undermined public unity. Official descriptions of Henri IV's instruction also underscored, as had earlier supplications, the incompatibility of heresy and monarchy.[36] The king's catechism thus restated the refrain of past years that to truly be king, Henri IV had to be Catholic. As his Catholic supporters saw it, Henri IV's decision to convert reaffirmed the normative value of confessional unity for the individual, the monarchy, and Catholic society.

In echoing these jaundiced views of Protestantism, official descriptions of Henri IV's instruction demonstrated to a skeptical public the king's commitment to Catholic doctrines as well as prejudices. They also emphasized the voluntary nature of the king's conversion in order to defend the royal penitent from attacks on his sincerity. Beneath these pictures of kingly resolve and piety there lurked fears about the conversion's acceptability. This concern even became manifested in such mundane matters as food. When Henri IV's private audience with the four prelates ended around one o'clock, for example, the king straightaway notified his household staff that, it being Friday, they were not to serve that evening or any Friday in the future any of the meats prohibited by the Church. This return to the dietary codes of the Catholic Church meant, symbolically at least, that Henri IV would no longer tolerate at his table any of the new eating habits Huguenots had used to flaunt their disregard for Catholicism. After the midday repast, Henri IV apparently decided to fast for the remainder of the day to deprive his body of pleasure while his mind concentrated on godly pursuits. The king began these penitential exercises immediately after catechism without any apparent prompting by his spiritual directors. This underlined anew that all such acts, like the conversion, flowed freely from the king's desire to return to the Catholic Church.[37]

The four prelates who had passed the morning with the king returned to the assembly of clergy around three o'clock. Renaud de Beaune told them that the king expected the final drafts of his abjuration and profession of faith to be ready that evening. Another dispute, again led by Vendôme, broke out because the cardinal believed that the amendments submitted by the king weakened the provisions against heresy. Several other prelates agreed with him this time and voted against acceptance of the drafts in their new form.[38] Discussions later that afternoon failed to bring a compromise. With Sunday less than two days away, the assembly had little choice but to send their complaints—and perhaps their prayers—to the king for consideration.

Henri IV wasted little time in dealing with the dispute. The next morning he called together several judges and crown officers, explained to them the unreasonableness of the clergy's refusal, and then warned that he could not go through with the conversion unless the clergy complied with his wishes. Henri IV accepted Achille de Harlay's offer to discuss the matter with the clergymen, hoping "they [would] take up this matter with earnest zeal."[39] Later that afternoon, the judges managed to persuade Vendôme and his followers to withdraw their objections and accept the documents with the king's amendments. The judges then returned with the two texts, which Henri IV read and signed, again in his royal council. This imbroglio on the eve of the king's conversion reminded Catholics that Henri IV still reserved the right to reconsider his decision to embrace Catholicism. The problem of the conversion's acceptability was already difficult enough without dissenters at St. Denis, even if only a small minority, sullying the project from the outset.

After signing the two texts that he was to deliver the next day, Henri IV went to read them before the assembly of clergy. This concluded his catechism, whereupon the clergy applauded his pious resolve and René Benoist brought the assembly to an end with a sermon on God's bountiless mercy for the sincere penitent—a sermon the king reportedly found quite pleasing.[40] Henri IV then declared St. Denis an open city welcome to all who wished to attend the following day's festivities. He sent a herald to Paris to tell its good people that the only passport they needed to gain entry into St. Denis was a joyful heart. After this gesture of goodwill, Henri IV accompanied the clergymen to the abbey church, where they together celebrated a triumphant *Te Deum*. That night Henri bade farewell to the handful of Huguenot retainers who had come with him to St. Denis. They then quietly departed from the town, leaving Henri IV alone one last time as a Protestant among Catholics.

Paris on the Eve

On July 24, League authorities in Paris, fearful of what the next day held in store for them and their cause, did their best to dampen the enthusiasm of the city's inhabitants, many of whom openly announced their intention to go to St. Denis on the morrow.[41] Seize officials ordered requiem masses to be held to mark the dark day which loomed ahead for Catholicism. At the prompting of the legate-cardinal of Piacenza, parish priests in the city declared the immediate excommunication of anyone who dared to take part in the "comédie de la conversion." Mayenne bolstered these spiritual punishments with physical threats. He made it a capital offense for anyone to leave the city during the next twenty-four hours, ordering the guards along the walls to shoot all such persons on sight. That ardent champion of the League, Madame de Nemours, delivered a sullen speech at the Hôtel de Ville in which she sadly deplored that "the king of Navarre will make himself over into a Catholic tomorrow, of that we cannot doubt." [42] It seemed that God was again putting them to the test by permitting the Béarnais to go through with his feigned conversion. The League's measures proved largely ineffectual, however, as several hundred *bourgeois et manans* stole out of the city under cover of night to St. Denis, where they joined the throngs of joyful witnesses gathered to receive Henri IV back into the Church and their hearts as *roi très chrétien.*

The Day of the Conversion

There was nothing casual about the choice of July 25 as the day for Henri IV to convert to Catholicism. It fell on the seventh Sunday after Pentecost, a time in the liturgical year when "there is signified and expressed this regenerated life, which is to be spent on the model of Christ's, and under the direction of his Spirit." [43] Henri IV's conver-

The Abjuration of Henri IV (Courtesy of Bibliothèque Nationale, Paris)

sion thus took place at a time in the liturgical cycle when the entire body of the faithful, after careful preparation, reaped the benefits of communion with Christ. The homiletic theme for the seventh Sunday after Pentecost further underscored the submission of the believer to Christ; the sermon of the day called for the supplicant to renew knowledge of the fear of the Lord, for "fear of the Lord was the beginning of wisdom."[44] The liturgy for the seventh Sunday after Pentecost enriched and deepened the meaning of the king's experience in ways that bolstered belief in his sincerity and thus acceptability as Catholic king.

Before rising that morning, Henri IV met privately in his bed-chamber with the Protestant minister, La Faye. Why La Faye had not left the previous night with other Huguenots cannot be determined. The pastor asked God to keep the king safe in the years ahead; he also promised to serve Henri IV as faithfully in the future as he had in the past. According to Estoile, the king thanked La Faye for this touching remembrance and assured him that as king, he "[would] never permit any wrongs to be committed against them, nor violence against their religion."[45] After a tearful embrace, La Faye left the room through a rear door, perhaps to spare Henri IV the embarrass-ment of being seen publicly with a Huguenot on the day of his con-version.

The conversion ceremony officially got under way around nine o'clock with a solemn procession of the clergy from the abbatial palace to the abbey church. The decision to hold two processions, one ecclesiastical and the other lay, reflected the separation of the religious and temporal spheres which eventually became joined later that morning when Henri IV knelt before the assembled prelates on the abbey steps. As the clergymen assembled outside the abbatial pal-ace, a brief dispute broke out between monks of St. Denis and royal chaplains as each group competed for the signal honor of carrying the cross, the holy water, and the bible to be used during the conver-sion ceremony.[46] Although head of the royal chapel, Beaune settled the disagreement in favor of the monks; in subsequent years, how-ever, royal chaplains were able to prevail in these and other such claims.[47] Once organized, the ecclesiastical cortege proceeded in an orderly fashion from the abbatial palace, located on the south side of the abbey compound, west along the rue de la Cordonnerie, which eventually widened into the large Place Pannetière, lying directly in front of the abbey church's west portals. There the procession ended. Several monks led the way into the square, bearing incense and ringing small bells which carried aloft in smoke and sound the good news of the king's conversion. Following them was the Cardinal de Vendôme, resplendently dressed in his abbatial robes and holding his jeweled crozier. Just behind him came Renaud de Beaune, whose long, flowing pontifical vestments signified his high honor as primate of Aquitaine. In his train were the bishops and abbots invited to St. Denis. Each group wore the special garb and insignia denoting its place in the church hierarchy. After them came the monks of St. Denis, who bore the sacred objects to be used during the conversion ceremony. Unlike the prelates, who represented the splendor of the Gallican church, the monks wore their regular choir robes in an effort to "keep at a minimum the pomp and solemnity ordinarily used in royal receptions." [48] The monks' modest dress signified that Henri IV came to the church as a simple penitent, not as *roi très chrétien*. The remaining clergymen brought up the rear of the procession, though nothing is known about the precise order in which they marched. In all, more than one hundred clergymen of the Gallican church took part in the ecclesiastical procession which wended its way that morning through the hot and dusty streets of St. Denis. [49]

According to most accounts, the crowds which lined the streets and square remained relatively subdued as these good shepherds passed them. This restrained attitude gave way to delirium, however, when around ten o'clock Henri IV finally set forth from the abbatial palace to begin his pilgrimage to the church. He and the other members of the much larger royal procession retraced the clergymen's route, only they trod upon a thick carpet of flowers thrown by the throngs of well-wishers who wildly cried "Vive le roi!" with the king's every step. [50] Henri IV's attire said much about how he approached his day of reckoning with God. The dominant motif was white, a symbol of purity and innocence which reflected the penitent's readiness to receive God with an open heart. Henri IV wore a simple white doublet with gold brocade and white stockings set off by a black cape, black shoes, and a black plumed hat. These garments had none of the usual insignia, such as *fleurs-de-lis* and crowns, normally found on the king's clothing in royal ceremonials. Significantly, the only emblem of royal authority that Henri IV bore during the procession was his sword, a sign of justice which testified to the righteousness of his conversion. [51] Yet the king gave up even this solitary symbol of royal authority to the Seigneur de Bellegarde before he made his way up the steps of the church. Stripped of the signs of kingship, Henri IV went to the abbey church as a humble penitent in search of divine forgiveness and salvation.

The royal procession which accompanied the modestly clad king more than made up for this absence of royal emblems on his person. In many respects, it resembled other triumphant royal entries of the Renaissance as dignitaries and court officers assumed their customary positions before and after the king. The *grand prévôt de l'hôtel du roi* led the way as master of court ceremonies, his baton raised high. Next came two hundred archers, each wearing green jerkins trimmed in gold, followed by the serried ranks of nearly five hundred royal guardsmen. On their heels marched some eight hundred lavishly dressed *gentilhommes* of the royal household. Then came representatives of the royal courts, first the Châtelet, then the Chambre des Comptes and Parlements, each draped in the rich red robes of judicial office. After them strode the Chancellor, François d'O, and other members of the royal council. Directly in front of the king came twelve trumpeters who signaled Henri IV's arrival. In his train followed an indeterminate number of princes, *grands,* knights of the Orders of St. Michel and the St. Esprit, *seigneurs,* and other assorted noblemen and officers. This impressive array of notables assumed their appointed places along the Place Pannetière directly in front of the abbey church as Henri IV slowly made his way up the steps to the prelates gathered at the doors of St. Denis.[52]

Bereft of the usual symbols of royalty, Henri IV became something of an anomaly in this otherwise traditional processional expression of monarchy. Whereas each group reflected various attributes of royal sovereignty, such as force and justice, Henri IV came as a simple penitent set apart by dress and space from the full panoply of French kingship. The symbolism of these ceremonies conveyed a much clearer separation of the king's *dignitas* from his person than most loyalist Catholics were ever willing to admit, given their notions of respectful obedience. They nonetheless found this distinction acceptable when expressed through ritual. This disparity also revealed the ongoing ambivalence they felt toward the twin image of Henri IV as the humble penitent and the absolute king. Many Leaguers, of course, shared this qualm but dealt with it through the language of suitability and election considered anathema by loyalists.

This disparity between religious rite and political thought continued during Henri IV's encounter with the prelates and clergymen gathered at the entrance of the abbey church. After removing his sword and hat, Henri IV left his entourage and climbed alone up the church steps. He stopped some six paces in front of Beaune and the others, and there knelt to the ground. In this way, he publicly displayed his willingness to submit to the Church's authority. As he lifted his head he witnessed a startling scene. Beaune's pontifical vestments left no doubt that he had the power to bind and loosen. Yet the chair upon which he remained seated represented the temporal realms which Henri IV hoped to receive after his conversion. Covered with white damask embroidered with golden *fleurs-de-lis,* the chair had carved in its rear corners the coats of arms of France and Navarre. This makeshift throne clearly belonged to the Church while Henri IV made amends, to be surrendered to him only after he had received absolution. The velvet carpets emblazoned with more *fleurs-de-lis* that were strewn about the reception area also echoed these royal motifs. Arrayed next to the enthroned archbishop were the prelates and other clergymen there to help him welcome the king back into the Church. This expression of the Church's supremacy over the crown is unprecedented in the annals of French history.[53]

As Henri IV gazed above the clerics, he beheld a similar scene sculpted on the arch of the main portal. There he saw the regal figure of an enthroned Christ, his arms spread outward as if to receive the royal penitent. The Twelve Apostles stood at Christ's side surrounded by a galaxy of saints and angels, one of whom carried a kingly crown while another brought down from heaven a crown of thorns. The columns which supported the arches contained reliefs of kings and queens from the Old Testament, thus signifying that the glory of kingship lay in service to the Church. A Latin inscription over the portal invited the onlooker to exalt in this depiction of triumphant Christianity. As Georges Duby wrote, referring to an earlier time, the imagery "serves the function of a profession of faith, the true faith, and repudiation of heretical deviations."[54] The clergymen on the abbey steps thus consciously emulated the sculpted vision of the Kingdom of Heaven which God had set over the earth, the entry into which they alone controlled as His ordained ministers.

Henri IV remained kneeling before the enthroned Beaune during the course of his interrogation on the church's steps. This exchange began with another poignant reminder that Henri IV came to the

Church as a simple Christian in search of God's mercy. Without any outward signs of his royal dignity, he heard Beaune ask him, "Who are you?" to which Henri IV simply responded, "I am the king," thus establishing his otherwise unknown identity. "What do you want?" the archbishop then tersely asked. "I want to be received into the bosom of the Roman Catholic Church," Henri IV solemnly replied. "Do you wish to do so freely?" Beaune then inquired in order to discover the nature of the king's intention. "Yes, I desire it freely," Henri IV proclaimed. Immediately after this brief interview, Henri IV delivered into the archbishop's hands the texts of the abjuration and profession of faith he had signed the previous day. With tears reportedly in his eyes—a sure sign of contrition—Henri IV then turned to the crowd in the plaza and, with his hand on a bible, recited a shorter version of his abjuration and profession of faith:[55]

> I, Henri, king of France and Navarre by the grace of God, do hereby recognize the Roman Catholic Church to be the true Church of God, holder of all truth and without error. I promise before God to observe and uphold all decrees established by its saintly Councils and all canons of the Church, following the advice given to me by prelates and doctors as contained in statements earlier agreed to by me wherein I swear to obey the ordinances and commands of the Church. I also hereby disavow all opinions and errors contrary to the holy doctrines of the Church. I promise as well to obey the Apostolic See of Rome and our Holy Father, the Pope, as have all my predecessors. I will never again depart from Catholicism, but instead persevere in its profession with the grace of God until I die. For this I implore His assistance.

Henri IV's address apparently touched off a wave of enthusiastic applause from the crowd in the square, after which Beaune and the assisting prelates sang the customary pontifical prayers of thanks to God. Then Beaune rose from his chair and, according to one account, again read the king's abjuration and profession of faith.[56] He then blessed the penitent king, who kissed the prelate's ring in return. Henri IV thereafter remained kneeling for some time, his head bowed in prayer. Beaune finally lifted him to his feet and led him into the church, "not without difficulty given the huge multitude of people within, all the way up to the rafters and windows" of the sanctuary.[57]

As the Swiss Guards beat their drums in solemn cadence, Henri IV made his way to the main altar with Beaune and Vendôme at his sides. The clergymen who had assisted on the steps entered next, followed by the lay dignitaries and crown officers who had accompanied the king in the royal procession. Henri IV knelt before the altar, it too draped in "ornements royaux," and with his hands placed on a bible reaffirmed his pledge to live and die a Catholic. The sound of the congregation's joyous cry of "Vive le roi!" then apparently filled the church. The oath that Henri IV swore at the altar sacralized the one he had just made on the steps of the church. Beaune intoned another prayer of thanks, after which he and Vendôme again helped the king to his feet and led him up to the altar—a holy place usually reserved to the priests. There, before God, Henri IV made the sign of the cross and tearfully embraced the altar, thus sealing his loving pact with the Lord. The king then walked behind the altar to the confessional that had been moved there specially for the occasion. The sacred space of the altar stood between the world and Henri IV as he confessed his sins to Beaune, which reportedly took about twenty minutes. Beaune imposed on the royal supplicant certain unrevealed penitential exercises and then absolved him for his past offenses against God. Meanwhile, some fifty cantors from the royal chapel sang the triumphant *Te Deum laudamus* to the crowd's by now constant refrain of "Vive le roi!" which resonated through the abbey church.[58]

His soul cleansed, Henri IV left the confessional and went to the special pew arranged for him in the main oratory. Elevated on a dais covered with rich velvet brocade embroidered with white *fleurs-de-lis* and draped with golden cloth, Henri IV sat above the congregation during the High Mass which followed his confession. This royal pew represented a public reintegration of Henri's person and royal *dignitas*, effecting a sort of spiritual enthronement of the now Catholic king. Beaune and Vendôme again took their places next to the kneeling king. Behind them in the abbey choir stood the assisting clergymen, while in the nave filed the princes, noblemen, and ladies, as well as court officers, all "mixed in together without any consideration of rank."[59] Some fifteen feet in front of the prayerful king stood Philippe du Bec, who celebrated the Mass, which Henri IV reportedly heard with "grande reverence." Two monks from the abbey, Nicolas Esselin and Jean de Lisle, assisted Du Bec by delivering that day's Epistle and Gospel readings. The first came from Romans, in which St. Paul admonished all believers not to yield to sin but instead to surrender themselves to God, to become "servants to righteousness unto holiness" (6:19). While the Epistle selection dealt with the glory of true conversion, Lisle's Gospel reading from Matthew dwelt on the dangers of hypocrisy and "false prophets" (7:4). Both addressed fundamental questions about the believer's sincere commitment to the Church—concerns that weighed heavily in the conversion of Henri IV.[60]

After the Gospel reading, Du Bec raised the bible toward heaven and then handed it to Vendôme, who brought it before Henri IV to be kissed—an act again otherwise reserved to the officiating priest. The cardinal then took the king's hand and led him to the Communion table directly in front of the altar. Behind the king came the Comte de St. Pol holding the royal sword, thus signifying that the consecrated Henri IV approached the Lord as king. Only Henri IV partook of the holy repast, receiving both the bread and the wine. This reflected not only a holdover from traditional notions about sacerdotal kingship, but also the Catholic practice of giving the new convert access to both the body and blood of Christ upon his return to the Church.[61]

After Communion, as the cantors sang the hymn *Agnus Dei,* Henri IV's chief rival in the past, Vendôme, fittingly offered the king the kiss of peace. The Mass now concluded, Vendôme turned to the congregation and declared that the consecrated Host would remain exposed on the chevet, to be used only in the subsequent Masses celebrated with the king over the next three weeks at St. Denis.[62] This meant that every time Henri IV returned to the Communion table, he would partake of the Host transubstantiated during his conversion; he would therefore reenact his conversion experience each time he approached the altar at St. Denis, thus reinforcing the mysterious bond forged between him and Christ. The decision to expose the Host used during the king's conversion also appealed to the popular revivalist practice of perpetual adoration of the Holy Sacrament by allowing the congregation to view and venerate the sacred repast destined for the king.[63] This permitted the faithful to approach, but not touch, the Host reserved for the king, for no one else could eat from that plate while Henri IV remained in St. Denis. For the people, the king's conversion became an event to be viewed only from a prescribed distance, lest they interfere in the holy relationship between the royal penitent and God.

No sooner had the king taken Communion, thus completing his

reunion with the Church, than a flock of white doves flew from the abbey's belfry. This "miracle," though no doubt planned to coincide with the king's reception of the Host, became the subject of excited comment after the conversion. Gabriel de Lurbe, a barrister from the Parlement of Bordeaux, for example, pointed out that among all the animals, the dove most typified the virtues of innocence and chastity; the gentle bird thus symbolized Henri IV's total devotion to the Catholic Church. The dove was also a harbinger of worldly peace, God's way of announcing his clemency and goodwill here on earth.[64] This obviously presaged a return to civil harmony, the barrister argued. Moreover, the Holy Spirit often took the form of a dove to aid a fallen individual's ascent to God. It had appeared at Christ's baptism (John 1:32) as well as at the celebrated conversion of Clovis. In Lurbe's opinion, the doves at St. Denis, "these beautiful messengers from heaven," likewise proved that the conversion of Henri IV was the work of God and no other.[65]

After Mass, as the doves still circled the Place Pannetière, Henri IV rose to rejoin the dignitaries, after which they all returned to the king's lodgings in the same order in which they had come earlier that morning. The humble penitent left the church as king, taking up his sword again and returning it to his side; he also exchanged his plain black cape for a crimson one emblazoned with *fleurs-de-lis*. During the ensuing procession, the converted king distributed some four hundred silver écus as alms to the enthusiastic crowd; he also instructed almoners from the royal chapel to dole out to the poor three thousand loaves of bread and three thousand sous in a munificent act of royal charity and penance.[66] Trumpets blared and tambours sounded as he strode through the streets, while cannonades from the town walls announced to the world Henri IV's return to Catholicism.

Upon returning to the Hôtel de Ville, Henri IV and an indeterminate number of clerics and notables sat down to enjoy the midday meal. Beaune solemnly blessed the dinner as cantors from the royal chapel sang *grâces en musiques*. A large throng gathered outside became so insistent in its shouts that Henri IV "was several times constrained to go outside or show himself at the window to appease his poor people."[67] Following the meal, René Benoist gave a sermon, after which the king and his guests repaired to the abbey church for yet another sermon, this time by Beaune. Regrettably, no details of these sermons have survived. At four o'clock, Henri IV attended vespers at the abbey church, during which "the Magnificat was alternately sung in plain chant or to the accompaniment of instruments played by the monks and cantors" in yet another attempt to mollify the squabbling clerics of St. Denis and the royal chapel. All remarked on the king's pious demeanor during the service as he remained kneeling before the altar, his hands clasped in earnest prayer.

At five o'clock, Henri IV left the abbey church and went by horse with a huge escort to the parish church of Montmartre, where he rendered thanks to God among the martyrs' tombs. A large crowd of townspeople apparently turned out to cheer him as he rode through the hilly streets. He eventually stopped at the promontory which overlooked Paris, where he remained in full view of his rebellious capital—a scant quarter mile away—as cannonades and fireworks in his honor lit up the evening sky. One sympathetic observer wrote that the converted king had but to ride down the hill to take the city.[68] After these festivities, Henri IV wended his way through the valley of Montmorency, occasionally stopping at other village churches enroute to render public thanks to God amidst more fireworks and the enthusiastic applause of spectators. This royal tour in miniature showed the converted king to the world at large as word rapidly spread throughout the Île-de-France and then beyond of Henri IV's glorious return to the Catholic Church. This short expedition also demonstrated to a country still at war the freedom of movement and courage of the new Catholic king. Henri IV wearily returned to St. Denis around eight o'clock to eat and rest after the long, eventful day. Many of those who had remained in the town, however, continued to toast the king long into the night. Raucous revelry replaced the solemn pomp and circumstance of the day on which Henri IV at last fulfilled his promise to convert to Catholicism.

What the Conversion Meant

The conversion of Henri IV was an extraordinary act of Christian submission and royal triumph that lent itself to numerous interpretations. Even loyalist Catholics disagreed over its meaning given the disputes that marred the king's formal instruction at St. Denis. Official transcripts of the conversion ceremony, documents that might be expected to convey a coherent picture of the king's experience, betrayed a conflict between the impression of royal initiative and contemporary expectations of penitential contrition during catechism. As a result, they left unanswered many important questions about Henri IV's sincerity and, thus, his acceptability as Catholic king.

One of the most controversial points was the validity of the episcopal absolution that Henri IV received from Beaune. The canonicity of the absolution was crucial, because without it Henri IV still remained in a state of mortal sin. Absolution thus held one of the keys to Catholic acceptance of him as a true believer and king. Loyalist clergymen argued that any bishop could absolve a heretic who abjured his misbeliefs. Besides this episcopal privilege, there was the question of the crown's exemption from sentences pronounced by the pope. The League's claim that the papacy alone and not the clerics at St. Denis possessed the right to forgive Henri IV flew in the face of the traditional liberties of the Gallican church. It is interesting, however, that loyalist clergymen chose not to cite these liberties to justify the absolution that Henri IV received at St. Denis, though defenders of the king, such as the lawyer Pierre Pithou, later did.[69] The clergy opted instead to rely on the special canonical case of absolution *ad cautelam,* recognized by Trent, which upheld episcopal jurisdiction if the penitent faced the peril of imminent death.[70] Although suffering under a papal ban, Henri IV could nonetheless licitly receive pardon from lesser priests since, as Claude d'Angennes noted, "the king continually takes part in patrols, sieges, battles, and ambushes which threaten his precious life."[71] Loyalist clergymen had offered similar arguments to justify the absolution Henri III had received shortly before his death. In both cases, steps had to be taken to win the full pardon of the pope because, as loyalist clergymen frankly admitted, absolution *ad cautelam* was only a temporary measure to be used under extraordinary circumstances. It was thus politically necessary to reach an understanding with the pope in order to render the conversion uncontestable. Loyalist clergymen also hoped thereby to reduce the possibility of a schism with Rome.

Official transcripts of the king's conversion also gave conflicting interpretations of the genesis of Henri IV's decision to embrace Catholicism. At times, they presented it as the result of months of intensive inquiry by the king who, guided by his catechizers, delved deeply into Catholic doctrine. The impromptu discussions, staged conferences, and then formal instruction he received on July 23 all meant that Henri IV had returned to Catholicism for its own sake, not in response to political pressure by his enemies. This emphasis on the voluntary nature of Henri IV's conversion left little room for divine inspiration, though transcripts and the king's letters all attributed the conversion to God's irresistible grace. The conversion of Henri IV reflected but could not settle the worrisome problem of free will and grace which had long perplexed Catholic theologians and, at the time, raised doubts about the king's sincerity.

These twin themes of kingly initiative and divine guidance moved from theology to a political defense of the rights of the royal conscience. This was perhaps best seen in Henri IV's unusual request to be instructed privately in the royal council, rather than publicly in a church. The special status of the royal soul simply demanded that certain aspects of Henri IV's experience, in this case his instruction, be removed from public view. This made belief in his sincerity turn more on the notion of respectful obedience than on acts of penitential satisfaction. To protect his royal dignity, the king and not his confessor determined his acts of atonement. The special latitude conceded to the royal conscience found its own unique limitations in Henri IV's responsibility as king to promote the welfare of both the Church and *estat*. After 1593, the pursuit and celebration of kingly *gloire* thus became expiatory acts for France's first Bourbon king, whose apotheosis would come seventeen years later as a result of an assassin's blade.

Another significant aspect of the king's instruction concerned his relations with the Church. Traditionally, a penitent's catechism heightened the sacerdotal authority of the priests. When the penitent happened to be the king, however, the clergy's duty to reprove the errant became intertwined with their civil obligation to obey God's lieutenant on earth. Although Henri IV's instruction and atonement made certain concessions on this score, other parts of the conversion ceremony returned quite forcefully to the Gregorian tradition of sacerdotal supremacy over kings. Although largely confined to ritual and imagery, this brief recrudescence of a very old debate perhaps helps to explain why champions of royal Gallicanism became so combative in the years ahead.[72] However discordant, the conversion of Henri IV was simultaneously an act of penitential submission by the king and a glorification of absolute monarchy.

Another source of ambivalence lay in attempts by loyalist Catholics to express in nonpartisan ways an act they alone controlled. They took special care to avoid statements, particularly in the king's abjuration and profession of faith, which could jeopardize Henri IV's future dealings with the Huguenots and the papacy. This conciliatory attitude never found its way to the peace talks carried on immediately before and after Henri IV's return to the Church, however. Many loyalist Catholics still held out for a victorious peace which would vindicate their principles of respectful obedience. Above all, they sought a settlement which would assure them primacy of place in the regime of the Catholic Henri IV. Only later did Henri IV begin to realize that partisan use of his conversion threatened to undermine his efforts to pacify the realm.

The conversion of Henri IV did not end on July 25, nor the next day when he met with Vendôme and the monks of St. Denis to reconfirm the abbey's privileges.[73] Neither did it end at any of the subsequent Masses which the king attended at the abbey church over the next three weeks. These acts and gestures merely reflected the full return of Catholic ritual and routine to court, a reestablishment in effect of the *la religion royale*. It might be said that the conversion of Henri IV continued for the remainder of his life, for he—like all Christians—had to wage a perpetual war against sinful temptation. The ceremonial expression of the royal conversion staged at St. Denis, though a crucial first step, paled before this deeper concern with conversion as an ongoing process of spiritual renewal. The ensuing debate between loyalist Catholics and Leaguers over Henri IV's sincerity gradually became part of a much wider inquiry into the nature of religious belief and action characteristic of the next century's Catholic revival in France. Years later, in fact, the funeral orations pronounced for Henri IV replayed the drama of his conversion as the potent image of the Gallic Hercules became merged with the Christian king's victory over sin in death.[74] Soon after the assassination, Henri IV's conversion entered the annals of royal historiography as infallible proof of God's eternal tutelage over France and its kings. All who found inspiration in the conversion of Henri IV perpetuated its salutary consequences for the realm. In this age of profound belief in God and reverence toward the throne, the grand gestures of kings— like the kings themselves—never really died but instead became immortalized.

8

The Catholic King
and Pacification

THE CONVERSION OF Henri IV provided no quick and easy end to the French Wars of Religion. Although divisions in the League widened after July 25, they were not strong enough to prompt a mass exodus to the Catholic king.[1] Other assurances besides conversion had to be given to Leaguers before they would formally recognize Navarre. For many Leaguers, the ceremonies performed at St. Denis left open not only the question of the king's sincerity, but also the question of what place, if any, he reserved for them in his court and government. Even members of Henri IV's coalition, from the royal council to officers in the field, differed sharply over how best to pacify the country. Some urged leniency toward the rebels, while others called for stern treatment. How the king's conversion would eventually lead to an end of the wars hinged on which of these different perceptions of Henri IV would prevail in the years ahead.

The Limits of League Resistance

Radical Leaguers wasted no time in attacking the king's conversion. The cardinal-legate of Piacenza set the tone on July 26, when he condemned the conversion as both feigned and injurious to papal authority.[2] Taunts and abuses poured forth from pulpits and presses in Paris and other Leaguer cities as radical Leaguers tried desperately to rally Catholic opinion against the converted king. Not surprisingly, the prolific Jean Boucher provided the most thorough critique of Henri IV's conversion in his *Sermons de la simulée conversion et nul-*

lité de prétendue absolution de Henry de Bourbon. Boucher delivered these sermons in the church of St. Benoît in Paris in early August 1593, and reportedly drew large crowds. Six months later, he returned to the sermons and prepared them for publication as the Seize's position in Paris rapidly disintegrated. Ironically, the first copies of the *Sermons* appeared only a week before Paris fell to Henri IV on March 22, 1594, after which Boucher fled for his life to the Spanish Netherlands.[3] Much the same fate befell Louis Dorléans, author of the witty tract *Le banquet et après disnée du conte d'Arète.* Estoile noted its existence in manuscript form as early as August 1593, though Dorléans delayed its publication until 1594; he, too, fled north after Henri IV entered the capital.[4] The brilliant *Dialogue d'entre le Maheustre et le Manant,* probably composed over the summer of 1593, also circulated as a manuscript before it finally appeared as a pamphlet in December. In this piece, a loyalist nobleman called the Mahuestre debated with the Manant, a pro-League townsman, the reasons for the recent wars and their possible resolution as a result of the king's conversion. Although the lag time between composition and publication certainly lessened the impact of these tracts, their authors raised serious questions about Henri IV's confessional change which could not be left unchallenged.

In many ways, Catholic attacks on *la comédie de la conversion* marked the efflorescence of League political theory, the logical culmination and restatement of nearly a decade of polemical struggle. For ardent Leaguers, it only stood to reason that Navarre had faked his conversion to realize his evil ambition to rule Catholic France; his present exploits thus constituted but another sorry episode in his life of heresy and immorality. The Manant, for example, asked why anyone should believe that Navarre now spoke the truth when the Béarnais had secretly remained a heretic after his conversion of 1572.[5] After all, every Catholic knew that Calvin encouraged his followers to lie and cheat in the pursuit of worldly fortune. Jean Porthaise, a canon doctor of theology in the diocese of Poitiers, claimed that Henri IV still attended clandestine Calvinist services as well as consorted with heretics.[6] It was obvious to Boucher that Navarre had consented to enter the Church only out of fear, not out of concern for his soul. He cited the betrayal contemplated by the Tiers Parti conspiracy and the Estates' efforts to elect a Catholic king as proof that

Henri IV succumbed to worldly pressures, not divine grace, when he went to Mass on July 25.

Radical Leaguers thought it only a matter of time before every Catholic realized, like them, that Navarre had converted for reasons other than religion. Censors pointed to the clumsy, contrived symbolism used during the king's conversion: Navarre's white tunic, the doves, and the copious tears of contrition, only served—in their opinion—to cloak the insincerity of the Béarnais. Anyone who accepted Navarre's sincerity had to have his head examined, never mind his soul. Critics of the king's conversion therefore determined to expose Navarre's true motives so that readers could understand "the consequences of this hopelessly sudden conversion."[7] To know a man's thoughts, let alone those of a king, meant passing judgment on matters of the heart—a province usually reserved to God. Boucher dealt with this problem ingeniously. To believe that God had actually moved Navarre to convert was nothing but a conjecture, for man—unlike God—had only the external signs or "fruits" by which to gauge the conversion's authenticity. The same held true for the Leaguers' assumption of insincerity. Yet in these times of turmoil and spiritual danger, the *bon françois catholique* had to judge as best he could the nature of Navarre's commitment to Catholicism and then use that knowledge, however uncertain, to determine his proper duty to the Church and France. For Boucher, all signs confirmed the suspicion that Henri IV merely pretended to embrace Catholicism. As the Manant snidely observed, going to Mass does not make one a Catholic.[8]

Among the signs which attested to a convert's sincerity was a willingness to perform notable acts of penance. Such was not the case with Henri de Navarre, critics charged. His confessor had failed to impose on him penitential works lest they detract from his supposed royal dignity. Such hesitation struck detractors as proof of Navarre's refusal to atone for his sins—a fact further seen, they claimed, in the glaring absence of regret and mortification normally expected in a new convert. Navarre's insincerity could be seen as well in the dissolute lifestyle he had pursued since the conversion, they argued. The Gascon wit so often admired in Henri IV became for his critics a sign of a blasphemous nature; his adulterous love affair with Gabrielle d'Estrées scandalized them as well. With satire and invective, they laid bare the worldly—and thus religiously suspect—side of the loyalists' *bon Henri*.[9]

Henri IV's instruction also became a subject of Leaguer complaint and derision. Some critics noted its alarming brevity, while others impugned the officiating prelates. Moreover, many of the crucial points in Navarre's supposed instruction had taken place behind closed doors, not openly in church. For Leaguers, the loyalist decision to catechize the king privately obscured the nature of the convert's new beliefs and commitment to the Church. As a result, these irregularities dashed whatever vain hopes Navarre had of being accepted as Catholic king of France.[10]

Leaguer attacks went beyond the issue of personal change because Catholic opposition to Henri IV rested on his unsuitability to occupy the throne, not on his capacity to become a Catholic. Even if valid, Henri IV's rehabilitation through conversion had no effect on his permanent exclusion from the royal succession, critics argued. Navarre's supposed royal dignity required him to adhere even more strictly to the forms of true conversion, not bypass them. A related concern was the attempt by loyalist Catholics to make any inquiry into the king's motives for conversion a treasonable offense, a case of *lèse majesté*. Boucher and others thought the troubling oversights which marred the conversion undermined the king's ability to perform his sacred duty of upholding public morality. For them, loyalist Catholic efforts to remove the king's conscience from his subjects' gaze corrupted the public nature of the royal office. For the sake of public safety, a prince's reasoning had to be scrutinized "not only with regard to his actions, but even his thoughts," Dorléans wrote.[11] Echoing his 1585 tract *L'anglois catholique*, he pointedly added that the rise and fall of past monarchies was nothing more than the story of the piety or impiety of the princes who governed them. Catholics should therefore withhold recognition from Navarre until he had proven his love for his subjects and the Church. The best way this could be shown, according to ardent Leaguers, was for Navarre to abdicate any claim he had to the throne.

However brilliantly rendered, the case which these champions of Catholic resistance built against the king's conversion failed to arrest, let alone reverse, the steadily growing disunity in the League. The radical attack on the conversion may very well have accelerated the movement's disintegration because it failed to heed the extent to which war-weariness and approaching economic collapse had undermined the Leaguers' will to believe Navarre insincere. Few alternatives apart from reconciliation existed, given the inability of the Estates General of 1593 to translate Leaguer elective theory into practice. The threat of Spanish intervention along with rising social tensions, seen so vividly, for example, in the *Dialogue d'entre le Maheustre et le Manant,* made defection an increasingly honorable choice for Leaguer *bons françois* in the nobility and the magistracy. Recognition of the converted Henri IV soon became synonymous in the loyalist press with opposition to foreign aggression and the craven ambitions of social inferiors.

In the end, the perception of insincerity so crucial for further Catholic resistance required an even greater commitment to the movement's principles than during the time of Navarre's overt heresy. The conversion had altered the frames of reference that had earlier shaped how both parties dealt with the question of the king's faith. In the past, the burden of proof concerning Henri IV's willingness to convert had lain with loyalist Catholics; after July 1593, it shifted to radical Leaguers whose critique assumed that it was only a matter of time before Navarre's insincerity became obvious to all. But time was a commodity in short supply for Catholics still pledged to resistance after Henri IV's day of reckoning at St. Denis.

The Politics of *Douceur*

A variety of options existed for the converted Henri IV as he turned to the problem of pacification. He could step up pressure on the League to force its surrender—a policy long advocated by Huguenots and Catholic hardliners before the conversion; or he could treat the Leaguers leniently—an approach which appealed to advocates of a negotiated settlement. In the past, Henri IV had usually sided with the proponents of a harsh peace, though necessity had at times compelled him to allow talks with the League. After his conversion, however, Navarre slowly gravitated toward a lenient accord for reasons that are not difficult to fathom. A conciliatory approach could help dispel the warnings of apocalyptic doom sounded by radical Leaguers by extending to all his subjects the mercy God had shown the king during his conversion. After all, it was highly impolitic to treat the Leaguers in ways which contradicted the very spirit of his reconciliation with the Church. In this way, the exigencies of propaganda entailed in validating his sincerity helped shape how Henri IV approached pacification.

Fittingly enough, Henri IV opened the campaign for his acceptance as a sincere Catholic by sending dozens of circular letters to loyalists who had not been present at St. Denis. These letters allowed the general populace to participate vicariously in his conversion by ordering public processions and prayers to be held to thank God. Celebrating the abjuration also offered the community and its leaders an occasion to demonstrate their loyalty to the converted king. Henri IV furthermore enjoined local curates to read his letters to their congregations so that "everyone will dutifully praise God." [12] After the fall of Paris on March 22, 1594, such prayers for the king served as a test of loyalty for Paris curates. [13] The traditional Gallican invocation for the king during Mass was also reintroduced to signify the confessional unity of Navarre and his Catholic subjects. [14]

Henri IV's letters and declarations after July 25 proposed no startling new measures, but rather fulfilled previous expectations about the conversion's nature and motives. His conversion, for example, satisfied his promise at St. Cloud to be instructed in Catholicism. As evidence of his sincerity, Henri IV reiterated in an abbreviated form his abjuration and profession of faith; he also renewed in each letter his sacred pledge to live and die a Catholic. All who accepted his sincerity helped to secure the lasting peace and prosperity which France deserved after so much suffering. Acknowledgment of the king's sincerity also vindicated past Catholic support of his claim to the throne. Henri IV thus made it clear that all Catholics could share in the glory of the conversion by accepting his sincerity as a Catholic and his authority as king. [15]

Henri IV took the initiative in the brewing debate over his sincerity not only in words, but in actions. It became widely advertised, for example, that he attended Mass daily at St. Denis for most of August. The king also made it a point to tour neighboring churches in the Île-de-France, liberally dispensing alms to the enthusiastic crowds who greeted him. The thaumaturgical rite of the king's touch, infrequently performed during the years prior to his conversion, reemerged in Henri IV's encounters with the populace after July 1593. The forgiveness he had received from God also moved him to release a number of petty criminals from prison—a departure from the previous practice of granting such pardons almost exclusively during royal coronations.[16]

Paranoid fears that crazed assassins—some real, such as Pierre Barrière and Jean Chastel, and others imagined—stalked the converted king began to circulate among his supporters during the weeks following his conversion. These scares continued to recur periodically for the remainder of his reign until, as prophesied, Henri IV perished by an assassin's knife. The seven or eight plots reputedly discovered between 1593 and 1595 revealed not only the malefic intentions of hardened Leaguers, but also the divine protection enjoyed by the converted Henri IV. In fact, according to the *procès-verbal* composed after his arrest, Pierre Barrière had momentarily lost heart after he saw the king praying devoutly during Mass, though his courage eventually returned on August 12, 1593, when he finally struck.[17] This time Henri IV escaped with only a minor flesh wound. Although relieved, his supporters fully expected another attack in the near future. When it came sixteen months later, it was God who diverted "the murderous blade" held by Chastel. Henri IV's survival thus attested to his sincerity and invited his loyal subjects to implore God to save him from a martyr's fate.[18]

The potent image of Henri IV as a devout and clement king emerged strongly in the subsequent campaign to win his acceptance as Catholic king. For weeks after his conversion, in fact, he purposely abstained from military maneuvers in and around Paris, because he thought it unseemly to tarnish his newfound faith with martial pursuits. Henri IV perhaps best advertised his openness to peace in the general truce he concluded with Mayenne on August 1, 1593. Henri IV had previously refused to make such a pact with Mayenne lest it revive the duke's wavering authority over the rebellion. That political concern faded after July 25, however, as conciliatory Catholics urged the king to promote a connection between his conversion and the growing desire for peace evident throughout the country. On July 31, the king finally gave in to Mayenne's insistent demands for a treaty and, on the next day, agreed to a general truce for three months.[19]

On paper, at least, the general truce of August 1 marked a significant step forward on the road to pacification. The truce called for an immediate ceasefire and enjoined both sides to set up a joint commission to work out a lasting settlement. The truce even proposed topics for future discussion, such as amnesty provisions and guarantees for the Church. Though the commission met in September, it soon became incidental as the truce broke down and the war resumed its bloody course. After the general truce of August 1, Henri IV never again departed from his long-standing policy of dealing separately with each Leaguer, and never under any circumstance did he afford Mayenne the luxury of acting in their names. A world of difference existed between such public shows of peaceful intentions and Henri IV's readiness to compromise with his adversaries, however. He used the general truce, in fact, to prepare for his brand of pacification; since assuming the guise of the clement monarch, he was in a much stronger position than before the ceasefire to return to his familiar policy of divide and conquer.

Although the general truce hardly signaled a return to normalcy, it helped to encourage the slow but steady drift of Catholic opinion toward the converted king. It was an extraordinary public relations coup for loyalists because it allowed the king to maintain his current military advantage while portraying Leaguers, many of whom seemed genuinely open to rapprochement, as treacherous warmongers. It also further isolated Mayenne. The more conciliatory Leaguers in the Parlement of Paris and among the nobility pressed the duke to continue along the path of peace, while the more refractory Catholics, led by the preachers, refused to be party to an accord negotiated in their name, but without their consent. During the autumn of 1593, radical Leaguers denounced Mayenne and his followers as traitors to the holy cause of Catholic resistance. These disputes soon made it impossible for any of them to challenge the growing loyalist monopoly on the language of peace and order so crucial to swaying public opinion.[20]

Mayenne's acceptance of the truce proved that it was indeed possible for Leaguers to conclude a peace treaty with the converted king which, at least on paper, protected them and the Church. The duke's inability to rally his fellow Leaguers behind the truce permitted Navarre's supporters to blame him personally for subsequent violations of the ceasefire, however.[21] Mayenne's predicament made Henri IV's frequent avowals that he sought peace seem all the more credible by allowing him to maintain the public fiction that he prosecuted the war for the sake of peace.[22] Henri IV meted out swift punishment to those whom he thought guilty of violating the ceasefire, though in several instances the loyalists clearly acted as the aggressors.[23] This fact mattered little because in print Henri IV almost always emerged as the aggrieved party. After the conversion, the politics of peace seemed ineluctably to favor the king's cause as he and his publicists skillfully offered to the war-weary country the panacea of peace, only to withdraw it when they thought the rebels unworthy of it.

Although cynically used by both sides, the general truce served as a model for the accords which Henri IV later concluded with Leaguers in 1594 and 1595; in fact, many of its clauses reappeared word for word in these later treaties.[24] Henri IV certainly allayed much anxiety among Leaguer notables when in article II, for example, he recognized all appointments made by Mayenne during the war. Besides confirming the notables in their offices and privileges, Henri IV allowed them to continue to collect taxes and surcharges levied in areas under League control. The king matched this restraint toward Leaguer notables with measures designed to win him the favor of Catholic merchants and peasants. The peace he offered held out the promise of renewed prosperity in its call for a resumption of free trade *(libre commerce)* and in its guarantees for the orderly gathering and marketing of the harvest that autumn. The king also vowed to reduce the current tax burden to its pre-war levels; indeed, the later Croquant revolts have been linked to such unfulfilled promises.[25] He dealt with the problem of local law and order by proscribing duels and empowering judicial officers to bring criminals to justice. Moreover, Henri IV inserted provisions which allowed local officials considerable latitude in tailoring the truce to fit local conditions. In these ways, the general truce of August 1 seemed a solid step in the direction of a lasting peace; what it lacked was the requisite commitment by both sides to put its provisions into practice.

Peace and Obedience

This commitment to peace took time to develop. Above all, it required further clarification of what Henri IV's conversion meant to a public long suspicious of his motives. This task fell to loyalist Catholic writers, who over the next several months elaborated on the themes of clemency and peace in their defenses of the king's sincerity. Some emphasized the religious meaning of Henri IV's experience at

St. Denis, while others concentrated on its political import. An example of the first approach came in an open letter by René Benoist to his parishioners in Paris, published in late August 1593. As a clergyman, Benoist naturally interpreted the rebellion largely in terms of the role played in it by men of the cloth. For him, Catholic opposition to Henri IV had sprung from the League preachers' misuse of the sacred authority vested in them by God. Rather than maintaining Church discipline, they had seduced the credulous populace into wrongly fearing that Henri IV sought the destruction of the true faith. They, not Navarre, therefore posed the most dire threat to the Church and realm. By fixing blame exclusively on League preachers, Benoist of course all but exonerated other Leaguers of responsibility for the rebellion, thus smoothing the way for their reconciliation.[26]

Catholics had to respect the integrity of Henri IV's new faith because only God possessed certain knowledge of its existence in the king's heart. Obedience to the converted king thus became a pious work, disobedience a sin. Benoist urged his readers to consider the many signs of Henri IV's sincerity. These included the king's clemency, the appearance of the white doves, and his miraculous survival of Barriere's assassination attempt. All these wonders clearly showed that Henri IV walked in the path of the Lord. To the standard *topoi* of personalized kingship, such as valor, courage, and magnanimity, Benoist added the sanctifying force of divine grace. In this way, Henri IV's person had become infused with holiness by the act of conversion. Once apprised of these "facts," the pope had to forgive the eldest son of the Church, Benoist reassured his readers. A new golden age was at hand for France and the Catholic Church, he exclaimed, now that God had answered their prayers for a Catholic king. Those who criticized the king's conversion only tempted God to revisit His wrath upon the country for its ingratitude. In the end, Benoist's case for Catholic acceptance of Henri IV rested on this precarious, yet optimistic, vision of future religious reform and renewal under the converted king.[27]

Benoist's pastoral letter interpreted the struggle for Catholic acceptance as a battle between good and evil. These bold tones became blurred, however, in Pomponne de Bellièvre's *Advertissement sur la conversion de Henry de Bourbon IIII*, which also appeared in late August.[28] As in the past, Bellièvre struck a conciliatory chord when he confessed that both sides shared some of the blame for the past conflict. He urged both parties to approach the peace talks, just then getting under way, in a spirit of Christian humility and forgiveness—a position which hardly sat well with hardliners in the king's council. With an eye to influencing crown policy, Bellièvre sent advance copies of his tract to a number of the king's councillors in an effort to elicit support for his conciliatory views.[29] His tract thus reflected as much as contributed to the critical shift then taking place in Henri IV's pacification policies.

Bellièvre considered it the duty of every *bon françois* to accept the king's sincerity; in this way, he lent Benoist's emphasis on charitable *douceur* a political twist. Whereas Benoist used a sermon to expound upon the religious duty of every good Catholic, Bellièvre sought through reference to historical events to establish the civic obligations of the good Frenchman. Bellièvre resorted to the recent past solely for didactic reasons, however, and did not hesitate to violate historical accuracy. He conveniently forgot, for example, to mention the large number of Catholics who, like himself, had withdrawn from court after Henri III's death; he also presented the promises extorted from Henri IV at St. Cloud as merely the humble requests of a complaisant Catholic nobility.[30] These distortions mattered little because Bellièvre never intended the *Advertissement* to mirror the past; rather, he selectively used it to reorient the Leaguers' political loyalties, which now, he argued, coincided with their long-standing duty to protect the Church.

Bellièvre's tract echoed a generation of political commentators who had treated the much cherished notion of the good French Catholic. His historical review made it clear that only loyalist Catholics had performed the dual obligations to throne and altar contained in the title of *bon françois catholique*. As a reward for their steadfastness, God had finally let the scales of error fall from the king's eyes. By converting, Henri IV had shown that he, too, belonged among the *bons françois catholiques*. Now only the Leaguers' voluntary submission to him stood between war-torn France and a lasting peace. Acceptance of Henri IV's sincerity offered Leaguers a chance—perhaps their last—to reaffirm their adherence to the code of the perfect Frenchman, to reclaim this venerable heritage and serve as an instrument of Providence.[31]

Bellièvre balanced his description of the *bon françois catholique* with a lengthy analysis of the recent wars. These passages shed light on the evolution of Henri IV's pacification program as well as his decision in 1595 to declare war on Spain. While criticized, the Leaguers hardly emerged as the chief villains in Bellièvre's account.[32] He instead reserved his opprobrium for Philip II of Spain. Although the Spanish menace had always figured significantly in loyalist literature about the war, it began to assume primacy of place only in 1593 as Henri IV moved toward the conversion. Antoine Arnauld's inflammatory tracts, such as *Les fleurs de lys* (1593), typified this new tendency to shift blame almost exclusively onto the king's foreign enemies.[33] In fact, Arnauld went so far as to transform the Leaguers into Spaniards, crudely arguing that their rebellion had stripped them of their ethnic identity. His call to arms tried to fan the almost racial enmity he saw existing between the French and the Spanish. He went beyond the familiar contention that Philip II used religion to cloak his ambitions; in his mind, the Spanish king was a dark-skinned Moor who secretly clung to the beliefs of the infidels.[34]

These venomous attacks on Spain set the stage for a crucial reinterpretation of France's civil wars. Conciliatory Catholics such as Bellièvre presented a vastly inflated picture of Spanish ambitions in an effort to lessen the domestic character of the conflict. In this way, the Leaguers became mere pawns in the larger national struggle between two peoples and historical traditions. As Bellièvre saw it, the Leaguers' principal crime lay not so much in willful sedition, as in their almost naive inability to distinguish between good and evil. Their otherwise laudable, if misplaced, concern for religion allowed them to be duped by France's hereditary enemies. Although such an explanation certainly did not exculpate the Leaguers entirely, it went a long way toward lessening the enormity of their crimes against the king. Like the later peace accords with Leaguers, Bellièvre reserved punishment for those directly implicated in the death of Henri III. As the Leaguers' role in the wars diminished, the loyalist Catholics no longer saw their end solely in terms of Leaguer submission. A lasting peace could instead come only with a complete Spanish defeat. Opponents of a *repos avec dignité* challenged this inordinate emphasis on the Spanish menace because it meant that the Leaguers could not be held responsible for the war.[35] Their harsh views went unheeded, however. Keenly aware of the benefits of benevolent rule, Henri IV apparently thought it better to treat the rebels as prodigal sons who could return home if they acknowledged his authority.

Benoist's homiletic letter on charitable *douceur* and Bellièvre's historicized account of the good Frenchman represented two different rhetorical approaches to the problem of Henri IV's acceptance as Catholic king. Antoine Séguier, *avocat général* in the loyalist Parlement of Paris in Tours, chose another familiar Renaissance genre, the panegyric, through which to broadcast the significance of the king's conversion. Unlike the tracts discussed above, Séguier's speech remained unpublished because it addressed an audience already firmly committed to the converted king. This explains why his harangue, delivered on November 13, 1593, to Henri IV and his fellow magistrates in Tours, dwelt more on the conversion's symbolic meaning than on its immediate political consequences. For him, Henri IV's experience at St. Denis represented a "rebirth of the French state and monarchy."[36] Rather than polemicize, Séguier strove through the language of exaltation to elevate the king's conversion to the august place he thought it deserved in the eternal memory of mankind. Without such literary monuments to preserve it, the king's conversion would risk fading into oblivion. Besides constituting a grievous disservice to the king, such an oversight withheld from future generations the vital lessons which Henri IV wished them to learn from his experience.

Like most panegyrists, Séguier often bordered on the commonplace because his desire to glorify the king's conversion did not embolden him to enter the debate over its validity. Indeed, to do so would somehow sully its miraculous quality. Henri IV's conversion had taken the world completely by surprise, he proclaimed; it was a "coup de salut" which heightened God's majesty by showing how the best-laid plans of men often went awry. Even so, Séguier's ingenious emphasis on the conversion's spontaneity served to strengthen the case for the king's sincerity. He warned loyalists not to take credit for the king's conversion, because any such claim detracted from the act's sacral quality. If Henri IV had been coerced, as his enemies so often contended, it was only by the will of God. Séguier wistfully recalled the absence of those loyal men whose deaths in the king's service had robbed them of the chance to witness the conversion at St. Denis. Rather than being mourned, they should be envied because "they reside where the prompting for the the king's impulse to convert first began."[37] The royal council which had catechized Henri IV thus extended to heaven; its members included not only God, but also the souls of departed servants. Séguier then went on to prophesy future blessings for France now that God had so visibly accepted the king back into the fold. Even more than the cleric Benoist, Séguier invested the king's conversion with the full panoply of religious mystery and the cult of kingship.

Loyalist defenses of Henri IV's conversion all shared certain qualities. All honored the unquestioning acceptance of Henri IV's right to rule France in what Séguier called "chaste silence." All three presented the conversion as a signal triumph of the Catholic reform movement, its first "coup de salut" against heresy, thus challenging the League's assertion that it alone embodied the spirit of militant Catholicism. They also linked the king's return to the Church with a thorough reform of the *estat*. Moreover, the arguments they used to defend the king's sincerity complemented Henri IV's own budding decision to pursue a lenient peace which would preserve the dignity of both parties. He chose peace based on *douceur*, not force, because it proved more compatible with the images of benevolence and piety that he wished to associate with his conversion. Just as the conversion had revolved around the question of Henri IV's sincerity, so the reestablishment of his authority ultimately depended on the voluntary submission of his subjects out of heartfelt affection, not fear.

Papal Absolution and Coronation

Catholic resistance after July 1593 derived much of its remaining strength from Pope Clement VIII's refusal to absolve the converted king. So long as papal acceptance was not forthcoming, the ceremonies performed at St. Denis could possibly be construed as schismatic. Once granted, however, papal absolution would make Catholics who still opposed Henri IV guilty of dividing the Church. Both parties, not to mention Spain, thus had much at stake in the diplomatic struggle over papal absolution. The Sieur de Sancy, a later convert to Catholicism, spoke for many when he wrote in October 1593 that "all our plans depend on what happens in Rome."[38] All found the road to Rome paved with many difficulties. The tortuous negotiations with the papacy over the issue of Henri IV's absolution dragged on for more than two years until Clement VIII finally consented in September 1595 to accept Henri IV into the Church.

Efforts to win papal absolution encountered obstacles from the outset. Rumors of the pope's joy upon learning of the king's conversion raised loyalist hopes, though Clement VIII could ill afford to ignore the formidable curial forces which Spain quickly rallied against talks with Navarre. Another stumbling block arose when Mayenne and other League leaders demanded an active role in these delicate negotiations, which—if successful—could improve their bargaining position with Henri IV. A pattern to the talks soon emerged as a result of this interplay between maneuvers in Rome and events in France. Leaguers often subverted the talks whenever they thought that papal absolution might be procured without them; likewise, the mere suggestion of League involvement in the negotiations so enraged Henri IV that he, in turn, undermined them whenever the pope consulted the Leaguers. The king also thought it best to delay talks with Rome as long as much of Catholic France still opposed his rule. He expected the pope to demand less onerous conditions for the absolution if he came to Rome as master of his realm, not its disputed leader.

Henri IV therefore waged his diplomatic offensive in Rome with an eye to the domestic problem of acceptance, rather than in any real hope of rapidly gaining papal forgiveness.[39] The day after his conversion, Henri IV sent the first of many letters to Clement VIII in which he humbly begged the pope to bestow on him the blessings due the eldest son of the Church.[40] A short time later, this letter went into print, as did numerous other documents associated with the mission to Rome undertaken by Nevers in August 1593. In fact, Nevers annotated these documents and had them published upon his return to France in February 1594.[41] Ossat and Duperron, who led the next, more successful delegation to Rome, employed the same rapporteur technique during their lengthy stay in Italy, thus affording Catholics in France a privileged—and one-sided—view of the trials and tribulations which beset the king in his efforts to win papal absolution.[42]

However dismal the prospects seemed in Rome, Henri IV and his Catholic supporters considered it imperative to publicize the king's readiness to submit to the pope. In time, these images of the humble king mattered more than the desultory negotiations in Rome. The news the king's supporters released about the talks made it clear that blame for their failure lay not with the repentant Henri IV, but rather with his enemies who held the Holy Father in thrall. Leaguer submission to Henri IV thus took the place of papal absolution once the rebels accepted the king's Catholicity; in this way, Henri IV prevented the papacy from mediating his reconciliation with his Catholic subjects.[43] As a result, when papal absolution finally came on September 22, 1595, it served more as a postscript to pacification than as its prelude. As Ossat playfully remarked to Henri IV in his description of the absolution ceremony in Rome, the pope's scepter felt no heavier than a fly when Clement VIII lowered it upon the king's shoulder as a sign of punishment.[44]

Even without papal absolution, Henri IV had another way in which to advertise his sincerity and authority as Catholic king: his *sacre* and coronation. At the time of his conversion, some advisers had urged Henri IV to proceed at once with a coronation to sanctify his authority even further. A variety of factors, particularly the League's control of Rheims, the traditional site of royal coronations, persuaded him to delay his *sacre* until the next year, when he finally decided to hold it in Chartres.[45] Opinion differed in the sixteenth century as to whether coronation rites helped constitute the king's authority or merely symbolized its sacred character. As could be expected, Leaguers tended toward the former viewpoint, whereas loyalists generally opted for the latter.[46]

French coronations had long reflected the monarchy's transcendent quality and close proximity to God. Official accounts of the coronation ceremony performed on February 17, 1594, at Chartres also presented Henri IV's anointment and investiture as sterling proof of his sincerity as a Catholic. Among the traditional oaths he swore as *roi très chrétien* was the solemn promise to extirpate heresy from the realm—a commitment many Leaguers still demanded before they would consider him legitimate. Along with the unquestioning service expected of the perfect subject went the special need to revere monarchical authority as a power which partook of the divine.[47] As during the king's conversion, sympathetic commentators highlighted the messages of peace and goodwill they saw contained in the rituals performed at Chartres. The holy oil used to anoint the king and the insignia of royal office symbolized "the peace we hope God will soon send us."[48] The coronation performed at Chartres thus lent more substance to the themes of clemency and benevolence which loyalists strove to associate with the converted Henri IV. Nicolas de Thou, bishop of Chartres, who officiated in place of the archbishop of

Rheims, later wrote the king that the coronation had done more to advance his cause than had the past four years of fighting.[49] Although this was an exaggeration, it is nonetheless true that Leaguer defections increased considerably after the king's *sacre* at Chartres.

Henri IV's promise at Chartres to insure a Catholic succession became a reality in the next few years as he commenced the slow, but quite deliberate recatholicization of the Bourbon household and its collateral lines, particularly the Condé family. Plans were already being made to arrange a divorce from Marguerite de Valois, with whom Navarre shared a mutual animosity rather than a conjugal bed.[50] Henri IV hoped he could then wed Marie de Medici of Florence. After considerable difficulty, the marriage finally took place in 1600. In the meantime, Henri IV entrusted the young Henri II de Condé, heir apparent until the birth of the future Louis XIII in 1601, to Catholic tutors who hoped to sow the seeds of another conversion. They were not disappointed.[51] Similar efforts in 1599 regarding the king's sister, Catherine de Bourbon, proceeded less smoothly, because she stubbornly clung to the Calvinist beliefs of her mother, Jeanne d'Albret. Like her mother, she became a symbol of respectability and a source of financial support for many leading lights of the Reformed movement until her sudden death in 1606.[52]

Henri IV's decision to recatholicize the royal family formed part of a larger confessional change taking place after 1593 at court and in the royal government. Although he had much less control in this arena, Henri IV nonetheless exercised an important influence over the growing number of Protestant officials and noblemen who embraced Catholicism. Among these converts were many of the king's Huguenot advisers, men such as Victor Pierre Palma Cayet (1593), Jean de Sponde (1593), the Sieur de Morlas (1594), and the Sieur de Sancy (1596). As Huguenot influence at the Bourbon court dwindled after 1593, relations between Navarre and the Reformed community deteriorated into mistrust and verbal abuse. Sully, of course, remained exceptional in this regard only because he refused to serve as the Huguenots' advocate at court.[53] All these converts cited high on their list of reasons for abjuration the sterling example set by the king. Other resonances of the king's conversion can be found in the apologia they wrote defending their decision to accept Catholicism. In them, they elaborated on many of the topics discussed during the king's Catholic instruction. These pamphlets gave Catholics a rare opportunity to examine the reasons behind the spate of conversions which began with the king's in 1593; they also helped deflect Protestant attacks on the king's sincerity. Conversions at court provided added proof of the Church's imminent victory over heresy under Henri IV.[54]

Peace with Honor

The campaign to win acceptance of Henri IV began to bear fruit in early 1594. Loyalists as well as Seize officials expected the Leaguer nobility to be the first to exchange its oath to the Holy Union for a new one to the Catholic Henri IV. Except for city governors such as Vitry and La Châtre, however, few Leaguer noblemen chose to recognize Henri IV before the summer of 1594. Many waited even longer. The Sieur de Libertat, who controlled Marseilles, for example, waited over two years before he submitted, and the League governor of Brittany, Mercoeur, did not come to terms with Henri IV until late 1597.[55] The accusations of betrayal leveled against Leaguer noblemen in, for instance, the *Dialogue d'entre le Maheustre et Manant,* hardly reflected the noblemen's complex attitudes toward Navarre. Nor did they serve as a blanket condemnation of the second estate. The antinobility sentiment of the Manant, which even the Maheustre occasionally shared, rested on the belief that League noblemen had abandoned Catholic resistance to secure favorable concessions for themselves and their clients. Critics failed to realize that League noblemen held out for such concessions to preserve the honor of their past actions; in fact, such concessions meant nothing without honor. League noblemen wanted to make it clear that their allegiance to Henri IV marked the culmination of their oath to defend the Church, not its betrayal.

Interestingly, the first breakthroughs came in the hotbeds of radicalism, the cities. The split in Paris between the Seize and the *ligueurs politiques,* whose strength lay in the law courts and the city council, existed in varying forms in many of the League's regional strongholds, such as Lyons, Meaux, Orléans, and Troyes. Since the 1580s, these urban factions in the provinces had regarded communal conflicts largely in terms of Henri IV's deviance. After the king's conversion, moderate Leaguers in the cities began to flaunt their sympathies for Henri IV, though they still withheld formal recognition of him.[56]

The first cities to submit were those in which city governors openly sided with moderates who called for negotiations with the converted king. Often the city governors initiated these talks and arranged conditions for submission. Vitry, the governor of Meaux, for example, entered into secret contact with Henri IV as early as September 1593; these talks eventually made him the first prominent nobleman to recognize Navarre four months later.[57] When he did so, he acted in conjunction with the city council; to seal this peace with dignity, Henri IV swiftly elevated Vitry to the rank of marshal when he entered Meaux on January 1, 1594.[58] This basic pattern of city governor and council acting together to recognize Navarre recurred over the months ahead. La Châtre and the city of Orléans submitted on February 1, while the Duc d'Aligncourt led Pontoise into Henri IV's camp on February 11.[59]

In cities where governors from the nobility, such as Nemours in Lyons and Carrouges in Rouen, had long since alienated moderate urban notables, the move to recognize Henri IV often proceeded without them, sometimes violently. The city fathers of Lyons, for instance, organized an armed revolt against Nemours in September 1593, quickly dismantling the various Leaguer councils in the city as well as imprisoning the duke and his followers for treason.[60] They then began talks with the Duc d'Ornano, the local loyalist commander. For a time, many expected Lyons to become the first Leaguer city to accept Henri IV; only a week after Nemours's downfall, however, the archbishop of Lyons, Pierre d'Épinac, arrived on the scene to persuade the city not to rush into the waiting arms of Henri IV. Without an eminent nobleman or prelate by their side, the city fathers approached the negotiations more cautiously. It took another five months before the city council, purged of its radical members, finally agreed to recognize Navarre. One of the conditions that Henri IV demanded was for the city to release Nemours, who quickly fled north to rejoin his cousins in Lorraine. Épinac, on the other hand, declared for Henri IV in May, and soon after became a staunch supporter of the king's pacification policies both in word and in deed.[61]

Henri IV's greatest triumph came with the fall of Paris in late March 1594. It, too, followed the pattern set earlier by other Leaguer cities and governors. Shortly after the royal coronation in Chartres, Henri IV began plotting with the Comte de Brissac whom, ironically, Mayenne had appointed to replace the untrustworthy Belin. If they knew of the brewing conspiracy, radical preachers and Spanish officials in Paris took no steps to forestall it. At four o'clock in the morning of March 22, Brissac and Pierre Lhuillier, the *prévôt des marchands,* opened the Porte Neuve to loyalist troops led by Timoléon d'Espinay, Sieur de Saint-Luc, and François d'O, the king's titular governor of Paris.[62] Martin Langlois, a prominent *échevin* and former *avocat de la cour,* opened the Porte St. Denis to Vitry, who provided living proof of Henri IV's forgiveness of Leaguers who recognized him. Loyalist troops held most of the strategic points by the time Henri IV finally entered the city about six in the morning. At eight o'clock, Navarre went to the cathedral of Notre Dame, accompanied by a large procession of the city's clergy who had apparently been prepared for his arrival. There the king heard Mass and celebrated a *Te Deum,* after which he repaired to the Louvre to begin pacification of the Leaguer capital.[63]

Henri IV Entering Paris (Courtesy of Bibliothèque Nationale, Paris)

The Mass celebrated during Henri IV's entry addressed the kinds of concerns that Parisians had heard raised by preachers about Navarre's sincerity as a Catholic. Many crowded into the cathedral to catch a glimpse of the triumphant king and demonstrate their acceptance of him by worshipping by his side.[64] What they saw then and during the Easter festivities which followed the city's fall did not disappoint them. Henri IV displayed the fervency of his new faith through numerous acts of royal piety: he washed the feet of the poor on Maundy Thursday; visited the sick in the Hôtel-Dieu; granted pardons to prisoners held in the Châtelet; and on Easter Sunday bestowed the royal touch on several hundred victims of scrofula, including several Spaniards.[65] These acts of royal charity extended to his treatment of the city as well. Loyalist troops passed out leaflets which conveyed the king's promise to pardon everyone, including members of the Seize, not implicated in the regicide.[66] Wishing to appear true to Christ's teaching to forgive one's enemies, Henri IV banished surprisingly few from Paris. He reserved that punishment for only some one hundred and twenty of the League's most notorious ringleaders, men such as Jean Boucher, Louis Dorléans, and Bussy-Leclerc.

The orderly takeover of Paris admirably illustrated Henri IV's policy of offering the Leaguers honorable conditions for submission in return for a promise to obey him. On the afternoon of his entry, Henri IV personally assured the Duke of Feria, the cardinal-legate of Piacenza, Madame de Nemours, and a host of other leading Leaguers who resided in Paris that they would suffer no harm unless they opposed him. He also allowed the some three thousand foreign troops under Spanish command garrisoned in Paris to withdraw peacefully from the country. Over the next few days, Henri IV reconfirmed the offices and titles of nearly all members in the Parlement and other law courts, as well as most municipal officials. On March 28, the king formally reunited the judges from Tours and Châlons-sur-Marne with their colleagues who had remained in Paris, an occasion which Antoine Loisel compared to the rebirth of the Phoenix.[67] Like Vitry and La Châtre, Brissac received the marshal's baton from Navarre, though unlike them he had to cede his post as governor to François d'O. Brissac apparently shed no tears. During Easter week, Renaud de Beaune assembled the king's closest clerical advisers in the episcopal palace, where they began an inquest into the past conduct

and present sympathies of the city's religious community. This ecclesiastical commission demanded that every cleric in Paris participate
with the king in the round of paschal services held throughout the
city and grant full absolution to Catholics who prayed for the king's
soul. Any infractions were to be reported to the commission immediately.[68] On April 2, after a debate over why the pope wrongfully withheld absolution from the king, the Sorbonne solemnly swore allegiance to Henri IV, enjoining all French Catholics to lay down their
arms and accept the king as ordained by God.[69] The swift and surprisingly smooth pacification of Paris led Revol to predict the rapid
disappearance of whatever resistance still remained in the provinces.[70]

And Revol proved to be right. The early wave of city submissions
that climaxed with the fall of Paris continued over the next several
weeks as Troyes (March 29), Rouen (March 30), Le Havre (April 8),
and Riom (May 3)—to mention only a few—opened their gates to
the converted king. What the *bonnes villes* perhaps lost in independence they more than made up for financially, at least in the short
run.[71] Not only did the fall of Paris insure the king's speedy triumph
elsewhere, it also enabled him to pursue pacification as a strictly local
affair arranged between the crown and the numerous individuals and
corporate groups which held regional power. These settlements usually included huge indemnities to League leaders to cover their war-
time losses. In a letter to Sully shortly after the fall of Paris, Henri IV
recognized that this piecemeal approach might possibly cost him
twice as much as one based on force. That price would be more than
worth it, the king observed, as long as he resisted the foolhardy advice
to conclude a general treaty with a *seul chef*, such as Mayenne, "who
might thereby be able to maintain a party in my State."[72] Henri IV
instead hoped to conquer the realm with kindness, which he meted
out in measured doses over the years ahead.

By negotiating separate settlements, Henri IV also reknit personal
bonds of *amitié* with local Catholic leaders in the towns and, eventually, in the countryside. In the scores of edicts and hundreds of letters
which Henri IV wrote to former Leaguers over the next five years he
always took care to address them as "my very dear and faithful
friends." These were not empty salutations; on the contrary, the
detailed accords which Henri IV concluded with former Leaguers
displayed a remarkable degree of consistency. Many of the treaties

contained identically worded provisions worked out in earlier submissions, all of which demonstrated the king's decision after July 1593 to treat Catholics honorably after they swore him obedience.

Contemporaries recognized this important role played by *amitié* during pacification. According to Loisel, for example, civil unity in France found its strength in the affective ties of *amitié* that bound people together to form a society under God and the king. The credo of the *bon françois catholique* championed by loyalists such as Loisel defined *amitié* as a bridge between respectful obedience and charitable *douceur*. Though based on affection, this concept of *amitié* departed from the earlier humanist emphasis on mutual obligations between equals, and instead defined it in terms of command and obedience. True *amitié*, loyalists argued, preserved rather than undermined the social hierarchy; it made each person accept and cherish his place in the world. *Amitié* gave the monarchy a comely image which made its subjects more willing—indeed enthusiastic—to obey its commands. It thus helped to internalize the need for discipline in every individual.[73]

People formalized this hierarchical notion of *amitié* in the public oaths they swore before God and the king to observe the basic tenets of religion and morality established by the crown. The public oaths that Henri IV required of former Leaguers stood as lasting proof of their adherence to the accepted code of the *bon françois catholique*. During pacification, Henri IV usually made the oath the sole requirement to regain his favor, because it marked a realignment of society around the pillars of piety and justice that he represented as monarch. A public oath to the converted king appealed to Leaguer noblemen, prelates, and judges because it elevated them above their social inferiors.[74] Pacification thus reaffirmed, indeed re-created, the traditional social order in France after a generation of armed strife.

Henri IV's peace treaties with Leaguers also contained guarantees for the Catholic faith and Church. In most preambles, Henri IV lauded God for his conversion and the miraculous disappearance of sedition from the country. Like the king, reconciled subjects served as instruments of Providence. Subsequent statements and provisions in the treaties portrayed Henri IV as the defender of the faith in France; some enthusiastic supporters even claimed that his protectorate extended to all of Christendom, calling upon him to lead a crusade against the Infidel.[75] After he became *rex sacerdotus* as a result of the coronation, Henri IV sometimes went so far as to include in the treaties phrases which sound deceptively like his oath to wage war against heresy. In his accords with Leaguer cities, for example, Navarre forbade the exercise of any religion but Catholicism within a radius of ten *lieux*.[76] He also ordered the return of all Church goods seized by Protestants during the wars and the restoration of clerical immunities. His agreements with Leaguer noblemen frequently placed even severer restrictions on the exercise of the Reformed religion. The obedience now given him by former Leaguers thus marked what many believed to be an important step toward the confessional reunification of the realm.[77]

Alarmed by these developments, French Calvinists prepared for the worst as Henri IV's pacification policies unfolded after 1593. Over the next five years, Protestant assemblies, which had seldom convened since 1589, began to meet regularly again after the defection of their erstwhile Protector. Militants among the Huguenot nobility and *consistoriaux* even suggested that they choose a powerful foreign prince, such as the Elector Palatine or Elizabeth I of England, to be their Protector. Although these plans came to naught, the Huguenot assemblies did agree in 1595 to withhold all military assistance from Henri IV during his struggle to expel Spanish troops from Amiens.[78] Ironically, these agitations by French Calvinists, while understandable given past experience, brought about precisely what they feared most: Henri IV's increasing reliance on Catholics. Some observers thought it likely that the converted king, after he had dealt with the Spanish menace, would turn his attention to the internal threat posed by the Huguenot "state within the state."[79]

The French Reformed community thus faced an uncertain future until Henri IV helped restore a measure of calm among its members in the Edict of Nantes, issued in April 1598. Although certainly crucial for his overall pacification of the realm, the Edict of Nantes was not the momentous breakthrough for toleration that historians have often assumed it to be. It must be seen in light of the king's worsening relations with the Huguenots as well as his earlier treaties with Leaguers. In these accords, Henri IV reinforced many of the barriers that had long separated Catholic France and the Huguenot minority, barriers that virtually foreclosed any eventual integration of the two except by conversion to the dominant religion. Far from toleration,

Henri IV predicated confessional coexistence on separation and exclusion mitigated only by those liberties specifically guaranteed for the Huguenots by the crown. The most immediate objective achieved by the Edict of Nantes was to allay Huguenot fears of the conversion's repercussions. It was a definite improvement compared with the past treatment that Huguenots had received from France's Catholic kings. Yet dependence on the crown was the price they had to pay for protection from the Catholic majority, even though the concessions made in the Edict of Nantes perhaps were greater than the *réformés* could realistically have expected under the circumstances. By presenting them with an offer they could not refuse, Henri IV was able to quarantine, not liberate, the Reformed community in Catholic France. As a result, the Edict of Nantes institutionalized rather than resolved the underlying conflict between Huguenot loyalism and religious dissent that had plagued French Calvinists ever since their Protector became heir to the throne in 1584. French Calvinists remained safe as long as the crown refused to exploit this implicit contradiction. Luckily for them, the Huguenots' *bon Henri* never pushed the issue; under his successors, however, they would not be so fortunate.[80]

Henri IV's eventual success in managing the Huguenot problem depended on his giving Catholics more reasons to accept such concessions than to oppose them. Here again his peace treaties with Leaguers proved instrumental. His treatment of League officeholders offers a case in point. In nearly every accord, Henri IV reconfirmed the rights and privileges which Leaguers claimed. Indeed, in sixteenth-century parlance, a peace with honor and dignity necessarily entailed the preservation of the tangible signs of rank and office expressive of one's personal worth. Leaguers avidly entered the Catholic king's service to preserve their goods and rights, and thus their families' place in society. Henri IV's accommodating treatment of robe officeholders typified this approach. After declaring all appointments made by Mayenne and League provincial leaders during the war null and void, the king then usually appended a series of exceptions that readmitted, after the payment of certain fees, virtually all League officials to their posts. Later, he frequently offered to sell these same offices to current incumbents, thus cementing their loyalty to him through the venality of office. Besides filling the king's coffers with ready cash, this sudden influx of officials led to an immediate increase in the size of the royal bureaucracy at Henri IV's disposal when he later tackled the problems of domestic reform and the war with Spain. The Leaguer nobility also fared well in their accords with the converted king, receiving in most cases large cash payments and pensions in exchange for submission. In a recent study of provincial governors, Harding has noted that during Henri IV's pacification many of these posts finally became recognized as the hereditary possessions of the various aristocratic families who controlled them.[81] Many former League noblemen fought with distinction against Spain, gallantly showing that they, too, belonged among the *bons françois catholiques.*

During pacification, virtually all Leaguer cities saw their ancient privileges and franchises ostensibly restored, commerce revived, and "prosperity and abundance return[ed] as before the wars." The reestablishment of order after the wars also allowed wealthy bourgeois to regain their country houses and again breathe the "gentle sweet air of the fields" after their long, unpleasant sojourn in the cities.[82] City officials demonstrated their newfound affection for Henri IV in a variety of ways, from celebratory parades and fireworks to triumphal arches and panegyrics which immortalized the king's deeds. As part of his general policy of amnesty, Henri IV undertook to expunge from public memory any reminders of the rebellion. He rejected the idea of a simple pardon because it implied wrongdoing, thus robbing the recipient of his honor and commitment to peace.[83] By royal fiat, he consigned the past to oblivion *(oubliance),* and in the process wiped clean the public memory as well as reaffirmed the crown's authority. To be complete, amnesty had to include the burning of "all memoranda, papers, and written instructions which testify to our past divisions and hatred," together with the "insignia and badges worn by the various factions."[84] Former Leaguers often took this advice to heart. During the formal submission of Lyons on February 22, 1594, city officials demonstrated their "affection for the king's service" by burning all tangible reminders of the League in the public square.[85] Many municipal registers as well as records from the royal courts underwent drastic alteration during pacification as conciliated Leaguers tried to erase from them every shameful trace of involvement in the rebellion. In every edict of pacification, Henri IV lent the force of royal authority to this wholesale expurgation of public memory, promising to punish anyone who violated the total amnesty which he granted to former rebels. Through selective recollection, the only past deemed worthy of preservation was the one which promoted the swift reestablishment of affective ties between the king and his people.[86]

But the past could not be so easily forgotten, even by those who profited most from *oubliance*. Despite the generous grant of amnesty, many former Leaguers felt compelled to accompany their flowing professions of loyalty to Henri IV with vigorous defenses of why they had opposed him in the past. Many included subtle reminders that had the king not converted, they would never have contemplated recognizing his right to the throne. In an open letter dated January 1, 1594, and addressed to other cities in the League, the city fathers of Meaux explained that they had gladly accepted past sacrifices as necessary to resist "a king whose religion was contrary to our own." That dreadful situation no longer existed as a result of Navarre's conversion at St. Denis. The city fathers unabashedly appropriated the credit for the king's conversion, attributing it to their "fervent prayers" to God to end the miseries that afflicted France.[87] For them, the king's return to the Church was a victory for the League—a victory, moreover, which could only be consummated by their oath to obey Henri IV as Catholic king.

Few resisted the chance to promote the continuity between their past reasons for joining the League and their present motives for embracing Henri IV. Noblemen, in particular, expressed sentiments similar to those of the townspeople of Meaux. Vitry's manifesto to the French nobility, issued in early 1594, defended as honorable his past adherence to the League and his present decision to accept Navarre as king. Far from a betrayal of the League's stand against heresy, obedience to Henri IV now vindicated the past struggle to uphold Catholicism.[88] The Sieur de Chillaud carefully emphasized in his letter of submission to Henri IV that it was "holy sentiments, not ambition" which had moved him to join the League.[89] Even loyalist clergymen, such as Adam de Hurtelou, bishop of Mende, linked the king's conversion with "his power and authority to rule," thus implying that had Navarre not converted, his reign would lack the divine sanction necessary to win the allegiance of Catholics.[90]

The vast majority of Leaguers who decided to test the king's offer of peace with honor quickly became fluent in the language of respectful obedience and charitable *douceur*. This growing harmony of viewpoints hid an essential difference, however: most former Leaguers insisted that their past opposition to the Protestant Henri IV was consistent with their present desire to serve him. Henri IV overlooked this unsettling implication, no doubt trusting that time would eventually render such matters irrelevant. After all, to do otherwise would contradict his express policy of amnesty and *oubliance*. Henri IV usually bestowed on his old adversaries the honorable title of *bon françois catholique*. He even volunteered excuses that absolved his once rebellious people of blame for France's past misery. In his declaration to the city of Beauvais, for example, Henri IV drew the startling analogy between his earlier reluctance to convert and the city's decision to resist him until he did. Both were questions of conscience, he argued, and as such merited special consideration.[91]

Leaguer Catholics who submitted after 1593 often took up arguments that loyalists had earlier used to defend the king's sincerity. Like loyalists, they regarded the recent windfall of unforced submissions as "irrefutable proof of the true, not feigned, character of the king's conversion."[92] Surely it was God who had made possible the sudden progress of Henri IV's cause since his conversion and coronation, the city fathers of Riom wrote in June 1594.[93] Speaking for the Catholics of Lyons, the city's clergy prayed for Henri IV to fulfill his destiny by delivering the Church from the disorder and disunity that plagued it, while the good citizens of Meaux averred that the godly conversion of Henri IV, "grandson of Saint Louis," made it imperative for all Catholics to lay down their arms and obey him.[94] The act of submission soon became a sort of conversion not unlike Henri IV's; many of the same terms and metaphors of sin and salvation, regret and forgiveness, found in loyalist accounts of the king's conversion recurred in descriptions of League reconciliation. These allowed former Leaguers to associate their change of allegiance with that of the king, thus lending it more legitimacy. Recognition of Henri IV as Catholic king was not only a political act, but also a religious one that helped advance God's honor and the Church.

These concessions helped make the king's conversion the key to ending the French Wars of Religion. The commitment of former Leaguers to Henri IV, like that of loyalists before them, rested on more than the pursuit of status and power, though those concerns certainly came into play. Deeper motives moved them to accept his rule—they hoped thereby to banish from the kingdom, much as they had from the king's person, the contagions of heresy and immorality, avarice and ambition, which they believed had been the root causes of

France's past ordeal. Henri IV's conversion thus provided much-desired peace and order, the struggle for which had ironically incited the past thirty-five years of strife. The king's conversion at St. Denis broke this vicious cycle by restoring public confidence in the crown newly sanctified by God. As the sole guarantor of order in France, Henri IV embodied the hopes and aspirations of a generation scarred by the horrors of civil war. Bourbon absolutism sprang from this new, widespread conviction that the only thing standing between Catholic France and the chaos of the past was the converted Henri IV.

Conclusion

THE TRAGEDY OF the French Wars of Religion lay in the shared desire of all parties to establish peace and order by force of arms and religious persecution. Yet violence only bred disorder, which in turn brought greater insecurity for men and women in late sixteenth-century France. This cruel contradiction was, of course, not immediately apparent to contemporaries. Historical tradition had not prepared the French for the emergency created by Calvinist dissent and the eventual dynastic failure of the Valois house. These twin crises in the body politic, which economic collapse and social misery compounded, merged after 1584 in Henri de Navarre's stubborn refusal to convert to Catholicism. The ensuing war of words over the king's faith dominated public discourse as did no other issue during the early modern period in France, and made the struggle over public opinion a critical one during the 1580s and 1590s. Yet public opinion meant something very different then from what it later became in the eighteenth century. Rather than affirming a sense of critical independence from the monarchy, the country's Catholic elites reconfirmed the integral relationship between king and community. As they saw it, independence meant anarchy, not civic renewal. In the process, they helped create a new type of political culture in which public opinion eventually became more consciously subsumed in the royal will.

This crucial change turned on the halting efforts by French Catholics to come to grips with the dilemma posed by a Protestant king. Despite their divisions on the conversion question, Catholic elites in the country remained captive to ancient myths about the sacred character of French kingship and the special relationship which they believed existed between the French people and God. After 1584, however, these moral bonds between king and subject clashed with the long-standing identification of confessional unity with social harmony. It was not a question of which of the two was to prevail in the struggle over Henri IV's deviance; it was rather a matter of how to realign the dictates of piety and justice which all considered necessary to achieve peace and godliness.

This traumatic crisis shook the confidence which Catholic elites had in the monarchy, and helps to account for both the violence of the conflict and the nature of the settlement that eventually emerged after Henri IV's abjuration at St. Denis. Popular unrest after 1589 in the cities and countryside reflected the widening scope of the crisis and contributed, once Henri IV reaffirmed the Catholic character of the monarchy, to a renewed sense of elite solidarity behind the converted king. The common heritage of the *bon français catholique,* which Catholic publicists on both sides reclaimed as the monarchy broke down, seemed all the more precious given the peril of Navarre's heresy. A civic identity so conceived alloyed cultural conceits with sectarian religion, and took various forms according to different social groups. Contained within the debates over Navarre's conversion were thus struggles to redefine what it meant to be a nobleman, a cleric, and a royal judge. This soul-searching among members of the political nation, to borrow the term used by British historians, shaped public discourse about the king's conscience in ways which caused Catholics on both sides to reaffirm—and in the process redefine—their cherished notions about God, the Church, royal authority, and the estates of the realm. With widespread violence and the accompanying war of words, these touchstones of French political consciousness in effect became internalized as a consequence of the crown's flagging credibility during the 1580s and early 1590s. Public discussion about the French polity—both its history and its providential origins—along with the accompanying attack on all that perverted it, such as heresy, immorality, and demonic evil, provided Catholic elites with an opportunity to reconceptualize in ideal form those characteristics which seemed woefully lacking in the monarchy and church. Although harrowing and bloody, this search to create a new order during the struggle over Henri IV's faith forged a new sense of unity and purpose among Catholic elites which made possible the later growth of Bourbon absolutism.

As we have seen, the key here lay in how French Catholics grappled with the nagging problem of the king's sincerity, that Gordian knot which so complicated the crisis. With no way to verify the king's conviction completely, the subject could only rely on his own willingness to believe Henri IV sincere and thus acceptable as Catholic king. This leap of faith entailed a further reification of royal authority in which Navarre's conscience, like other areas of royal statecraft, became shielded from public view as part of the *arcana imperii* of monarchy. Inherited from Roman law, this venerable tradition forbade public scrutiny or comment on decisions by the king which touched his authority, *estat,* and, now, conscience. The *arcana imperii* of kingship shielded Henri IV's special relationship with God from public view by reinforcing the absolutist claim that the first duty of every loyal subject was unquestioning acceptance of the inherent justice of every royal act, beginning with Henri IV's momentous return to the Catholic Church in July 1593. The decision at St. Denis to catechize the king privately *in camera,* not publicly *in ecclesia,* meant that future reconciliation with the king and subsequent readmission to the privileged estates of the realm required a disavowal by Leaguers of any claim to judge the king's motives. Most Leaguers eventually decided to make this critical leap of faith because they, like loyalist Catholics before them, became convinced after 1593 that only the monarchy, newly sanctified by Henri IV's encounter with God at St. Denis, stood between them and the horrors of the past. Acceptance of Henri IV's sincerity demanded that every subject willingly abdicate any claim to participate in public affairs unless framed exclusively by reference to the royal will and conscience. This act, more than anything else, crystallized the new relationship that later developed between the Bourbons and France's Catholic elites during the next century.

The enormous appeal of this new type of royal absolutism after the Wars of Religion rested on this call for a suspension of ethical inquiry by subjects into the king's motives and the *arcana imperii* of royal office. Such inquiry, so common during the Renaissance and Reformation, had come to be seen as detrimental to public order and social harmony, and therefore as a transgression of the bounds of legitimate public discussion. This new political culture represented a conscious retreat from the ideologies of resistance and assertive royalism that had held sway in the recent past. In the future, political power would lie only with those individuals who voluntarily resigned the responsible exercise of authority to an absolute king sanctioned by a Catholic God. This simple formula and solution to the past troubles animated the renewed commitment of Catholic elites to the crown after 1593. In exchange for order, they embraced the new discipline that reserved the perquisites of power and status to those who participated in the cult of monarchy and the self-abnegating doctrine of *service du roi*.

Seventeenth-century French absolutism thus did not derive its initial strength primarily from laws and institutions; indeed, these only came later, during Richelieu's ministry. Rather, absolutism began in the minds and hearts of those groups whose powerful positions in society had been most threatened during the Wars of Religion. These were the Catholic elites, whose divisions, more than anything else, had contributed to the strife, and whose newfound unity after 1593 helped make possible the Bourbon achievement. For Catholics all across France, the conversion of Henri IV at the abbey church of St. Denis was thus more than a ripple in *l'histoire événementielle*. They saw it at the time and for years afterward as a transcendent act of public and private redemption, an act that preserved the crown's sacred character and cleansed the king's person of the taint of heresy. Most important, the conversion of Henri IV reminded all French men and women that they would be truly among God's chosen people if they abandoned sedition and experienced a reconversion to *la religion royale*. The monarchy thereafter went on to reach new heights under Henri IV's successors, only to start its slow descent a century later when another series of prolonged wars and the secularizing ideas of the *philosophes* began to foster new notions about the nature and ends of human government.

Abbreviations

Notes

Bibliography

Index

Abbreviations

AC	Archives Communales de St. Denis
AESC	*Annales économies, sociétés, civilisations*
AN	Archives Nationales
BA	Bibliothèque de l'Arsenal
Berger de Xivery	*Lettres missives et correspondance d'Henri IV*, ed. Jules Berger de Xivery and Joseph Gaudet, 8 vols. (Paris, 1846–1858)
BM	Bibliothèque Mazarine
BN	Bibliothèque Nationale
BSG	Bibliothèque St. Geneviève
BSACP	*Bulletin de la société des amis du château du Pau*
BSHPF	*Bulletin de la société d'histoire du protestantisme français*
CCC	Cinq Cent Colbert
CD	Collection Dupuy
CG	Collection Godefroy
FF	Fonds Français
FI	Fonds Italien
IF	Institut Français
NA	Nouvelle Acquisition
nd	date of publication unknown
np	place of publication unknown
PUF	Presses Universitaires de France
SCJ	*Sixteenth Century Journal*

Notes

Introduction

1. Norbert Elias, *The Court Society,* trans. Edmund Jephcott (New York: Pantheon, 1983), pp. 146–213; Ernst Koosman, "The Singularity of Absolutism," in *Louis XIV and Absolutism,* ed. Ragnhild Hatton (Columbus: Ohio State University Press, 1976), pp. 4–17; G. Durand, "What Is Absolutism?" in same, pp. 18–36; Georges Pagès, *La monarchie d'ancien régime en France de Henri IV à Louis XIV* (Paris: Hachette, 1928), pp. 56–59; Roland Mousnier, *La vénalité des offices sous Henri IV et Louis XIII,* 2nd ed. (Paris: PUF, 1971), pp. 579–604; Richard Bonney, *Political Change in France under Richelieu and Mazarin, 1624–1661* (Oxford: Oxford University Press, 1978).

2. Sharon Kettering, *Judicial Politics and Urban Revolt in Seventeenth-Century France* (Princeton: Princeton University Press, 1978), and *Patrons, Brokers and Clients in Seventeenth-Century France* (Oxford: Oxford University Press, 1986); William Beik, *Absolutism and Society in Seventeenth-Century France: State Power and Provincial Aristocracy in Languedoc* (Cambridge: Cambridge University Press, 1985); Daniel Hickey, *The Coming of French Absolutism: The Struggle for Tax Reform in the Province of Dauphiné, 1540–1640* (Toronto: University of Toronto Press, 1986); Roger Mettam, *Power and Faction in Louis XIV's France* (Oxford: Oxford University Press, 1988).

3. Pierre Mesnard, *L'essor de la philosophie politique au XVIe siècle,* 2nd ed. (Paris: Vrin, 1971), pp. 473–482; William F. Church, *Constitutional Thought in Sixteenth-Century France: A Study in the Evolution of Ideas* (Cambridge, Mass: Harvard University Press, 1941); Julian Franklin, *Jean Bodin and the Rise of Absolutist Theory* (Cambridge: Cambridge University Press, 1973), pp. 41–53; Donald Kelley, *Foundations of Modern Historical Scholarship: Language, Law and History in the French Renaissance* (New

York: Columbia University Press, 1970); Nannerl Keohane, *Philosophy and the State in France: The Renaissance to the Enlightenment* (Princeton: Princeton University Press, 1980), pp. 15–18, 108–123.

4. Ralph Giesey, *The Royal Funeral Ceremony in Renaissance France* (Geneva: Droz, 1960); Sarah Hanley, *"The Lit de Justice" of the Kings of France: Constitutional Ideology in Legend, Ritual and Discourse* (Princeton: Princeton University Press, 1983); Richard A. Jackson, *Vive le Roi! A History of the French Coronation from Charles V to Charles X* (Chapel Hill: University of North Carolina Press, 1984); Lawrence M. Bryant, *The King and the City in the Parisian Royal Entry Ceremony: Politics, Ritual and Art in the Renaissance* (Geneva: Droz, 1986).

5. For a general survey, see J. H. M. Salmon, *Society in Crisis: France in the Sixteenth Century* (New York: St. Martin, 1975); Henry Heller, *Iron and Blood: Civil Wars in Sixteenth-Century France* (Montreal: McGill-Queen's University Press, 1991); Peter Clark, ed., *The European Crisis of the 1590s* (London: G. Allen & Unwin, 1985).

6. Frederic J. Baumgartner, *Radical Reactionaries: The Political Thought of the French Catholic League* (Geneva: Droz, 1976); Myriam Yardeni, *La conscience nationale en France pendant les guerres de religion* (Louvain: Nauwelaerts, 1971); Donald Kelley, *The Beginning of Ideology: Consciousness and Society in the French Reformation* (Cambridge: Cambridge University Press, 1981), pp. 307–336.

7. See Edmund H. Dickerman, "The Conversion of Henri IV: 'Paris is Worth a Mass' in Psychological Perspective," *The Catholic History Review,* 63 (1977), pp. 1–13, and David Buissert, *Henry IV* (London: G. Allen & Unwin, 1984), pp. 44–46.

The Search for God

1. Oscar Cullmann, *Baptism in the New Testament,* trans. J. K. S. Reid (London: SCM Press, 1964); John Baille, *Baptism and Conversion* (New York: Scribner, 1963). For the early modern period, see Jean Delumeau, *Le catholicisme entre Luther et Voltaire* (Paris: PUF, 1971); Pierre Chaunu, *Le temps des réformes: Histoire religieuse et système de civilisation, la crise de la chrétienté—l'éclatement, 1250–1550* (Paris: Gallimard, 1976); John Bossy, *Christianity in the West, 1400–1700* (Oxford: Oxford University Press, 1985).

2. Frances A. Yates, "The Hermetic Tradition in Renaissance Science," in *Art, Science and History in the Renaissance,* ed. Charles S. Singleton (Baltimore: Johns Hopkins University Press, 1967), pp. 255–274.

3. Pierre Dumonceaux, "Conversion, convertir: Étude comparative d'après les lexicographes du XVIIe siècle," in *La conversion au XVIIe siècle: Actes du XIIe colloque de Marseille,* ed. Roger Duchêne (Marseilles, 1983), pp. 7–15. For background, see Arthur Doby Nock, *Conversion: The Old and New in Religion from Alexander the Great to Augustine of Hippo* (Oxford:

Oxford University Press, 1933), pp. 17–32; Herbert B. Workman, *The Evolution of a Monastic Ideal from Earliest Times down to the Coming of the Friars* (Boston: Beacon Press, 1962); Robert Ellrodt, ed., *Genèse de la conscience moderne* (Paris: PUF, 1983); J. Wirth, "La naissance du concept de croyance (XII-XVIIe siècle)," *Bibliothèque d'humanisme et Renaissance,* 45 (1983), pp. 7–58; J. Bonduelle, "Conversi," in *Dictionnaire du droit canonique* (Paris, 1948), vol. 6, pp. 562–588; Paul Aubin, *Le problème de la conversion* (Paris: Beauchesne, 1962).

4. J. Patout Burns, *The Development of Augustine's Doctrine of Operative Grace* (Paris: Études augustiniennes, 1980), pp. 141–158. See also L. J. Daly, "St. Augustine's Confessions and Erik Erikson's Young Man Luther: Conversion as 'Identity Crisis,'" *Augustiniana,* 31 (1981), pp. 183–196; Peter Brown, "St. Augustine's Attitude to Religious Coercion," in *Religion and Society in the Age of Saint Augustine* (New York: Harper and Row, 1972), pp. 160–178.

5. See Henri Bouillard, *Conversion et grâce chez S. Thomas d'Aquin* (Paris: Éditions Montaigne, 1941).

6. See Marilyn J. Harran, *Luther on Conversion: The Early Years* (Ithaca: Cornell University Press, 1983).

7. For Calvin's own conversion experience, see Harro Höpel, *The Christian Polity of John Calvin* (Cambridge: Cambridge University Press, 1982), appendix I, pp. 219–226.

8. Hubert Jedin, *A History of the Council of Trent,* trans. Dom Ernest Graf, O.S.B., 5 vols. (St. Louis: B. Herder, 1957); Victor Martin, *Le gallicanisme et la réforme catholique* (Paris: A. Picard, 1919); Thomas I. Crimando, "Two French Views of the Council of Trent," *SCJ,* 19 (1988), pp. 169–186.

9. Pierre Deyon, "Sur certaines formes de la propagande religieuse au XVIe siècle," *AESC,* 36 (1981), pp. 16–25. On education, see René Bady, *L'homme et son 'Institution' de Montaigne à Bérulle, 1580–1625* (Paris: Société d'édition "Belles Lettres," 1964), pp. 91–103.

10. Joseph R. Stayer, "France: The Holy Land, the Chosen People, and the Most Christian King," in *Action and Conviction in Early Modern Europe: Essays in Memory of E. H. Harbison,* ed. Theodore K. Rabb and Jerrold E. Seigel (Princeton: Princeton University Press, 1969), pp. 3–16.

11. Elizabeth L. Eisenstein, *The Printing Press as an Agent of Cultural Change: Communications and Cultural Transformations in Early Modern Europe,* 2 vols. (Cambridge: Cambridge University Press, 1979); Roger Chartier, *Lectures et lecteurs dans la France d'ancien régime* (Paris: Éditions du Seuil, 1982).

12. Edmond Auger, *Formulaire de prières catholiques avec plusieurs advertissements pour tous estats et manières de gens* (Paris, 1585). In general, see A. Lynn Martin, *Henri III and the Jesuit Politicians* (Geneva: Droz, 1973), and *The Jesuit Mind: The Mentality of an Elite in Early Modern France* (Ithaca: Cornell University Press, 1988).

13. *Les décrets du concile de Trente,* ed. A. Michel, pp. 324–332; Jean Delumeau, *Le péché et la peur: La culpabilisation en Occident (XIIIe–*

XVIIIe siècles) (Paris: Fayard, 1983); Thomas N. Tentler, *Sin and Confession on the Eve of the Reformation* (Princeton: Princeton University Press, 1977).

14. Jean Boucher, *Sermons de la simulée conversion, et nullité de prétendue absolution de Henry de Bourbon, Prince de Béarn, à S. Denys en France, le dimanche 25 juillet 1593* (Paris, 1594), p. 37.

15. *Les décrets du concile de Trente,* ed. A. Michel, p. 334. See also Carl J. Peter, "Auricular Confession and the Council of Trent," *Jurist,* 28 (1968), pp. 280–297; Nicole Lemaître, "Pratique et signification de la confession communitaire dans les paroisses au XVIe siècle," in *Pratiques de la confession* (Paris: Cerf, 1983), pp. 139–157.

16. Thomas N. Tentler, "The *Summa* of Confessors as an Instrument of Social Control," and the rejoinder by L. E. Boyle, "The *Summa* of Confessors as a Genre and Its Religious Intent," in *The Pursuit of Holiness,* ed. Charles Trinkaus and Heiko Obermann (Leiden: Brill, 1974), pp. 103–137; Edmund Leites, ed., *Conscience and Casuistry in Early Modern Europe* (Cambridge: Cambridge University Press, 1988).

17. See *La prière au moyen âge: Littérature et civilisation. Communications présentées au colloque du CUER-MA, Aix-en-Provence* (Paris, 1981); Friedrich Heiler, *Prayer: A Study of the History and Psychology of Religion,* trans. Samuel McComb (Oxford: Oxford University Press, 1958); P. Apollinaire, *Les prières pour le roy en 1593* (Nîmes, 1892), pp. 4–8; BN FF Mss 3363, fol. 223–224, "Résolution de ceulx de la Sorbonne pour oster la prière du canon de la messe pour le roy," April 5, 1589.

18. Pierre de Villars, *Traicté sommaire et invectif contre les vains sermens, fréquents juremens et autres vices* (Lyon, 1596), pp. 3–7; Peter Bayley, *French Pulpit Oratory, 1598–1650: A Study in Themes and Styles* (Cambridge: Cambridge University Press, 1980), pp. 14–21.

19. Roland Mousnier, *L'assassinat d'Henri IV* (Paris: Gallimard, 1964), pp. 11–25.

20. A. K. Pugh, "The Development of Silent Reading," in *The Road to Effective Reading: Proceedings of the Tenth Annual Studies Conference of the United Kingdom Reading Association,* ed. W. Latham (Totley: Thornbridge, 1973), pp. 111–114.

21. Robert Mandrou, *Magistrats et sorciers en France au XVIIe siècle* (Paris: Plon, 1968); Joseph Klaits, *Servants of Satan: The Age of the Witch Hunts* (Bloomington: Indiana University Press, 1985); A. Soman, "Les procès de sorcellerie au Parlement de Paris (1565–1640)," *AESC,* 32 (1977), pp. 790–814; Robin Briggs, "Witchcraft and the Community in France and French-Speaking Europe," in *Communities of Belief: Cultural and Social Tension in Early Modern France* (Oxford: Oxford University Press, 1989), pp. 7–65.

22. See W. H. C. Frend, *Martyrdom and Persecution in the Early Church* (Oxford: Blackwell, 1965).

23. Maurice Causse, "La 'Familière Exposition' de Gérard Roussel et l'aventure 'nicodémite' en Guyenne," *BSHPF,* 130 (1985), pp. 5–33, and "Les

dissimulations de Marguerite de Navarre et l'aventure nicodémite," *BSHPF,* 132 (1985), pp. 346–389. See also Albert Autin, *La crise du nicodémisme, 1535–1545* (Toulon: P. Tissot, 1917).

24. "Excuse de Jean Calvin à messieurs les nicodémites," (Geneva, 1544), in *Opera quae supersunt omnia,* ed. Eduard Cunitz (Brunswick, 1963–1900), vol. 6, pp. 589–614; Carlo M. N. Eire, "Calvin and Nicodemism: A Reappraisal," *SCJ,* 10 (1979), pp. 45–69; Jean Delumeau, "Prescription and Reality," in *Conscience and Casuistry,* ed. Edmund Leites, pp. 134–158.

25. Carlo Ginzburg, *Il nicodemismo: Simulazione e dissimulazione religiosa nell'Europa del '500* (Turin: G. Einaudi, 1970); Delio Cantimori, "Submission and Conformity: 'Nicodemism' and the Expectation of a Conciliar Solution to the Religious Question," in *The Late Italian Renaissance,* ed. Eric Cochrane (New York: Harper & Row, 1970), pp. 233-265; Albano Biondo, "La guistificazione della simulazione nel cinquecento," in *Eresia e riforma nell'Italia del cinquecento. Miscellanea 1* (Chicago: Northern Illinois University Press, 1974), pp. 7–68.

26. Nathaniel Weiss, *La Chambre Ardente: Étude sur la liberté de conscience en France sous François I et Henri II (1540–1550)* (Paris, 1889), pp. 214–222; Raymond A. Mentzer, Jr., *Heresy Proceedings in Languedoc, 1500–1560, Transactions of the American Philosophical Society,* 74 (Philadelphia, 1984), pp. 44–57, 113–118.

27. Janine Garrisson-Estèbe, *Protestants du Midi, 1559–1598* (Toulouse: Privat, 1980), pp. 71–82.

28. Michel Peronnet, ed., *La conversion religieuse (XVIe–XVIe siècles) colloque,* 2 vols. (Montpellier, 1981); Marie-Christine Varachaud, "La conversion au XVIIe siècle," Thèse du 3e Cycle, Paris-Sorbonne, 1975.

29. Jean-Robert Armogathe, "De l'art de penser comme art de persuader," in *La conversion religieuse,* vol. 1, pp. 29–41. For Neostoicism, see Léontine Zanta, *La renaissance du stoïcisme au XVIe siècle* (Paris: H. Champion, 1914); Julien Eymard d'Angers, *Recherches sur le stoïcisme au XVIe et XVIIe siècles* (Hildesheim: G. Olms, 1976); Gerhard Oestreich, *Neostoicism and the Early Modern State,* trans. David McLintock (Cambridge: Cambridge University Press, 1982).

30. Robert M. Kingdon, "Problems of Religious Choice for Sixteenth-Century Frenchmen," *The Journal of Religious History,* 4 (1966), pp. 105–112; J. Parkin, "Montaigne's *Essais* 3:1: The Morality of Commitment," *Bibliothèque d'humanisme et Renaissance,* 41 (1979), pp. 41–62.

31. Hugues Sureau du Rosier, *Confession de foy faicte par H.S. du Rosier avec abjuration et détestation de la profession* (Paris, 1573), p. 2; G. W. Sypher, "'Faisant ce qu'il leur vient à plaisir': The Image of Protestantism in French Catholic Polemics on the Eve of the Religious Wars," *SCJ,* 9 (1980), pp. 59–84.

32. Matthieu de Launoy, *Défense de Matthieu de Launoy et d'Henry Pennetier, naguère ministres de la prétendue religion réformée, et maintenant retournez au giron de l'église chrestienne et catholique* (Paris, 1577), pp. 42–43. Launoy went on to become one of the League's most vocal supporters.

33. Sureau du Rosier, *Confession de foy*, p. 18. See Geoffrey Wainwright, *Eucharist and Eschatology* (New York, 1981); Rémi Snoeks, *L'argument de tradition dans la controverse eucharistique entre catholiques et réformés français du XVIIe siècle* (Louvain: Publications universitaires de Louvain, 1951), pp. 3–14.

34. Hugues Sureau du Rosier, *Confession et recognoissance de Hugues Sureau, dict du Rosier, touchant sa cheute en la papauté, et les horribles scandales par luy commis* (Basel, 1574), p. 6. In general, see M. Reulos, "Controverses entre catholiques et réformés à l'occasion des conversions," in *La conversion religieuse*, vol. 1, pp. 116–130; Michael Shortland, "The Figure of the Hypocrite: Some Contours of an Historical Problem," *Studies in the History of Psychology and the Social Sciences*, 4 (1987), pp. 255–274.

35. Boucher, *Sermons*, pp. 21–22; Jean Porthaise, *Cinq sermons esquels est traicté tant de la simulée conversion du roy de Navarre que du droict d'absolution ecclésiastique* (Paris, 1594), p. 13.

36. *Forme d'abjuration d'hérésie et confession de foy que doivent faire les desvoyez de la foy, prétendans estre receu en l'église* (Paris, 1572); BN FF Mss 15811, fol. 87, "Articles d'abjuration pour adjouster à la profession de foy du concile de Trente."

37. BN FF Mss 3364, fol. 153. See James K. Farge, "Self-Image and Authority of Parisian Theologians in Early Reformation France," in *Social Groups and Religious Ideas in the Sixteenth Century*, ed. Miriam Usher Chrisman and Otto Grundler (Kalamazoo: Western Michigan University Press, 1978), pp. 68–75.

38. *Abjuration de plusieurs huguenots et hérétiques du païs de Provence et Languedoc* (Paris, 1586), pp. 4–8.

39. *Célèbre conversion de la personne et famille de M. Geoffroy de Vaux après avoir esté ministre de la doctrine Calvinienne de Dauphiné* (Paris, 1597), p. 25.

40. See Chapter 7.

41. Denis Crouzet, *Les guerriers de Dieu*, 2 vols. (Paris: Champs Vallon, 1990); Terence Cave, *Devotional Poetry in France, c. 1570–1613* (Cambridge: Cambridge University Press, 1969), pp. 259–269; Terence Cave and Michel Jeanneret, *Métamorphoses spirituelles: Anthologie de la poésie religieuse française, 1560–1630* (Paris: Gallimard, 1972), pp. 3–18; Andrew E. Barnes, "Religious Anxiety and Devotional Change in Sixteenth-Century French Penitential Confraternities," *SCJ*, 19 (1988), pp. 389–405. For religious language, see Ronald E. Santoni, ed., *Religious Language and the Problem of Religious Knowledge* (Bloomington: Indiana University Press, 1968).

Into the Maelstrom

1. R. J. Knecht, *Francis I* (Cambridge: Cambridge University Press, 1982); Frederic J. Baumgartner, *Henri II, King of France, 1547–1559* (Dur-

ham: Duke University Press, 1988); N. M. Sutherland, *The Huguenot Struggle for Recognition* (New Haven: Yale University Press, 1980); R. M. Kingdon, *Geneva and the Coming of the Wars of Religion* (Geneva: Droz, 1956); D. J. Nicholls, "The Nature of Popular Heresy in France, 1520–1542," *The Historical Journal*, 26 (1983), pp. 261–275; J. K. Farge, *Orthodoxy and Reform in Early Reformation France: The Faculty of Theology of Paris, 1500–1543* (Leiden: Brill, 1985).

2. Henri was born December 18, 1553, and baptized March 15, 1554, with Charles, Cardinal de Bourbon, as one of his godfathers. BN CD Mss 88, fol. 18, "Journal des naissances et morts des princes de Béarn"; Eugène Halphen, *Enquête sur le baptême d'Henri IV (1599)* (Paris, 1878). Henri's childhood and family history can be found in Nancy L. Roelker, *Queen of Navarre, Jeanne d'Albret, 1528–1572* (Cambridge, Mass.: Harvard University Press, 1968). For the spiritual development of Henri's sister, see C. Lafon, "Catherine de Bourbon, duchesse de Bar," *Bulletin de la société historique et archéologique de Périgord*, 93 (1966), pp. 29–53, 92–152, 174–189; J. Fonda, "L'infortunée Catherine de Bourbon, soeur unique d'Henri IV," *Revue de l'Agenais*, 93 (1967), pp. 137–150; Raymond Ritter, ed., *Lettres et poésies de Catherine de Bourbon* (Paris: H. Champion, 1927).

3. Pierre de Salefranque, "Histoire de l'hérésie en Béarn," ed. V. Dubarat, in *Bulletin de la société des sciences, lettres et arts de Pau* (1921), pp. 39–40, 68–69, 74–80; Duc d'Aumale, *Histoire des princes de Condé pendant les XVIe et XVIIe siècles*, 2 vols. (Paris, 1885), vol. 1, pp. 42–68; N. M. Sutherland, "Antoine de Bourbon, King of Navarre and the French Crisis of Authority, 1559–1562," in *Princes, Politics and Religion, 1547–1589* (London: Hambledon Press, 1984); Robert M. Kingdon, *Geneva and the Consolidation of the French Protestant Movement* (Geneva: Droz, 1967), especially for the influential role played by Jean de Morély.

4. Louis de Gonzague, Duc de Nevers, *Mémoires*, 2 vols. (Paris, 1665), vol. 2, pp. 585–586; E. M. Beame, "The Limits of Toleration in Sixteenth-Century France," *Studies in the Renaissance*, 13 (1966), pp. 250–265.

5. Pierre Hurtubise, "Marriage mixte au XVIe siècle: Les circonstances de la première abjuration d'Henri IV à l'automne de 1572," *Archivium historicae pontificiae*, 14 (1976), pp. 103–134; Charles Hirschauer, "La politique de St. Pie V en France (1566–1572)," *Bibliothèque des écoles d'Athènes et de Rome*, 120 (1922), pp. 13–43.

6. BN FF Mss 3950, fol. 84–86, "Trois discours fait par le duc de Nevers et baillés au duc d'Anjou sur les propositions que monsr. l'admiral volloit [*sic*] faire pour induire le roy à faire la guerre en Flandre," dated June 19, 1572; fol. 91–92, "Avis motivé du duc de Nevers au roi Charles IX pour le détourner d'entreprendre la guerre en Flandre," dated June 26, 1572.

7. BN FF Mss 2746, fol. 258–266, "Contrat du mariage entre Marguerite de Valois et Henri de Navarre"; fol. 256–257, "Contrat du mariage entre Henri de Condé et Marie de Clèves"; *Article du pourparler d'entre M. le prince de Navarre et madame le princesse de Valois* (Blois, 1572), dated

April 11; A. Duval, "Contrat et sacrement de mariage au concile de Trente," *La Maison-Dieu,* 127 (1976), pp. 34–63. Condé's marriage to Marie de Clèves presented few problems because she was already a Protestant.

8. Bernard Abbatia, *Prognostication touchant le mariage du très-honoré et tresamé Henry par la grâce de Dieu roy de Navarre et de la très-illustre princesse Marguerite de France* (Paris, 1572), p. 6.

9. BN FF Mss 4337, fol. 123–126, "Mariage du roy de Navarre, 1572"; BN CD Mss 591, fol. 41–42, "Advis sur les cérémonies du mariage de M. le prince de Navarre et de madame, soeur du roy, en la convocation des ministres."

10. Barbara Diefendorf, "Prologue to a Massacre: Popular Unrest in Paris, 1557–1572," *American Historical Review,* 90 (1985), pp. 1067–1091; Janine Estèbe, *Tocsin pour un massacre. La saison des Saint-Barthélemy* (Paris: Le Centurion, 1968); *La Saint-Barthélemy ou les résonances d'un massacre,* ed. Philippe Joutard (Neuchâtel: Delachaux & Niestle, 1976); A. Soman, ed., *The Massacre of St. Bartholomew: Reappraisals and Documents* (The Hague: M. Nijhoff, 1974); N. M. Sutherland, *The Massacre of St. Bartholomew and the European Conflict, 1559–1572* (New York: Barnes & Noble, 1973); Robert Kingdon, *Myths about the St. Bartholomew's Day Massacres, 1572–1576* (Cambridge, Mass.: Harvard University Press, 1988).

11. *Dépêches des ambassadeurs vénitiens* (Paris, 1838), appendix 84.

12. Claude Haton, *Mémoires,* 2 vols. (Paris, 1754), vol. 2, pp. 606–607.

13. Gaspard de Saulx, seigneur de Tavannes, *Mémoires,* ed. Michaud and Poujoulat (Paris, 1881), pp. 390–391.

14. BN FF Mss 16140, fol. 33–35.

15. BN FF Mss 15555, fol. 80, Messieurs du Parlement to Charles IX, September 17, 1572, Toulouse.

16. Tavannes, *Mémoires,* p. 391; Cheverny, *Mémoires,* ed. Michaud and Poujoulat (Paris, 1881), p. 471; BN CCC Mss 397, fol. 755, Vulcob to Charles IX, November 8, 1572, Vienna. Henri's sister, Catherine de Bourbon, also briefly converted at that time—a move she always deeply regretted. Henri Zuber, "Henri de la Tour et Catherine de Bourbon (1576–1604). Affirmation et défense du protestantisme français," *Revue de Pau et du Béarn,* special number (1984), pp. 51–63.

17. Janine Garrisson, *Protestants du Midi,* pp. 71–82. Catholics even tried to evangelize Coligny's widow. A. Lynn Martin, "Une tentative ignorée de conversion de la veuve de Coligny par un Jésuite," *BSHPF,* 126 (1980), pp. 109–114.

18. *Copies des lettres du roy de Navarre et de M. le prince de Condé à nostre très sainct père le pape pour estre réunis à la saincte église* (Paris, 1572).

19. BM Mss 2590, unpaginated.

20. BN FF Mss 15555, fol. 110, Villars to Catherine de Medici, late September 1572, Bordeaux; BN FF Mss 3224, fol. 41, Henri de Navarre to

Villars, October 24, 1572, Paris; *Ordonnance du roy de Navarre, par laquelle il veult que la religion catholique, apostolique et romaine, soit remise en tous les endroictz de ses pays et royaume* (Paris, 1572).

21. Henri d'Anjou to Charles IX, May 9, 1573, camp at La Rochelle, in *Lettres missives de Henri III,* ed. P. Champion, 2 vols. (Paris, 1911), vol. 1, pp. 259–260.

22. *Registres du bureau de la ville de Paris,* ed. Fr. Bonnardot, 13 vols. (Paris, 1894), vol. 7, pp. 106–107, 252. In fact, Henri and Alençon were briefly imprisoned in March 1574 as a result of their activities. *Déclaration des très illustres princes les duc d'Alençon et roy de Navarre* (Paris, 1574). See Mack Holt, *The Duke of Anjou and the Politique Struggle during the Wars of Religion* (Cambridge: Cambridge University Press, 1986); J. J. Supple, "The Role of François de la Noue in the Siege of La Rochelle and the Protestant Alliance with the *mécontents,*" *Bibliothèque d'humanisme et Renaissance,* 42 (1981), pp. 107–122; Raymond Ritter, "Le roi de Navarre et sa prétendue fuite de la cour en 1576," *Bulletin philologique et historique,* 2 (1972), pp. 667–684.

23. P. Richard, *La papauté et la Ligue française. Pierre d'Épinac, archévêque de Lyon (1573–1599)* (Paris: A. Picard, 1901); Joseph Lecler, "Aux origines de la Ligue: Premier projets et premiers essais (1560–1571)," *Études,* 227 (1936); Mark Greengrass, "Dissension in the Provinces under Henri III, 1574–1585," in *The Crown and Local Communities in England and France in the Fifteenth Century* (Gloucester: University of Gloucester Press, 1981), appendix, pp. 162–182.

24. Aumale, *Historie des princes de Condé,* pp. 108–112.

25. In general, see I. A. A. Thompson, *War and Government in Hapsburg Spain, 1560–1620* (London: Athlone Press, 1976); R. B. Wernham, *The Making of Elizabethan Foreign Policy* (Berkeley: University of California Press, 1980), and *After the Armada: Elizabethan England and the Struggle for Western Europe, 1588–1595* (Oxford: Clarendon Press, 1983).

26. "Déclaration d'Henri de Navarre," November 30, 1585, Bergerac, in *Édits des guerres de religion,* ed. André Stegmann, 2 vols. (Paris: J. Vrin, 1979), vol. 2, pp. 214–216; Henri de Navarre to MM du clergé, January 1, 1586, Montauban, Berger de Xivery, vol. 2, pp. 165–168.

27. René de Lucinge to Charles-Emanuel, October 3, 1585, Paris, in *Lettres sur les débuts de la Ligue (1585),* ed. Alain Dufour (Geneva: Droz, 1964), pp. 201–202.

28. *Deux lettres du roy de Navarre à messieurs les gens tenans la cour de Parlement à Paris et à messieurs de la faculté de théologie du collège de Sorbonne* (np, 1586), dated December 1595; C. Blum, "De la méthode de résoudre les controverses: Le 'Traité de concile' de Duplessis Mornay," in *La controverse religieuse,* ed. B. Dompnier, 2 vols. (Montpellier, 1980), vol. 1, pp. 116–130.

29. Donald Nugent, *Ecumenism in the Age of the Reformation: The Colloquy of Poissy* (Cambridge, Mass.: Harvard University Press, 1974).

30. Léonce Anquez, *Histoire des assemblées politiques de la France, 1572–1622* (Paris, 1859); E. Haag, *La France protestante,* 10 vols. (Paris, 1846–1859).

31. Tadatake Maruyama, *The Ecclesiology of Theodore Beza: The Reform of the True Church* (Geneva: Droz, 1978), pp. 239–242; Marguerite Soulie, "Les idées politiques d'Agrippa d'Aubigné de 1580 à 1590," in *Les écrivains et la politique dans le sud-ouest de la France autour des années 1580. Actes du colloque de Bordeaux 6–7 novembre 1981* (Bordeaux: Presses Universitaires de Bordeaux, 1982), pp. 163–168; Étienne Vaucheret, "Le rôle politique et militaire de Duplessis-Mornay de 1580 à 1588," in same, pp. 147–160; Raoul Patry, *Philippe Du Plessis-Mornay: Un huguenot homme d'état (1549–1623)* (Paris: Fischbacker, 1933); Bouillon, *Mémoires,* ed. Michaud and Poujoulat (Paris, 1881), pp. 52–58; Henri Zuber, "Recherches sur l'activité politique et diplomatique de Henri de la Tour, vicomte de Turenne, puis duc de Bouillon," Thèse de l'École nationale des Chartes, 1982; Frank Delteil, "Henri de la Tour, duc de Bouillon: Recherche récente et complémentaire," *BSHPF,* 132 (1986), pp. 79–98.

32. See Robert Descimon, *Qui étaient les Seize?* (Paris: Fayard, 1984); Élie Barnavi and Robert Descimon, *La Sainte Ligue, le juge et la potence* (Paris: Hachette, 1985); Robert R. Harding, "Revolution and Reform in the Holy League: Angers, Rennes, Nantes," *Journal of Modern History,* 53 (1981), pp. 379–416; Denis Richet, "Aspects socio-culturels des conflits religieux à Paris dans la seconde moitié du XVIe siècle," *AESC,* 32 (1977), pp. 764–789.

33. Robert Descimon, "La Ligue à Paris (1585–1594): Une révision," *AESC,* 37 (1982), pp. 72–111.

34. *La ligue très saincte, très chrestienne et très catholique* (np, nd), pp. 11–16; Jean Boucher, *Le martyr de frère Jacques Clément de l'ordre S. Dominique* (Paris, 1590), pp. 9–10; Jehan Caumont, *De la vertu de noblesse* (Paris, 1585), pp. 3–5.

35. David A. Bell, "Unmasking a King: The Political Uses of Popular Literature under the French Catholic League, 1588–1589," *SCJ,* 20 (1989), pp. 371–386.

36. Charles Faye d'Espesses, *Discours des raisons et moyens* (Tours, 1591), pp. 44–46; Michel Hurault, *Discours sur l'estat de France* (np, 1591), pp. 69–74. In general, see Christopher Bettinson, "The Politiques and the Politique Party: A Reappraisal," in *From Valois to Bourbon: Dynasty, State and Society in Early Modern France,* ed. Keith Cameron, Exeter Studies in History, no. 24 (Exeter: University of Exeter Press, 1989), pp. 35–50.

37. BN FF Mss 3947, fol. 114.

38. Gaston Weill, *Les théories sur le pouvoir royal pendant les guerres de religion* (Paris, 1891), pp. 206–207.

39. Claude du Seyssel, *La grande monarchie de France,* ed. Jacques Poujol (Paris, 1961), I:8–12; II:11, 17; Jean Bodin, *Six livres de la république,* I:7. See also Julian Franklin, *Jean Bodin and the Rise of Absolutist Theory* (Cambridge, Mass.: Harvard University Press, 1973); André Stegmann, "Jean

Bodin, critique de Claude du Seyssel," in *Lyons et l'Europe, hommes et sociétés. Mélanges d'histoire offerts à Richard Gascon*, 2 vols. (Lyons, 1981), vol. 2, pp. 245–265; W. H. Greenleaf, "Bodin and the Idea of Order," in *Bodin Tagung* (Munich, 1973), pp. 23–38.

40. Louis Dorléans, *Apologie et défence des catholiques unis, les uns avec les autres contre les impostures des catholiques associés à ceux de la religion prétendue réformée* (np, 1586). A French translation of *Brutum Fulmen* can be found in *Mémoires curieuses de l'histoire de France*, ed. Cimber and Danjou, vol. 11, pp. 59–60.

41. François Hotman, *Antisixtus* (Geneva, 1586); Pierre de Belloy, *Moyens d'abus de rescrit et bulle Sixte V par un catholique apostolique et romaine, mais bon françois* (La Rochelle, 1586); H. Kretzer, "Remarques sur le droit de résistance des calvinistes français un début du XVIIe siècle," *BSHPF*, 73 (1977), pp. 54–75.

42. Roland Mousnier, "Comment les français ont voyé la constitution," in *La plume, la faucille, et le marteau* (Paris: PUF, 1970); Ralph Giesey, "The Juristic Basis of Dynastic Right to the French Throne," *Transactions of the American Philosophical Society* (Philadelphia, 1961); R. Villers, "Aspects politiques et aspects juridiques de la loi de catholicité (1589–1593)," *Revue d'histoire de droit*, 37 (1959), pp. 196–213; Martyn P. Thompson, "The History of Fundamental Law in Political Thought from the French Wars of Religion to the American Revolution," *American Historical Review*, 91 (1986), pp. 1103–1138.

43. See BN FF Mss 3612, fol. 64–65, "Mémoire de 'P. T.' tendant à prouver que la reconnaissance des droits de Henri 'roy de Navarre' à la couronne de France, est contraire à l'intérest de l'estat"; F. Melchior de Flavin, *Remonstrance de la vraye religion* (Paris, 1562), p. 28; *Déclaration des causes qui ont meu Mgr. le cardinal de Bourbon et les pairs . . . de s'opposer par armes à ceux qui veulent subvertir la religion* (np, 1588), dated May 31, 1585, at Péronne; *Remonstrance aux catholiques de tous les estats de France, pour entrer en l'association de la Ligue* (np, 1586), pp. 9–11.

44. Baumgartner, *Radical Reactionaries*, pp. 59–62.

45. *Déclaration de la bonne volonté du roy envers les villes et subjects qui tiennent son party* (Tours, 1589), p. 3.

46. Matteo Zampini, *De la succession du droict et prérogative du premier prince du sang de France, déférée par la loy du royaume à monseigneur Charles, cardinal de Bourbon* (Paris, 1588), and *Le droict de monseigneur le cardinal de Bourbon à la couronne de France défendu et maintenu par les princes et catholiques français* (Paris, 1589). See also Léon-Pierre Raybaud, "La royauté d'après les oeuvres de Matteo Zampini," in *La prince dans la France au XVIe et XVIIe siècles*, ed. Claude Bontems et al. (Paris: PUF, 1965), pp. 171–186; Frederic J. Baumgartner, "The Case for Charles X," *SCJ*, 4 (1973), pp. 87–98.

47. Eugène Saulnier, *Le rôle politique du cardinal de Bourbon, 1523–1590* (Paris: H. Champion, 1912), pp. 103–104, cites other instances when the *droit de proximité* took precedence over the *droit d'aînesse*, as in the

cases of Charles IV, Philippe IV, Louis XII, François I, Charles IX, and Henri III. See also *Traité sur la déclaration du roy pour les droits le prérogative de monseigneur le cardinal de Bourbon* (Paris, 1588); Pierre de Belloy, *Examen du discours publie contre la maison royale de France, et particulièrement contre la branche de Bourbon, seule reste d'icelle, sur la loy salique et succession du royaume* (np, 1587).

48. Rossaeus, *De Justa Respublicae Christianae Authoritate* (Paris, 1590), pp. 46–53. See C. H. McIlwain, "Who was Rossaeus?" in *Constitutionalism and the Changing World* (Cambridge: Cambridge University Press, 1939), pp. 178–182.

49. Several tracts justified the Estates General's right to alter the succession to defend public welfare. See for example, *Le dispositif avec advertissement et advis à MM les députés des estats de France* (np, 1588); *Discours sur les calomnies imposées aux princes et seigneurs catholiques par les politiques* (np, 1588). For the proposal to exclude Navarre from the throne, see *Articles pour proposer aux estats et faire passer en loy fundamentale du royaume* (np, 1588); *Advertissement à messieurs des estats pour la condemnation du roy de Navarre* (np, 1588).

50. *Déclaration des causes qui ont meu monseigneur le conte de Soissons, de prendre les armes, avecques la copie des lettres dudict conte, tant au roy, qu'au cardinal de Bourbon, et autres* (np, 1587).

51. André Maillard, *Lettre d'un catholique françois au roy de Navarre pour l'induire à se retourner à l'église apostolique et romaine* (np, 1586), p. 4; *Conférence chrestienne de quatre docteurs théologiens, et trois fameux advocats, sur le faict de la Ligue* (np, 1586).

52. See Keith Cameron, *Henri III: Maligned or Malignant King?* (Exeter: University of Exeter Press, 1978); Jacqueline Boucher, *Société et mentalités autour de Henri III*, 4 vols. (Paris: PUF, 1981), vol. 4, pp. 1393–1398.

53. J. Boucher, *Société et mentalités*, vol. 4, pp. 1400–1412. See also Bernard Dompnier, "Pastorale de la peur et pastorale de la séduction, la méthode de conversion des missionaires capucins," in *La conversion au XVIIe siècle*, pp. 257–273.

54. Henri de Navarre to M. de Pérul, July 3, 1584, Pau, Berger de Xivery, vol. 1, pp. 672–673. See also Pierre Champion, "La légende des mignons," *Humanisme et Renaissance*, 4 (1937), pp. 31–52; René Lucinge to Charles-Emanuel, duc de Savoie, April 17, 1585, Paris, in *Lettres sur les débuts de la Ligue*, ed. Alain Dufour (Geneva: Droz, 1964), pp. 61–62; Yves Cazeux, "Les entretiens d'Henri IV avec le duc d'Épernon au cours de l'été 1584," *BSACP*, 72 (1977), pp. 41–50.

55. Sully, *Oeconomies royales*, p. 46. Other members of the royal delegation included Nicolas de Brûlart, Alphonse d'Elbène, and Jean Prévost. After 1589, the first declared for Henri, the second opted for neutrality, and the third joined the League.

56. For these meetings, see Brémond d'Ars, "Les conférences de Saint-Brice entre Henri de Navarre et Catherine de Médici, 1586–1587," *Revue des questions historiques*, 34 (1884), pp. 41–43; BN FF Mss 3958, fol. 270–

272, "Propos tenus entre Catherine de Médici et Henri, roy de Navarre," December 26, 1586; *Discours fait à la Royne Mère du Roy, par un sien fidèlle subjet [sic] pour le bien de la paix de ce royaume avant qu'elle partist pour aller traicter avec le roy de Navarre* (np, 1586); *Lettre d'un gentilhomme françois, à un sien ami estant à Rome. Contenant le discours du voyage de la royne mère du roy* (np, 1587). Montaigne also attended the meetings. D. Maskell, "Montaigne médiateur entre Navarre et Guise," *Bibliothèque d'humanisme et Renaissance*, 41 (1979), pp. 541–553.

57. Pierre Mathieu, *Histoire de France* (Paris, 1631), vol. 2, pp. 541–547. For a contemporary account of the battle, see *Lettre d'un gentilhomme catholique françois à messieurs de la Sorbonne de Paris sur la nouvelle victoire obtenue par le roy de Navarre contre Monsieur de Joyeuse à Coutras le mardy 20 d'octobre 1587* (np, nd).

58. Théodore Beza said as much in a letter to Navarre dated March 15, 1588, Geneva. See "Henri de Navarre et 'Messieurs de Genève,' 1570–1589," *BSHPF*, 90 (1948), pp. 1–18, p. 14, note 2. Many suspected that Condé's new wife, Charlotte de la Trémouïlle, had had him poisoned. She was in fact arrested, and incarcerated for the next eight years before she received an acquittal from the Parlement de Paris in July 1596. Henri probably trumped up the charges against her to break up Condé's coterie of supporters; Condé's mother thought so, at least. BN FF Mss 4810, fol. 42–43, Françoise d'Orléans to Charlotte de la Trémouïlle, April 9, 1588, np.

59. See *Discours véritable sur ce qui est arrivé à Paris le douzième de May 1588* (Paris, 1588); Louis de Sainctyon, *Histoire véritable de ce qui est advenu en ceste ville de Paris depuis le VII may 1588, jusques au dernier jour de juin ensuyvant audit an* (Paris, 1588); "Le procès-verbal d'un nommé Nicolas Poulain, lieutenant de la prévosté de l'Isle de France, qui contient l'histoire de la Ligue, depuis ce second janvier 1585 jusques au jour des barricades, esceues le 12 may 1588," in *Archives curieuses de l'histoire de France*, ed. Cimber and Danjou (Paris, 1836), pp. 289–323.

60. For the Estates General of 1588, see Manfred Orléa, *La noblesse aux états-généraux de 1576 et de 1588* (Paris: PUF, 1980). In general, see J. Russell Major, *Representative Institutions in Renaissance France* (Madison: University of Wisconsin Press, 1960).

61. Renaud de Beaune, *Bref exhortation faicte aux estats de ce royaume* (Paris, 1588). See also Frederic J. Baumgartner, "Renaud de Beaune: Politique Prelate," *SCJ*, 9 (1978), pp. 99–114.

62. Orest Ranum, "The French Ritual of Tyrannicide," *SCJ*, 11 (1980), pp. 18–34. Henri III also had Pierre d'Épinac, the archbishop of Lyons, and the Cardinal de Bourbon placed under house arrest.

63. Étienne Pasquier, "Étude sur le roi Henri III," in *Lettres historiques*, pp. 438–442; Michel Hurault, *Discours sur l'estat de France* (np, 1591), p. 13.

64. Dozens of pamphlets attacking Henri III appeared within months of the murders. See, for example, André de Rossant, *Les meurs, humeurs et comportements de Henry de Valois* (Paris, 1589); *L'athéisme de Henry de*

Valois où est montré le vray but de ses dissimulations et cruautez (Paris, 1589); *De l'excommunication et censures ecclésiastiques encourues par Henry de Valois pour l'assassinat commis ès personnes de messieurs le cardinal et duc de Guise* (Paris, 1589).

65. *Édict et déclaration de monseigneur le duc de Mayenne, et le conseil général de la Saincte Union. Pour réunir tous vrais chrestiens françois à la défense et conservation de l'église catholique . . . et manutention de l'estat royal* (Paris, 1589). For Mayenne, see the classic study by Henri Drouot, *Mayenne et la Bourgogne, étude sur la Ligue en Bourgogne, 1587–1596*, 2 vols. (Dijon: A. Picard, 1937).

66. *Discours bref, mais trèssolide, monstrant clairement qu'il est loisible, honneste, utile et nécessaire au roy, de s'allier avec le roy de Navarre* (London, 1589).

To Convert a King

1. See François Dumont, "La royauté française vue par les auteurs littéraires au XVIe siècle," in *Études historiques à la mémoire de Noël Didier* (Paris: PUF, 1960), pp. 61–93; Michel Tyvaert, "L'image du roi: Légimité et moralité royales dans les histoires de France au XVIIe siècle," *Revue d'histoire moderne et contemporaine*, 21 (1974), pp. 521–547; Orest Ranum, *Artisans of Glory* (Chapel Hill: University of North Carolina Press, 1983); N. Ferrier-Caverivière, *L'image de Louis XIV dans la littérature française de 1660 à 1715* (Paris: PUF, 1981); Jacques Krynen, *Idéal du prince et pouvoir royal en France à la fin du moyen âge (1380–1440)* (Paris: A. & J. Picard, 1981).

2. Frances Yates, *The French Academies of the Sixteenth Century* (London: Warburg Institute, 1947); Eric Siegel, *The Palace Academy of Henry III* (Geneva: Droz, 1977). For background on these currents of thought, see René Bady, *Humanisme chrétien dans les lettres françaises, XVIe–XVIIe siècles* (Paris: Fayard, 1972); Marie-Madeleine La Garanderie, *Christianisme et lettres profanes, 1515–1535* (Lille: H. Champion, 1976); Jean Jehasse, *La Renaissance de la critique* (St. Étienne: Publications de l'Université de St. Étienne, 1976).

3. Roger Chartier, "Stratégies éditoriales et lectures populaires, 1530–1660," in *Lectures et lecteurs*, ed. Chartier, pp. 87–124.

4. Murray N. Rothbard, ed., *The Politics of Obedience: The Discourse on Voluntary Servitude by Étienne de la Boétie*, trans. Harry Kurz. (New York: Free Life Editions, 1975); *Lettre missive aux parisiens d'un gentilhomme serviteur du roy* (np, 1591), p. 24.

5. Samuel Kinser, "Agrippa d'Aubigné and the Apostasy of Henry IV," *Studies in the Renaissance*, 2 (1964), pp. 245–268.

6. Henri Hauser, ed., *Sources de l'histoire de France* (Paris: A. Picard, 1912), vol. 3, p. 291; Villeroy, *Mémoires d'estat*, 3 vols. (vol. 1, Sedan, 1622/

vol. 2–3, Paris, 1623), vol. 1, pp. 22–28; BN CCC Mss 489, fol. 181–207. I have relied on a manuscript copy entitled "Dialogue entre le sieur de Roquelaure et M. de Mornet," in BN FF Mss 4683, fol. 71–90.

7. BN CCC Mss 489, fol. 181–209; Jean Robert, "Voyages et séjours d'Henri de Navarre en 1584," *Revue de Pau et Béarn*, 12 (1984), pp. 67–94.

8. Both sides invoked this providential theme. See Duplessis Mornay, *Remonstrance à la France sur les maux qu'elle souffre, et les remèdes qui lui sont nécessaires* (np, 1587), and the anonymous Leaguer pamphlet entitled *Le vray discours sur la déroute et admirable disconfiture des reystres . . . par la vertu et prouesse de Mgr. le duc de Guise* (Lyons, 1587).

9. André Maillard, *Lettre d'un catholique français au roy de Navarre, pour l'induire à se retourner à l'église apostolique et romaine* (np, 1586). Maillard, a presidial judge in Burgundy, supported Navarre unequivocally after the regicide. See his *Le francophile ou très grand, très chrétien, très magnanime et très belliqueux Prince Henri Auguste IIII, roy de France et Navarre* (np, 1591).

10. *De la différence du roy et du tyran* (Paris, 1589), p. 9; François Grimaudet, *De la puissance royale et sacerdotale* (np, 1579), p. 55; François de la Rochefoucauld, *De l'état ecclésiastique*, 2nd ed. (Lyons, 1596), p. 25.

11. BN FF Mss 3952, fol. 277–287, "Advis au roy de Navarre," dated February 10, 1587.

12. BN FF Mss 3947, fol. 222, Bellièvre to Henri de Navarre, np, 1586; BN FF Mss 4028, fol. 1–6, "Lettre de Mon. de Villeroy au roy de Navarre pour l'induire à rechercher la bonne grâce du roy et penser à sa conversion à la religion catholique," May 12, 1588. The Day of the Barricades no doubt lent urgency to Villeroy's appeal. For Bellièvre and Villeroy, see Edmund H. Dickerman, *Bellièvre and Villeroy: Power in France under Henry III and Henry IV* (Providence: Brown University Press, 1971); N. M. Sutherland, *The French Secretaries of State* (London: Athlone, 1962).

13. See Jacques Hennequin, *La naissance d'un mythe: Henri IV à travers ses oraisons funèbres* (Paris, 1980); Christian Desplat, "Le mythe d'Henri IV: Nouvelles approches," *BSACP*, 72 (1977), pp. 81–103.

14. Étienne Pasquier, "Étude sur le roi Henri III," in *Lettres historiques*, ed. Dufour, pp. 438–442.

15. André de Rossant, *Les meurs, humeurs et comportements de Henry de Valois* (Paris, 1589), pp. 3–9; *L'athéisme de Henry de Valois où est montré le vray but de ses dissimulations et cruautez* (Paris, 1589), pp. 12–18.

16. *Discours sur les causes et raisons qui ont meu . . . les françois . . . contre Henry III* (Paris, 1589), pp. 5–11.

17. See P. Feret, "Nullité de mariage de Henri IV avec Marguérite de Valois," *Revue des questions historiques*, 11 (1876), pp. 77–114.

18. Sydney Anglo, "Henri III: Some Determinants of Vituperation," in *From Valois to Bourbon*, ed. Cameron, pp. 5–20.

19. A. Lloyd Moote, *Louis the Just* (Berkeley: University of California Press, 1988).

20. André Maillard, *Panégyrique à Henry IV, roy de France et de Navarre* (Tours, 1590), pp. 8–9.

21. *Le faux-visage descouvert du feu Renard de la France* (Paris, 1589), pp. 11–12; Pauline M. Smith, *The Anti-Courtier Trend in Sixteenth-Century France* (Geneva: Droz, 1961).

22. Denis Crouzet, "Henri IV, King of Reason?" in *From Valois to Bourbon*, ed. Cameron, pp. 73–106.

23. *Les propos lamentables de Henry de Valois, tirez de sa confession, par un remords de conscience, qui tousjours tourmente les misérables* (Paris, 1589).

24. J. V. D. Bechet, *Oraison funèbre prononcée aux obsèques de Henry III . . . le 1 septembre 1589* (Angers, 1589); Claude Paillot, *Les tristes airs et funèbres . . . en mémoire du feu roy à la postérité* (Tours, 1589); Pierre Allard, *Oraison funèbre et prononcée à Lyon . . . aux obsèques de Henry III* (Lyon, 1594); Claude Morenne, *Oraison funèbre faite sur le trespas de Henry III* (Paris, 1595). For funeral orations, see V. Saulnier, "L'oraison funèbre au XVIe siècle," *Bibliothèque d'humanisme et Renaissance*, 10–11 (1948), pp. 124–157.

25. Étienne Pasquier, *L'antimartyr de frère Jacques Clément* (np, 1590), pp. 2–9; BN FF Mss 14054, "Pièces originales du procès de Jacques Clément, dominican, assassin de Henri III."

26. Pasquier's tract was a rebuttal to Jean Boucher's *Le martyr de frère Jacque Clément de l'ordre S. Dominique* (Paris, 1590). See also Edme Bourgoin, *Discours véritable de l'estrange et subite mort de Henry de Valois, advenue par permission divine* (Paris, 1589). Bourgoin was later captured by loyalist forces and executed for complicity in the king's death in March 1590.

27. *Dernier propos du roy consolant avant sa mort à ses fidèles sujets* (np, 1589), p. 1; "Lettre d'un des premier officiers de la cour de Parlement escrite à un de ses amis sur le sujet de la mort du roi Henri III," in *Collection des mémoires relatifs à l'histoire de France*, ed. Michaud and Poujoulat (Paris, 1881), vol. 11, p. 469; BN FF Mss 3275, fol. 64, "Attestation sur les dernières paroles et actions du roy Henry III."

28. BN Cabinet des Estampes et Gravures, B 10700.

29. Cheverny, *Mémoires*, p. 495; *Discours de la divine élection du très chrestien Henry IV* (np, 1590), p. 62; François Billacois, "Du régicide: Matériaux pour une enquête sur la légimité dynastique," in *Études réunis en l'honneur de P. Goubert* 2 vols. (Paris: PUF, 1984), vol. 2, pp. 71–79.

30. Aubigné, *Histoire universelle*, pp. 79–80.

31. Sully, *Oeconomies royales*, p. 71.

32. Ralph E. Giesey, *The Royal Funeral Ceremony in Renaissance France* (Geneva: Droz, 1960); for provincial reactions, see BN CD Mss 61, fol. 40, Méry de Vic to Henri IV, August 28, 1589, Limoges.

33. In 1593, Leaguers in Paris occasionally used these items in processions to rally opinion behind the movement as the king's conversion became imminent. BN FF Mss 15699, fol. 327–328.

34. *Instructions envoyées au duc de Luxembourg* (Tours, 1589); H. Ferrière, "La mission du duc de Luxembourg à Rome (1589–1590)," *Revue des questions historiques,* 40 (1886), pp. 5–49; Bernard Barbiche, "L'influence française à la cour pontificale sous le règne de Henri IV," *Mélanges d'archéologie et histoire de l'école française à Rome,* 77 (1965), pp. 177–199.

35. *Bulle de nostre s. père le pape Sixte V contre Henry de Valois et ses complices* (Paris, 1589). A papal brief dated July 20, 1587, empowered the royal confessor to absolve the king in reserved cases. A. Tardif, *Privilèges accordés à la couronne de France* (Paris, 1855), p. 281. See also BN FF Mss 3386, fol. 41–42, "Partie d'un discours italien contre ce que le pape Sixte V avoit défendu de donner absolution au feu roy," delivered in Rome, October 25, 1589; André Maillard, *La fulminante pour feu très-grand et très-chrestien prince Henry III roy de France et de Pologne, contre Sixte V soy disant pape de Rome et les rebelles de la France* (np, 1590).

36. On September 22, 1595, Pope Clement VIII confirmed the episcopal absolution given to Navarre at St. Denis two years earlier. *Cérémonies observées à Rome* (Paris, 1595), pp. 3–12.

37. François Meglat, *Apothéose ou harangue funèbre de la royne douairière au roy, plus le paranymphe de justice, la parfaite amitié, et les consolations de la mort* (Paris, 1601).

38. Bechet, *Oraison funèbre,* pp. 3–8.

39. BN CD Mss 546, fol. 55–56. Duplessis Mornay put it more bluntly in a secret memorandum to Henri IV several days after the regicide: "The Catholics are alarmed about the fate of their religion; it is therefore necessary to issue a declaration if only to allay their fears." *Mémoires et correspondance,* vol. 2, p. 394. A letter from Henri IV to Duplessis Mornay, dated November 7, 1589, in same, p. 395, reveals the Protestants who helped him draft the Declaration of St. Cloud. They included Châtillon, La Noue, Beauvais-Canocle, Guitry, La Force, Sully, and Sancy.

40. *Le serment et promesse du roy à son avènement* (np, 1589), pp. 3–4; *Déclaration du roy portant déffense de ne toucher ès maisons des catholiques qui sont avec le roy de Navarre, esquelles ne se faict acte d'hostilité* (Paris, 1589). See in general Ronald S. Love, "Winning the Catholics: Henri IV and The Religious Dilemma in August 1589," *Canadian Journal of History,* 24 (1989): 361–379.

41. Auguste Poirson, *Histoire du règne de Henri IV,* 4 vols. (Paris, 1865), vol. 1, pp. 38–39.

42. "Extraict d'un discours d'estat," in Nevers, *Mémoires,* vol. 2, pp. 590–594.

43. BN CD Mss 698, fol. 488.

44. *Serment réciproque des princes du sang, et autres ducs, pairs etc. à sa majesté* (np, 1589), p. 7; BN FF Mss 10191, fol. 118, "Harangue au roy Henry IV sur l'assassinat de Henry III."

45. Norbert Elias, *La société de la cour,* trans. Pierre Kamnitzer and Jeanne Étore (Paris: Flammarion, 1985), p. 158.

46. *Discours entre le roy de Navarre et Marmet son ministre sur l'instruction par luy demandée en forme de dialogue* (Paris, 1590), p. 11. For Mermet, see Gabrielle Berthoud, "Le pasteur Antoine Mermet de Dombresson à Nérac (1536–1607)," in *Mélanges d'histoire du XVIe siècle offerts à Henri Meylan. Travaux d'humanisme et Renaissance* (Geneva: Droz, 1970), vol. 110, pp. 139–152.

47. *Le remerciement des catholiques unis faict à la déclaration et protestation de Henry de Bourbon* (Paris, 1589), pp. 5–7; *Lettre du roy de Navarre aux illustrissimes seigneurs de la république de Berne leüe publiquement en l'église cathédrale de Troyes le 20e de ce mois de septembre à fin que chacun cogneut clairement le but du Biarnois* (Paris, 1589). Henri wrote Elizabeth I, April 5, 1587, np, Berger de Xivery, vol. 2, p. 33: "Rest assured, Madam, that the preservation of true religion, which we must pass along unsullied to posterity, is as close to my heart as it is to yours."

48. *Advertissement des catholiques de Béarn aux catholiques françois unis à la Sainte Union, touchant la déclaration faicte par Henry roy de Navarre le 4e aoust 1589* (Paris, 1589); *Discours en forme de dialogue entre le sieur d'O et Claude Bourgeois de Paris* (np, 1591), pp. 18–19.

49. Jean Boucher, *Métamorphose d'Henry de Bourbon, jadis roy de Navarre, faussement et indignement prétendant d'estre roy de France. En laquelle se monstre ce qu'il fit l'an 1572 feignant d'estre converti à nostre religion catholique* (Lyons, 1589), pp. 11–15.

50. *Advertissement au roy où sont déduites les raisons d'estat pour lesquelles il ne luy est pas bien séant de changer de religion* (np, 1589). Alan Boase, in his *Vie de Jean de Sponde* (Geneva, 1979), p. 66, offers strong proof that it was written by Sponde. Palma Cayet, in his *Chronologie novenaire*, p. 169, states that the pamphlet was published in La Rochelle.

51. L. B., "Remonstrance au roy," delivered August 2, 1592, in Ernst Stähelin, *Der Übertritt König Heinrich IV zur römischen katholischen Kirche* (Basel, 1856), appendix 1, pp. 783–795. For atheism in sixteenth-century France, see Lucien Febvre, *Le problème de l'incroyance au XVIe siècle* (Paris: A. Michel, 1942); F. Berriot, *Athéismes et athéisties au XVIe siècle en France*, 2 vols. (Paris: Cerf, 1984).

52. Henri Hauser, "François de la Noue et la conversion du roi," *Revue historique* (1888), pp. 313–323; William H. Huseman, "François de la Noue (1531–1591) au service du libéralisme du XIXe siècle," *Renaissance and Reformation/Renaissance et Réforme*, 9 (1985), pp. 189–208.

53. Michel Hurault, *Discours sur l'estat de la France* (np, 1591), pp. 7–9.

54. A flurry of pamphlets defending the need for the king to be sincere appeared in 1591 to refute the call for accommodation put forth in *Remonstrance et supplication faicte au roy pour la religion catholique* (Bordeaux, 1591), p. 30. One rebuttal attributes this piece to Matthieu de Launoy, while Stähelin, *Der Übertritt*, p. 354, presents evidence that it was written by Yves Magistri, a Cordelier preacher and chaplain to the Spanish garrison in Paris. Among the anonymous responses are *Le vray catholique romain contre le ligueur couvert* (np, 1591); *Response à la supplication, contre celuy lequel*

faisant semblant de donner advis au roy de se faire catholique, veult exciter ses bons subjets de rébellion (np, 1591); and *Response à la blasphème et calomineuse remonstrance de Matthieu de Launoy* (Tours, 1591).

55. *Advertissement aux serviteurs du roy sur la supplication adressée à sa majesté pour se faire catholique* (np, 1591), pp. 2–3; M. B., *Lettre d'un ecclésiastique à un sien seigneur et amy, sur les difficultez que les ecclésiastiques d'Angers et autres Ligueurs font de prester serment de fidélité au roy Henry IIII* (Tours, 1589), pp. 9–11; Jean du Bec, *Bon augure au roy de Navarre, de sa grandeur en retournant au gyron de l'église catholique* (np, 1593). Du Bec had reworked a set of sermons he wrote during the 1580s in his work *Neuf sermons sur l'excellence de l'oraison de nostre seigneur* (np, 1586).

56. *Devis familier d'un gentilhomme catholique françois avec un laboureur* (np, 1590), pp. 102–103.

57. Du Bec, *Bon augure*, p. 33; M. D. M., *Remonstrance et supplication au roy de vouloir embrasser la foy de l'église catholique . . . sans craindre d'idolâtrer* (Melun, 1593), pp. 12–13.

58. BN FF Mss 4743, fol. 83–88, "Supplication et advis au roy de se faire catholique," 1591. Although the tract is attributed to Du Perron, its arguments closely resemble those in Pierre Ayrault, *Considérations des troubles et le juste moyen de les appaiser* (np, 1591). See also L. Perrottet, "Un exemple de polémique religieuse à la fin du XVIe siècle: La défense de la tradition par Robert Bellarmine (1542–1621) et la république calviniste," *Revue de théologie et de philosophie*, 114 (1982), pp. 395–413.

59. BN FF Mss 5808, fol. 73–75.

60. In general, see Jonathan Powis, "Gallican Liberties and the Politics of Later Sixteenth-Century France," *The Historical Journal*, 26 (1983), pp. 515–530.

61. BN CCC Mss 31, fol. 226, "Discours pour que sa majesté se fasse catholique," 1592. As Maillard put it to Navarre in his *Lettre d'un catholique français*, p. 12: "I am proud to say I am a Catholic, and would be ready to die a thousand deaths rather than change anything about its doctrines." See also *Remonstrance faite par quatre docteurs au roy de Navarre de se réunir à la foy catholique* (Bordeaux, 1585).

62. BN CD Mss 770, fol. 319–360.

63. Frances Yates, *Astraea: The Imperial Theme in the Sixteenth Century* (Boston: Routledge & Kegan Paul, 1975), pp. 208–214.

Piety and Politics

1. *Malheurs et inconveniens qui adviendront aux catholiques faisant paix avec l'hérétique* (Paris, 1590), p. 15; *Advis aux catholiques françois* (Paris, 1589), p. 3; *Advis sur ce qui est à faire conter les catholique simulez, que les ennemis ouverts de l'église catholique, apostolique et romaine* (Paris, 1589), p. 8.

2. Charles Faye, d'Espesses du, *Discours des raisons et moyens* (Tours, 1591), p. 95.

3. Jacqueline Boucher, "Catholiques et Ligueurs: Une même mentalité des frères religieuses," in *Religion et politique: Mélanges offerts à André Latreille* (Lyons: PUF, 1972), pp. 67–81.

4. J. Russell Major, "Noble Income, Inflation and the Wars of Religion," *American Historical Review*, 86 (1981), pp. 21-148; Denis Crouzet, "Recherches sur la crise de l'aristocratie en France au XVIe siècle: Les dettes de la maison de Nevers," *Histore, économie, société*, 1 (1982), pp. 7–50.

5. See D. Bitton, *The French Nobility in Crisis, 1560–1640* (Stanford: Stanford University Press, 1969); G. Huppert, *Les bourgeois gentilhommes* (Chicago: University of Chicago Press, 1977); A. Jouanna, *Ordre social, mythes et hiérarchies dans la France au XVIe siècle* (Paris: Hachette, 1977); E. Schalk, *From Valor to Pedigree: Ideas of Nobility in France in the Sixteenth and Seventeenth Centuries* (Princeton: Princeton University Press, 1986); K. Neuschel, *Word of Honor: Interpreting Noble Culture in Sixteenth-Century France* (Ithaca: Cornell University Press, 1989); F. Billacois, *The Duel: Its Rise and Fall in Early Modern France*, ed. and trans. Trista Selous (New Haven: Yale University Press, 1990).

6. See André Stegmann, *L'héroïsme cornelien: Genèse et signification*, 2 vols. (Paris: A. Colin, 1968); P. Benichou, *Morales du grand siècle* (Paris: Gallimard, 1948).

7. See, for example, the preface to B. de Salignac, *Le siège de Metz, en l'an MDLII* (Paris, 1553), unpaginated.

8. See R. Harding, *Anatomy of a Power Elite: The Provincial Governors of Early Modern France* (New Haven: Yale University Press, 1978).

9. Jacqueline Boucher, *La cour de Henri III* (Paris: Fayard, 1986), pp. 57–78.

10. Brantôme, *Discours sur les colonels,* p. 152, cited in A. M. Cocula, "Brantôme, un soldat et la politique," in *Les écrivains et la politique,* pp. 173–184.

11. M. Wolfe, "Piety and Political Allegiance: The Duc de Nevers and the Protestant Henri IV, 1589–1593," *French History*, 2 (1988), pp. 1–21.

12. *Response à la blasphème et calomnieuse remonstrance de Matthieu Launoy* (Tours, 1591), p. 8.

13. *Déclaration du roy sur les services qu'il attend de sa noblesse en la guerre ouverte contre les estrangers, ennemis anciens de la couronne de France* (Tours, 1591), pp. 6–9.

14. André Devyver, *Le sang epuré. Les préjugés de race chez les gentilhommes français de l'ancien régime, 1560–1720* (Brussels: Éditions de l'Université de Bruxelles, 1973).

15. Michel Hurault, *Discours sur l'estat de la France* (np, 1591), pp. 90–93.

16. Oudart Raynssant de Viezmaison, *Représentation de la noblesse hérétique sur le théâtre de France* (Paris, 1591), p. 4.

17. Jehan de Caumont, *De la vertu de noblesse* (Paris, 1585), p. 2.

18. Michel du Rit, *Le bon françois, ou la foy des gaulois* (Paris, 1589), pp. 45–46.

19. Matthieu de Launoy, *Remonstrance contenant une instruction chrestienne de quatre poincts à la noblesse de France* (Paris, 1590), pp. 5–6; P. Rousset, "L'idéologie de croisade dans les guerres de religion au XVIe siècle," *Schweizeriche Zeitschrift für Geschichte,* 31 (1981), pp. 174–184.

20. See Sharon Kettering, "Clientage during the French Wars of Religion," *SCJ,* 20 (1989), pp. 221–239; "Patronage and Kinship in Early Modern France," *French Historical Studies,* 16 (1989), pp. 408–435; Mark Greengrass, "Noble Affinities in Early Modern France: The Case of Henri I de Montmorency, Constable of France," *European History Quarterly,* 16 (1986), pp. 275–311.

21. See Chapter 5.

22. A. Dufour, "La paix de Lyon et la conjuration de Biron," *Journal des savants* (1968), pp. 428–455.

23. Frederic J. Baumgartner, *Change and Continuity in the French Episcopacy: The Bishops and the Wars of Religion, 1547–1610* (Durham: Duke University Press, 1986); Charles Labitte, *La démocratie chez les curés;* Arlette Lebigre, *La révolution des curés* (Paris: A. Michel, 1980).

24. A. Lynn Martin, *Henry III and the Jesuit Politicians* (Geneva: Droz, 1973), and *The Jesuit Mind: The Mentality of an Elite in Early Modern France* (Ithaca: Cornell University Press, 1988).

25. BN CD Mss 61, fol. 51, Hurtelou to Henri IV, September 19, 1589, np; Jean Roucaute, *Le pays de Gevaudan au temps de la Ligue* (Paris: A. Picard, 1900), pp. 183–257.

26. BN CD Mss 61, fol. 139, Hurtelou to Henri IV, June 20, 1590, np.

27. BN FF Mss 3914, fol. 106, Maury to Henri IV, September 14, 1589, Bayonne.

28. BN CD Mss 61, fol. 45, Sorbin to Henri IV, August 31, 1589, Nevers. A Leaguer tract that appeared the next year put Sorbin in a compromising position. See *Formulaire des prières pour l'extirpation de l'hérésie, délivrance du roy et paix de ce royaume: Ordonné par M. l'évêque de Nevers, pour être faictes tous les jours par toutes églises en son diocèse* (Paris, 1590). The king referred to in the title is Charles de Bourbon.

29. BN CD Mss 61, fol. 91, Prévost de Sansac to Henri IV, January 12, 1590, Bordeaux.

30. BN CD Mss 525, fol. 5–41, "Discours touchant la puissance du pape, composé par Messire Claude d'Angennes de Rambouillet, évesque du Mans," nd. D'Angennes probably wrote this treatise in the summer of 1591 for the upcoming Assembly of Chartres. See BN FF Mss 513, fol. 445–463, "Discours de la puissance de lier et délier, 1591."

31. BN CD Mss 525, fol. 19. See also J. Bréjon de Lavergnée, "Le serment de fidélité des clercs au roi de France pour le temporel relevant de la couronne," in *Mélanges offerts à Jean Dauvillier* (Toulouse, 1979), pp. 127–133.

32. *Le vray catholique romain contre le Ligueur couvert* (np, 1591), p. 5; M. B., *Lettre d'un ecclésiastique à un sien amy sur les difficultez que les ecclésiastiques d'Angers et autres Ligueurs font de prester serment de fidélité au roy Henry IV* (Tours, 1589), pp. 107–108.

33. BN FF Mss 3961, fol. 288–291, "Mémoire pour oster le scrupule de Monseigneur de Nevers, mai 1590."

34. René Benoist, *Troisiesme advertissement à la France, et principalement à la cour et la grande ville de Paris justement divinement punies* (Paris, 1591), pp. 19–20.

35. BN FF Mss 1509, fol. 392, Charles Faye d'Espesses to Bellièvre, July 22, 1591, Tours.

36. BN FF Mss 5045, fol. 306, "Les cardinaux, archevesques, évesques, abbez, chapitres et autres ecclésiastiques convoquez à Mantes, et depuis à Chartres, pour adviser et pourveoir aux affaires de l'église," September 22, 1591.

37. *Arrest de la cour de Parlement de Paris séant à Tours contre les prétendues bulles de nostre s. père* (Tours, 1691).

38. BN FF Mss 5045, fol. 306.

39. Leaguers also employed this notion of collective punishment and salvation, as in *Prières collectes et oraisons, avec un bel ordre de processions ordonnées, afin d'obtenir une heureuse victoire des ennemis de la foy et religion catholique . . . Aussi pour avoir un bon roy protecteur et défenseur d'icelle* (Paris, 1592).

40. Jean Orcibal, *Les origines du jansénisme,* 5 vols. (Paris and Louvain: J. Vrin, 1947), vol. 2, pp. 40–88.

41. BN FF Mss 3980, fol. 157–158, Aubespine to Piacenza, March 24, 1591, Orléans.

42. BN FF Mss 3980, fol. 165, La Châtre to Piacenza, March 26, 1591, Orléans.

43. *Response aux lettres envoyées par MM les cardinaulx de Vendôme et de Lenoncourt* (np, 1590).

44. BN FF Mss 3978, fol. 164–165, Hennequin to Vendôme and Lenoncourt, February 26, 1590, np; E. de Saint-Sauveur, "Note sur Aymar Hennequin, évêque de Rennes," *Bulletin de la société de l'histoire d'Ille et Villaine,* 23, pp. 93–100.

45. *Arrest de la cour de Parlement de recognoistre pour roy Charles dixiesme de ce nom* (Paris, 1589); *Arrest de la cour de Parlement de Paris contre Henry de Bourbon, ses fauteurs et adhérans* (Paris, 1589), dated October 14.

46. BN FF Mss 3978, fol. 161, Bouliers to Vendôme and Lenoncourt, February 24, 1590, Paris.

47. BN FF Mss 3978, fol. 158, Épinac to Vendôme and Lenoncourt, February 24, 1590, Paris; P. Richard, *La papauté et la Ligue française: Pierre d'Épinac* (Paris: A. Picard, 1901).

48. Richard Cooper, "The Blois Assassinations: Sources in the Vatican," in *From Valois to Bourbon,* ed. Cameron, pp. 51–72.

49. Jean Boucher, *Lettre missive de l'évesque du Mans, avec la response à icelle, faicte au mois de septembre passé, par un docteur en théologie de la faculté de Paris* (Paris, 1589), p. 14.

50. *Advis catholique sur le conciliabule d'aucuns prélats assemblez à Chartres, et les décrets d'iceluy* (np, 1591), pp. 2–9.

51. *Response aux lettres envoyées par MM les cardinaulx de Vendôme et de Lenoncourt* (np, 1590), pp. 22–23.

52. *État et église dans le genèse de l'état moderne* (Madrid: Casa de Velazquez, 1986); Maurice Barbier, *Religion et politique dans la pensée moderne* (Nancy: Presses Universitaires de Nancy, 1987); Henry Mechoulan, ed., *L'état baroque. Regards sur la pensée politique de la France du premier XVIIe siècle* (Paris: J. Vrin, 1985).

53. E. Maugis, *Histoire du Parlement de Paris de l'avènement des rois Valois à la mort d'Henri IV,* 2nd ed., 3 vols. (New York: B. Franklin, 1967), vol. 3; Arthur Desjardins, *Les parlements du roi (1589–1596)* (Paris, 1879); Frederic J. Baumgartner, "Party Alignment in the Parlement of Paris, 1589–1594," *Proceedings of the Western Society for French History,* 6 (1978).

54. S. Hanley, *The "Lit de Justice,"* p. 190, note 15.

55. Guillaume du Vair, *Exhortation à la vie civile* (np, 1594), and *Response d'un bourgeois de Paris* (np, 1594); Jean Bailbé, "Les guerres civiles de Rome dans la littérature française du XVIe siècle," *Actes Budé* (Rome, 1973).

56. BN FF Mss 4783, fol. 1–5, "Établissement du parlement en la ville de Tours par le roy Henri III, sa majesté séant en son lict de justice"; Jonathan Dewald, *The Formation of a Provincial Nobility: The Magistrates of the Parlement of Rouen, 1499–1610* (Princeton: Princeton University Press, 1980); Philip Benedict, *Rouen and the Wars of Religion* (Cambridge: Cambridge University Press, 1981); Mark Greengrass, "The Sainte Union in the Provinces: The Case of Toulouse," *SCJ,* 14 (1983), pp. 469–496.

57. BN CD Mss 61, fol. 85; François Gebelin, *Le gouvernement du Maréchal de Matignon en Guyenne (1589–1594)* (Bordeaux: M. Mounastre-Pecamilii, 1912); Géralde Nakam, *Montaigne et son temps* (Paris: Nizet, 1984), pp. 158–169, 204–207.

58. BN CD Mss 61, fol. 36, Matignon to Henri IV, August 18, 1589, Bordeaux. Like Matignon, the Duc d'Épernon ordered loyalist judges of the Parlement of Aix-en-Provence in exile in Pertuis to swear obedience to Henri IV shortly after news of the regicide arrived. Gustave Lambert, *Histoire des guerres de religion en Provence (1530–1598),* 2nd ed., 2 vols. (Nyons: Chantemerle, 1972), vol. 1, pp. 78–80. Not all provincial governors acted as promptly. See Poirson, *Le règne de Henri IV,* vol. 1, pp. 47–50.

59. BN CD Mss 61, fol. 85, "Arrest de la cour de Parlement de Bordeaux, par lequel il est déffendu à tous ceux du ressort d'icelle d'exercer, ès lieux catholiques, autre religion que la catholique"; P. Gouyon, *L'introduction de la réforme disciplinaire du concile de Trente dans le diocèse de Bordeaux, 1582–1624* (Bordeaux: Institut Catholique de Paris, 1945); C. Jouhaud, "Le

conseil du roi, Bordeaux et les Bordelais (1579–1610, 1630–1680)," *Annales du Midi*, 92 (1981), pp. 377–396.

60. *Arrest de la cour de Parlement de recognoistre pour roy Charles dix-iesme de ce nom* (Paris, 1589); Eugène Saulnier, *Le rôle politique de Charles, cardinal de Bourbon* (Paris: H. Champion, 1912), pp. 201–214.

61. Desjardins, *Les parlements*, pp. 22–23; Cheverny, *Mémoires*, p. 512.

62. E. Barnavi and R. Descimon, *La Sainte Ligue, le juge et la potence: L'assassinat du président Brisson, le 15 novembre 1591* (Paris: Hachette, 1985); Paul Gambier, *Le président Barnabé Brisson, ligueur (1531–1591)* (Paris: Perrin, 1957).

63. BN CD Mss 549, fol. 127–138, "Relation de ce qui se passa durant la Ligue lors de l'arrest pour la manutention de la loy Salique"; BN FF Mss 3646, fol. 62–63, "Extraict des registres du Parlement."

64. Maillard, *Lettre d'un catholique françois*, p. 1.

65. Guillaume du Vair, *De la constance* (Paris, 1594), pp. 18–33.

66. Colin Kaiser, "Les cours souveraines au XVIe siècle: Morale et Contre-Réforme," *AESC*, 37 (1982), pp. 15–31; J. Powis, "Gallican Liberties and the Politics of Later Sixteenth-Century France," *The Historical Journal*, 26 (1983), pp. 515–530.

67. See also Hugues de l'Estre's harangues in *Mémoires de la Ligue*, vol. 5, pp. 2–39, 115–145.

68. Roland Mousnier, "Les concepts d'ordres, d'états, de fidélité et de monarchie absolue en France de la fin du XVIe siècle à la fin du XVIIIe," *Revue historique*, 247 (1972), pp. 289–312; Pierre Goubert, "L'ancienne société d'ordres: Verbiage ou réalité?," *Clio parmi les hommes* (Paris and The Hague: Mouton, 1976); Armand Arriaza, "Mousnier, Barber and the Society of Orders," *Past and Present*, 89 (1980), pp. 39–57.

69. *Édict et déclaration de monseigneur le duc de Mayenne, et le conseil général de la saincte union. Pour réunir tous vrais chrestiens françois à la déffense et conservation de l'église catholique, apostolique et romaine, et manutention de l'estat royal* (Paris, 1589); Auguste Bernard, ed., *Procès-verbaux des États Généraux de 1593* (Paris, 1842), pp. xxxvii–xl.

70. Bernard, *Procès-verbaux*, pp. 16–17.

71. Isambert, *Recueil des anciennes loix françaises*, vol. 15, pp. 11–16; Bernard, *Procès-verbaux*, xxxiv; Angoulême, *Mémoires*, pp. 64–66; Cheverny, *Mémoires*, pp. 496–497; *Serment réciproque des princes du sang, et autres ducs, pairs etc à sa majesté* (np, 1589), pp. 4–5.

72. BN FF Mss 3430, fol. 28–39, "Procès-verbal de l'absolution du roy Henry IV lors de sa conversion à l'église catholique"; BN FF Mss 7774, fol. 258–264, "Relation des cérémonies qui furent faictes à St-Denis à la conversion de Henry IV."

73. BN FF Mss 15893, fol. 93, "Escrit de M. de Bellièvre, contre la convocation des prétendus estats de la Ligue et pour exciter ceulx de ce parti à se sousmettre au roy."

74. J. Russell Major, *Representative Institutions in Renaissance France: 1421–1559* (Madison, 1960), conclusion; Francine Leclercq, "Les états-

provinciaux et la Ligue en Basse-Auvergne de 1589–1594," *Actes 88e Congrès de la société des savantes Clermont-Ferrand, 1963*; H. Drouot, "Les conseils provinciaux de la Sainte-Union (1589–1595)," *Annales du Midi, 66* (1953), pp. 415–433.

75. A. Buisson, *Michel de l'Hôpital* (Paris: A. Picard, 1950), pp. 88–91.

76. BN FF Mss 3988, fol. 176–177, "Sur la nullité de convocation et assemblée des prétenduz estats généraux de France tenuz à Paris en l'an 1593, et des délibérations qui y ont este faictes."

77. François Dumont, "La noblesse et les états particuliers français," *Recueil de travaux d'histoire et de philologie, 45* (Louvain, 1952); Jean-Dominique Lassaigne, *Les assemblées de la noblesse de France aux XVIIe et XVIIIe siècles* (Paris: Éditions Cujas, 1965); Louis Serbat, *Les assemblées du clergé de France: Origines, organisation, développement (1551–1615)* (Paris: H. Champion, 1906); Pierre Blet, S.J., *Le clergé de France et la monarchie: Étude sur les assemblées du clergé de 1615–1666,* 2 vols. (Rome: Analecta Gregoriana, 1959); J. Russell Major, *Bellièvre, Sully and the Assembly of Notables of 1596* (Philadelphia, 1974), *Transactions of the American Philosophical Society.*

78. J. Michael Hayden, *France and the Estates General of 1614* (Cambridge: Cambridge University Press, 1972); Roger Chartier and Denis Richet, ed., *Représentation et vouloir politique autour des États-Généraux de 1614* (Paris: Éditions de l'École des Hautes Études, 1982); J. Apostolidès, *Le roi-machine* (Paris: Cerf, 1981), pp. 3–11; E. Le Roy Ladurie, "Auprès du roi, la cour," *AESC,* 38 (1983), pp. 21–41; Michel Antoine, *Le dur métier du roi* (Paris: PUF, 1986).

The Fight for the King's Faith

1. G. Joly, *Panégyrique au roy Henri IIII* (Paris, 1594), pp. 16–18.

2. Palma Cayet, *Chronologie novenaire,* p. 173.

3. Henri IV to Duplessis Mornay, November 7, 1589, Étampes, Berger de Xivery, vol. 3, pp. 70–73.

4. *Déclaration de M. le duc de Mayenne, lieutenant général de la couronne et de l'estat* (Paris, 1589), pp. 1–2; Palma Cayet, *Chronologie novenaire,* p. 171.

5. Jacques-Auguste de Thou, *Histoire universelle,* 16 vols. (London, 1734), vol. 11, pp. 27–31.

6. Henri IV to Elizabeth I, late September 1589, np, Berger de Xivery, vol. 3, pp. 50–51. See also John B. Black, *Elizabeth and Henri IV: Being a Short Study in Anglo-French Relations, 1589–1603* (Oxford: Oxford University Press, 1914).

7. BN FF Mss 15561, fol. 178–181, François le Mareschal, December 19, 1589, Bourges.

8. Drouot, *Mayenne et la Bourgogne,* vol. 2, pp. 10–33; De Lamar Jensen, *Diplomacy and Dogmatism, Bernardino de Mendoza and the French*

Catholic League (Cambridge, Mass.: Harvard University Press, 1964), pp. 205–206.

9. BN FF Mss 17281, fol. 241–242. Villeroy, *Mémoires d'estat*, ed. Michaud and Poujoulat (Paris, 1881), p. 139. BN FF Mss 4748, fol. 112–126, "Discours apolégetique . . . de sa conduite durant les troubles de la Ligue."

10. Villeroy, *Mémoires d'estat*, p. 194. The compromising disclosure can be found in BN CCC Mss 33, fol. 296, "Recueil sommaire des principaux points contenus en plusieurs lettres écrites en chiffre par les ennemis du roi en septembre et octobre [1589]."

11. Villeroy, *Mémoires d'estat*, p. 144. Henri IV thought he could force the League to recognize him after Arques. Henri IV to M. de Poyanne, October 7, 1589, np, Berger de Xivery, vol. 3, pp. 55–56.

12. Villeroy, *Memoires d'estat*, p. 144.

13. BN FF Mss 15909, fol. 270–272, Jeannin to Bellièvre, September 25, 1589, np.

14. BN FF Mss 4743, fol. 70–83, "Advis au M. le duc de Mayenne."

15. BN FF Mss 3386, fol. 41–42, "Partie d'un discours italien contre ce que le pape Sixte V avoit défendu de donner l'absolution au feu roy,"; BN FF Mss 3473, fol. 94–95, "Mémoire envoyé à Monseigneur d'Ossat sur la mort de Henri III," October 14, 1589.

16. *Négotiations diplomatiques de la France avec la Toscane*, vol. 60, Niccolini to Grand Duke, September 2, 1589, Rome; Martin, *Le gallicanisme et la la réforme catholique*, 253–259; Gregorio Leti, *La vie du pape Sixte V*, 2 vols. (Paris, 1758), vol. 2, pp. 411–472; Charles Giraud, "Sixte V, son influence sur les affaires de France au XVIe siècle," *Revue des deux mondes*, 101 (1882), pp. 462–486, 624–650, 848–877.

17. These instructions can be found in Caringi, "Sixte V et la Ligue, documents inédits," *Revue du monde catholique*, 17 (1923), pp. 449–453. See also Michel de Bouard, "Sixte Quint, Henri IV et la Ligue: La légation du cardinal Caetani en France," *Revue des questions historiques*, 20 (1932), pp. 59–140.

18. Caringi, "Sixte V et la Ligue," pp. 455–457; Franklin Charles Palm, *Politics and Religion in Sixteenth-Century France: A Study of the Career of Henry of Montmorency-Damville, Uncrowned King of the South* (Boston, 1927), p. 202.

19. Palma Cayet, *Chronologie novenaire*, p. 187; BN FF Mss 3490, fol. 14–15.

20. BN FF Mss 7764, fol. 343–355, "Propositions faictes au légat de la part du roy et refus du légat de l'escouter vers luy."

21. Jensen, *Diplomacy and Dogmatism*, pp. 201–203; BN FF Mss 3980, fol. 257–258, Anonymous to Nevers, January 19, 1590, Paris.

22. BN FF Mss 3978, fol. 92–93, Nevers to Villeroy, February 2, 1590, Nevers.

23. BN FF Mss 7764, fol. 247–253, La Guesle to Présidial de Saint Pierre-

le-Monstia [*sic*], January 20, 1590, Tours; BN FF Mss 15575, fol. 6, Cardinals and bishops at Tours to Caetani, February 11, 1590, Tours; and BN FF Mss 15575, fol. 5, Caetani to Vendôme, January 30, 1590, Paris.

24. Estoile, *Registre-journal*, p. 12. See also, *Les articles de la puissance donnée par N.S. père le pape à M. le cardinal Cajetan, légat en France* (Paris, 1590); *Résolution de messieurs de la faculté de théologie de Paris* (Paris, 1590), dated February 10.

25. *Response aux lettres envoyées par messieurs les cardinaulx de Vendosme et de Lenoncourt* (Paris, 1590).

26. BN FF Mss 7765, fol. 176–179, Mayenne to Saint-Luc, April 12, 1590, Soissons. For Nemour's appointment, see *Registre de l'Hôtel-de-Ville de Paris*, vol. 13, fol. 13.

27. BN FF mss 7765, fol. 181–195, "Nouvelles"; James W. Thompson, ed., *The Letters and Documents of Armand de Gontaut, Baron de Biron, Marshall of France, 1524–1592*, 2 vols. (Berkeley, 1936), vol. 2, pp. 692–711.

28. Charles de Navières, *Chant triomphal de la céleste victoire donnée au roy très chrestien près d'Ivry, le mars 1590* (Châlons-sur-Marne, 1590), p. 4; Henri IV spoke confidently of a brief siege in his "Lettre circulaire sur la bataille d'Ivry," Berger de Xivery, vol. 3, pp. 162–169; BN FF Mss 3615, fol. 44, François d'Orléans to Nevers, March 17, 1590, Vernon; BN FF Mss 3978, fol. 148, Revol to Vendôme, April 9, 1590, camp de Melun.

29. For the siege of Paris, see Estoile, *Registre-journal*, pp. 15–35; Pierre Corneio, *Bref discours et véritable des choses plus notables arrivées au siège mémorable de la renommée ville de Paris* (Paris, 1590); Alfred Franklin, ed., *Journal du siège de Paris en 1590 rédigé par un des assiégés* (Paris, 1876); BN FF Mss 5045, fol. 194–203, "Relation des affaires de France, faicte à Charles Emmanuel I, duc de Savoie, par François Panigarole"; Christopher Duffy, *Siege Warfare: The Fortress in the Early Modern Period, 1494–1660* (London: Routledge & Kegan Paul, 1979).

30. Corneio, *Bref discours*, pp. 26–27.

31. *Résolution des MM de la faculté de théologie de Paris sur les articles touchant la paix ou capitulation avec l'hérétique* (Paris, 1590); Estoile, *Registre-journal*, p. 17.

32. *Advis sur ce que est à faire contre les catholiques simulez* (Paris, 1589) had advocated such measures the year before.

33. Estoile, *Registre-journal*, pp. 30–32.

34. BN FF Mss 15909, fol. 307–308, Revol to Bellièvre, August 2, 1590, St. Denis.

35. *Épistre sur le fait de la paix avec la responce et advis sur icelle* (Paris, 1590), pp. 2–3; *Bref discours des inconviens qui ensuivront advenant qu'on face [sic] la paix prétendue avec Henry du Bourbon* (Paris, 1590), pp. 4–5; *Lettre escripte par le roy aux habitans de Paris* (np, 1590), pp. 23–24.

36. Palma Cayet, *Chronologie novenaire*, p. 241; M. D. P., *Response par le roy aux habitans de Paris* (np, 1590), pp. 23–24.

37. Estoile, *Registre journal*, p. 26; BN FF Mss 3996, fol. 157, "Résolution des prélats théologiens sur la question à eux posée par le cardinal de Gondy," August 2, 1590, Paris.

38. *Discours de ce qui s'est passé en l'armée du roy* (Paris, 1590), p. 27; *Recueil de ce qui s'est passé en la conférence des sieurs cardinal de Gondi et archevesque de Lion avec le roy* (Tours, 1590).

39. Henri IV to Tavannes, August 11, 1590, camp de St. Denis, Berger de Xivery, vol. 3, p. 237; BN FF Mss 17533, fol. 26–33, "Mémoires de Nicolas Brûlart, abbe de Joyenval," 1590–1593.

40. BN FF Mss 15909, fol. 318, Revol to Bellièvre, August 18, 1590, Noyons.

41. *Discours de ce que s'est passé en l'Armée du roy depuis que le duc de Parme s'est joinct à celle des ennemis* (Corbeil, 1590), p. 4; Franklin, ed., *Journal du siège de Paris en 1590,* pp. 160–163.

42. BN FF Mss 7765, fol. 365–366, "Acte et protestation du roy Henry IV pour la conservation de la religion catholique . . . Et protection de la ville de Paris en cas de soumission et obéissance," August 10, 1590; BN FF Mss 15591, fol. 149–153.

43. Théophile Frederick, *Le pacifique* (Geneva, 1590).

44. Du Bouchet, *Discours véritable de la victoire obtenue par le roy, en la bataille d'Ivry* (Tours, 1590), pp. 6–7.

45. *Déclaration véritable de la bataille faicte à Ivry la Chausée* (np, 1590), p. 2; *Discours véritable de la victoire obtenue par le roy sur la bataille donnée près le village d'Evry* (Tours, 1590); *Le vray discours de la victoire merveilleusement obtenue par le roy de France et de Navarre Henry IIII. En la bataille donnée contre les rebelles ligués pres le bourg d'Yvri* (London, 1590); "Lettre circulaire sur la bataille d'Ivry," Berger de Xivery, vol. 3, pp. 162–169.

46. As he put it: "Our king's prudence is such that the court's outward appearance has been in no way changed; only the prince's face is different." Duplessis Mornay to Beaulieu, August 10, 1589, Saumur, in *Mémoires*, vol. 4, pp. 392–393.

47. Duplessis Mornay to Henri IV, September 1, 1589, Saumur, in *Mémoires*, vol. 4, pp. 405–407.

48. BN FF Mss 7854, "État de la maison du roi, 1590–1593"; AN KK 150–153, "Officiers de la maison du roi, 1593–1601."

49. Cheverny, *Mémoires,* pp. 502–506; De Thou, *Histoire universelle*, vol. 11, pp. 168–170; BN FF Mss 15909, fol. 309, Cheverny to Bellièvre, August 7, 1590, Mantes. See Yves Durand, "Philippe Hurault de Cheverny, Chancelier de France (1528–1599)," in Roland Mousnier, ed., *Le conseil du roi de Louis XII à la Revolution* (Paris, 1970), pp. 69–86.

50. Cheverny, *Mémoires*, p. 506. See also Sebastien Rouillard, *Le grand aulmonsier de France* (Paris, 1607); Guillaume du Peyrat, *Histoire ecclésiastique de la cour* (Paris, 1645); abbé Étienne Oroux, *Histoire ecclésiastique de la cour de France,* 2 vols. (Paris, 1777), vol. 2, pp. 224–226. For changes in the royal household, see Jacqueline Boucher, "L'évolution de la maison du

roi des derniers Valois aux premiers Bourbons," *XVIIe siècle*, 34 (1982), pp. 359–379.

51. Cheverny, *Mémoires*, p. 506.

52. BN FF Mss 7767, fol. 435–439, "Mémoires escripts de la main de Mgr. de Chartres pour déliberer de ce qui seroit à faire sur la reception du roy entrant en la ville de Chartres," April 1591.

53. BN FF Mss 3275, fol. 133, "Articles accordez par le roy aux habitants de la ville de Chartres," April 10, 1591; BN FF Mss 3422, fol. 59, Henri IV to the Cardinal de Vendôme, December 10, 1589, Laval.

54. Nevers, *Mémoires*, vol. 2, pp. 118–148. The hot-headed Comte de Soissons made his intentions known in early August 1589 when he refused to sign the Catholic oath of loyalty at St. Cloud. Soissons found little support among loyalist Catholics, however; they considered a Tiers Parti risky enough without the count's arrogant indiscretions. Soissons deeply resented Henri IV's opposition to his marriage to Catherine de Bourbon, the king's sister.

55. J. A. de Thou, *Memoires*, vol. 11, p. 351.

56. BN FF Mss 7762, fol. 159–163, François le Mareschal to Nevers, December 8, 1589, Bourges.

57. Estoile, *Registre-journal*, p. 46.

58. Sully, *Oeconomies royales*, p. 80.

59. Henri IV to Montmorency, October 8, 1590, Marguy, Berger de Xivery, vol. 3, pp. 263–268.

60. BN FI Mss 851 fol. 1–12, "Discorso intorno l'ambasciera mandata dal Cardinal di Vandomo alla Sta. di No. Ste. Gregorio xiiii"; BN CCC Mss 500, fol. 173–175, Desportes to Mayenne, April 5, 1591, Rome.

61. BN FF Mss 3980, fol. 300–302, "Discours du duc de Nevers à Henri IV," June 21, 1591, Mantes.

62. Villeroy, *Mémoires d'estat*, pp. 182–183; Sully, *Oeconomies royales*, pp. 105–109.

63. *Bulles de nostre sainct père le pape Grégoire XIV, d'une contre toutes personnes ecclésiastiques, suyvants le party de Henry de Bourbon, jadis roy de Navarre, l'autre aux princes, seigneurs, nobles et autres personnes laïques suyvans le mesme party* (Paris, 1591), p. 6.

64. *Déclaration du roy confirmative d'autre déclaration par luy faicte à son advènement à la couronne de vouloir maintenir et conserver la religion catholique* (Tours, 1591).

65. BN FF Mss 7765, fol. 305–311, "Résultat du conseil tenu par Henri IV sur la révocation de l'Édit d'Union," July 6, 1591; *La dispute d'un catholique de Paris contre un politique de la ville de Tours* (Paris, 1591).

66. Groulart, *Mémoires de la Ligue*, vol. 4, p. 37; BN FF Mss 15909, fol. 409, Charles Faye d'Espesses to Bellièvre, August 24, 1591, Chartres.

67. BN FF Mss 5045, fol. 306, "Les cardinaulx, archevesques, évesques, abbez, chapitres et autres ecclésiastiques convoquez à Mantes, et depuis à Chartres, pour adviser et pourvoir aux affaires de l'église," September 21, 1591; BN FF Mss 5755, "Journal du secrétaire de M. Philippe du Bec, év-

esque de Nantes et archevesque de Rheims (1599–1603)," esp. fol. 13–16 for an insider's view of the Assembly. Charles Faye d'Espesse wrote the Parlement's rebuttal in *Discours des raisons et moyens pour lesquels MM du clergé . . . ont déclaré les bulles . . . nulles et injustes* (Tours, 1591); Matteo Zampini, *Défence pour les bulles* (Paris, 1591).

68. BN FF Mss 3996, fol. 279–289, "Procès-verbal des députés de l'assemblée du clergé tenue à Chartres envoyés ver le roy," (November 5–December 19, 1591).

69. *Brief discours des choses advenues en la ville de Rouen durant le siège mis devant par Henri de Bourbon, prétendu roi de Navarre* (Rouen, 1592); Ivan Cloulas, "L'armée pontificale de Grégoire, Innocent IX et Clément VIII pendant la seconde campagne en France d'Alexandre Farnese (1591–1592)," *Bulletin de la Committée d'Histoire Belgique,* 126 (1960), pp. 83–102.

70. See Élie Barnavi and Robert Descimon, *La Sainte Ligue, le juge et la potence* (Paris, 1985); Paul Gambier, *Le président Barnabé Brisson, ligueur (1531–1591)* (Paris, 1957); Jean Tournemille, "Le ligueur B. Brisson (1531-1591) ou les dangers d'un double jeu," *Cahier Ouest,* 16 (1957), pp. 23–28.

71. BN FF Mss 15893, fol. 2, Bellièvre to Revol, January 14, 1592, Grignon.

72. Villeroy, *Mémoires d'estat,* p. 180.

73. Duplessis Mornay to Fleury, March 16, 1592, Mantes, in *Mémoires et correspondence,* vol. 4, p. 231; Villeroy to Fleury, 23 March 1592, np, in same, pp. 236–238.

74. Henri IV to Duplessis Mornay, March 25, 1592, camp near Rouen, Berger de Xivery, vol. 3, p. 587; Duplessis Mornay to Bouillon, April 3, 1592, Buhi, in *Mémoires et correspondence,* vol. 5, pp. 266–268.

75. "Mémoire au roy," April 4, 1592, Mantes, in *Mémoires et correspondence,* vol. 5, pp. 268–272; BN FF Mss 15893, fol. 24, Bellièvre to anonymous, April 12, 1592, Mantes.

76. Duplessis Mornay to Henri IV, April 20, 1592, Mantes, in *Mémoires et correspondence,* vol. 5, pp. 310–312; Henri IV to Duplessis Mornay, April 26, 1592, Fontaine-de-Bourg, Berger de Xivery, vol. 3, p. 621.

77. Villeroy, *Mémoires d'estat,* p. 189; Henri IV to Montmorency, March 26, 1592, camp near Rouen, Berger de Xivery, vol. 3, pp. 591–594.

78. BN FF Mss 23195, fol. 53–55, Biron to Henri IV, May 28, 1592, camp near Fourmoy.

79. "Mémoire envoyé à M. de la Fontaine par M. Duplessis Mornay," May 29, 1592, np, in *Mémoires et correspondence,* vol. 5, pp. 334–335; La Fontaine to Duplessis Mornay, June 19, 1592, np, in same, pp. 339–345.

80. BN CD Mss 61, fol. 281–282, Revol to Henri IV, July 6, 1592, St. Denis.

81. BN FF Mss 6552, fol. 92, Revol to Maisse, October 6, 1592, np; BN FF Mss 3982, fol. 58–69, "Instructions à M. le marquis de Pisany," October 7, 1592, np; BN CCC Mss 31, fol. 258–261, "Instruction du roi Henri IV a M. de la Clièlle," October 12, 1592, camp near the Marne.

82. BN FF Mss 17533, fol. 42–47, "Mémoires de Nicolas Brûlart"; BN

FF Mss 3996, fol. 265–266, "Déliberation faicte aux cordeliers sur la requisition qui fut faicte au roy Henry IIII de se rendre catholique," October 20, 1592.

83. BN FF Mss 5045, fol. 411–412, "Récit de choses qui depuis peu se sont faicts à Paris." This piece covers October through November, 1592.

84. BN CD Mss 88, fol. 156, "Procès-verbal de l'assemblée des bourgeois, manans et habitants de la ville de Paris," October 30, 1592.

85. BN FF Mss 5045, fol. 413, "Response faicte par M. de Mayenne en l'assemblée générale tenue en la maison de ville," November 5, 1592, Paris.

86. BN FF Mss 4019, fol. 207–210, "Response de la part du roy," np, nd; BN FF Mss 4505, fol. 363, "Mandement du roy envoyé par lettres de cachet à ses cours de Parlement," November 22, 1592.

87. BN FF Mss 4019, fol. 217–225, Villeroy to Bellièvre, December 16, 1592, château de Villeroy; BN CCC Mss 31, fol. 289, "Créance donné par le pape à frère Alexandre Franceschi et qu'il a baillé par escrit au cardinal Gondy."

The Move to Convert

1. BN FF Mss 3624, fol. 12, anonymous to Nevers, January 12, 1593, Chaource; BN CD Mss 546, fol. 56–57, "Au roy venu à Tours en janvier 1593"; Villeroy, "Harangue faicte par M. de Villeroy, pour estre prononcée en l'assemblée des prétendus estats de Paris, 1593," in *Mémoires d'estat,* pp. 235–259.

2. Auguste Bernard, ed., *Procès-verbal des États-Généraux de 1593* (Paris, 1842), pp. 16–17.

3. BN FF Mss 15910, fol. 1, Revol to Bellièvre, January 1, 1593, Chartres.

4. *Déclaration faicte par M. le duc de Mayenne, lieutenant général de l'estat et couronne de France, pour la réunion de tous les catholiques de ce royaume* (Paris, 1593), pp. 2–3.

5. Ibid., p. 5.

6. Bernard, *Procès-verbal,* pp. 1–14.

7. Bernard, *Procès-verbal,* p. vii.

8. BN FF Mss 15910, fol. 4, Revol to Bellièvre, January 13, 1593, Chartres.

9. BN FF Mss 15910, fol. 8–9, Bellièvre to Villeroy, January 19, 1593, Grignon.

10. BN FF Mss 3983, fol. 23, Revol to Nivernois, January 15, 1593, Chartres; Henri IV to Maisse, January 29, 1593, Chartres, Berger de Xivery, vol. 3, pp. 719–722.

11. BN FF Mss 15893, fol. 68–96, "Escrit de M. de Bellièvre. Contre la convocation des prétendus estats de la Ligue et pour exciter ceulx de ce parti à se sousmettre au roy."

12. BN FF Mss 3988 fol. 176–177, "Sur la nullité de la convocation et

assemblée des prétendus estats généraux de France tenuz à Paris en l'an 1593, et des délibérations qui ont estés faictes"; Richard A. Jackson, "Peers of France and Princes of the Blood," *French Historical Studies,* 7 (1971), pp. 27–46.

13. BN CD Mss 549, fol. 136–137; *Déclaration du roy contre les prétendus estats de la Ligue* (Tours, 1593), pp. 4–5.

14. BN FF Mss 15910, fol. 14, Revol to Bellièvre, February 6, 1593, Chartres.

15. "Proposition des messieurs les princes, prélatz, officiers de la couronne, seigneurs, gentilhommes et autres catholiques estans au party du roy de Navarre," in Bernard, *Procès-verbal,* pp. 40–42.

16. BN FF Mss 15910, fol. 15–16, Jacques-Auguste de Thou to Bellièvre, February 25, 1593, Chartres.

17. BN FF Mss 20153, fol. 11, anonymous to anonymous, February 10, 1593, Paris; Bernard, *Procès-verbal,* pp. 45–64.

18. Bernard, *Procès-verbaux,* pp. 63–64.

19. "Responce du duc de Mayenne, princes, prélatz, seigneurs et députés des provinces assemblez à Paris à la proposition de messieurs les princes . . . du party du roy de Navarre," in Bernard, *Procès-verbaux,* pp. 73–79.

20. BN FF Mss 15910, fol. 19, Revol to Bellièvre, March 15, 1593, Chartres.

21. BN FF Mss 6552, fol. 154, Bellièvre to Épinac, early March 1593, Grignon; BN FF Mss 4743, fol. 113–114, Villeroy to Bellièvre, March 17, 1593, np; Duplessis Mornay to Buzenval, April 3, 1593, np, in *Mémoires et correspondance,* vol. 5, pp. 394–396; BN FF Mss 15910, fol. 22, Épinac to Bellièvre, March 20, 1593, Paris; BN FF Mss 15910, fol. 24, Revol to Bellièvre, March 24, 1593, Chartres.

22. "Réplique à la responce," in Bernard, *Procès-verbaux,* pp. 115–116.

23. "Responce à la susdicte réplique," in Bernard, *Procès-verbaux,* pp. 123.

24. BN FF Mss 15910, fol. 25, Revol to Bellièvre, March 28, 1593, Chartres; BN FF Mss 15910, fol. 26, Perrot to Bellièvre, March 31, 1593, Chartres.

25. BN FF Mss 4719, fol. 11, Schomberg to Nevers, April 3, 1593, Compiègne; BN FF Mss 15910, fol. 27, Angennes to Bellièvre, April 3, 1593, Rambouillet.

26. BN FF Mss 15910, fol. 29, Perrot to Bellièvre, April 4, 1593, Chartres.

27. Sully, *Oeconomies royales,* p. 105.

28. Ibid., p. 108.

29. Ibid., p. 109. Duplessis Mornay, in a letter to La Fontaine, April 20, 1593, La Rochelle, in *Mémoires et correspondance,* vol. 5, pp. 399–401, wrote that Henri IV was "still committed to the Reformed religion."

30. D'Aubigné, *Confession catholique du sieur de Sancy* (np, 1597), p. 5.

31. Duperron, *Oeuvres completes,* 2 vols. (Paris, 1624), vol. 2, pp. 146–151.

32. Palma Cayet, *Chronologie novenaire,* p. 445.

33. BN FF Mss 20154, fol. 879–880, De Thou to Bouillon, April 11, 1593, Suresnes.

34. BN FF NA Mss 7774, fol. 127–135, Commander of Diou to Guillaume Rose, July 3, 1593, Rome; P. Richard, *La papauté et la Ligue française. Pierre d'Épinac, archevêque de Lyon (1573–1599)* (Paris, 1901), pp. 488–507.

35. Villars and Belin both recognized Henri IV early the next year, while Jacques Le Maître helped gain passage of a resolution on the Salic Law in the Parlement of Paris on June 28. Bernard was an *avocat* in the Leaguer Parlement of Dijon and closely tied to Mayenne. Drouot, *Mayenne et la Bourgogne*, vol. 2, pp. 245–252. Laurens was a *premier président* in the Parlement of Aix-en-Provence and compiled the most complete account of the conference, apparently at the behest of Épinac to parry charges of collusion. BN FF Mss 3984, fol. 195, Épinac to Rubis, July 24, 1593, Paris.

36. Palma Cayet, *Chronologie novenaire*, pp. 446–447.

37. Honoré de Laurens, *Discours et rapport véritable de la conférence de Suresnes* (Paris, 1593), p. 32.

38. *Articles baillez par les députez de la part des princes catholiques au party du roy pour la conférence aux députez du party contraire* (np, 1593).

39. Laurens, *Discours et rapport véritable*, p. 61.

40. Ibid., p. 67.

41. Ibid., p. 70; De Thou to Nevers, BN FF Mss 4719, fol. 114, May 2, 1593, Mantes.

42. Laurens, *Discours et rapport véritable*, p. 72.

43. BN FF Mss 3626, fol. 25, Henri IV to Nevers, May 8, 1593, np.

44. The earliest explicit reference I have found of his decision to begin Catholic instruction is in a letter to the Prince de Conti on May 10, 1593, Mantes, Berger de Xivery, vol. 3, pp. 768–771.

45. BN FF Mss 3634, fol. 1, "Advis relatifs aux démarches de MM. de Revol et Schombert [*sic*] envers le roy."

46. Palma Cayet, *Chronologie novenaire*, p. 467; BN CD Mss 322, fol. 295–297, Gabriel Damours to Henri IV, June 20, 1593, St. Jean d'Angely.

47. A printed version appeared a few weeks later entitled *Déclaration faicte en l'assemblée tenue à Suresnes le dixseptiesme jour de may 1593* (np, nd); Laurens, *Discours et rapport véritable*, p. 92.

48. Estoile, *Registre-journal*, p. 134.

49. Ibid., p. 136.

50. Ibid., p. 137.

51. BN FF Mss 3997, fol. 71; BN FF Mss 3984, fol. 124, Creilly to the *curé* of St-Germain-de-l'Auxerois, July 6, 1593, np; BN FF Mss 3984, fol. 177–178, Philippe Desportes to Clement VIII, July 22, 1593, np.

52. BN CD Mss 549, fol. 127–138, "Relation de ce qui se passa durant la Ligue lors de l'arrest pour la manutention de la Loy Salique." A printed version can be found in the *Nouvelle collection des mémoires relatifs à l'histoire de France*, ed. Michaud and Poujoulat (Paris, 1881), vol. 11, pp. 541–548,

though curiously it omits the reference to the Tiers Parti contained in the original manuscript. See also BN FF Mss 3646, fol. 63–74, "Extraict des registres du Parlement"; BN FF Mss 5045 fol. 404, Henri IV to Buzanval, July 10, 1593, Mantes.

The Conversion at St. Denis

1. BN FF Mss 7774, fol. 17–18, Potier de Gesvres to Nevers, June 9, 1593, Mantes.

2. BN CD Mss 770, fol. 225–226, "Copie de la lettre du roy aux évesques pour sa conversion, une pour toutes," May 18, 1593; BN FF Mss 5045, fol. 396, Henri IV to Parlement of Normandy in Caen, May 1593, Mantes; Henri IV to Épernon, June 10, 1593, np, Berger de Xivery, vol. 3, pp. 799–803; BN FF Mss 3625, fol. 12, Henri IV to Nevers, July 14, 1593, St. Denis.

3. BN FF Mss 3997, fol. 877, Vendôme to Piacenza, np, nd.

4. BN CD Mss 770, fol. 226; BN CD Mss 119, fol. 10, Henri IV to Beaune, July 8, 1593, Dreux.

5. Palma Cayet, *Chronologie novenaire*, p. 689; BN FF Mss 3631, fol. 37, D'Escars to Nevers, June 26, 1593, Mussy; Henri IV to d'Abain, June 4, 1593, Mantes, Berger de Xivery, vol. 3, p. 787.

6. *Lettre missive du roy escrite à Monsieur Benoist* (Angers, 1593); E. Pasquier, *René Benoist, le pape des Halles* (Paris: A. Picard, 1901); "Épitre envoyée par M. Claude de Morenne, curé de St-Médéric, aux catholiques de la ville de Paris," August 10, 1593, St. Denis, in *Mémoires de la Ligue,* vol. 5, pp. 414–422; BN FF Mss 17533, fol. 78, Henri IV to Louis Séguier, July 7, 1593, encampment near Dreux.

7. BN FF Mss 3625, fol. 15, D'Escars to Nevers, July 16, 1593, Langres.

8. Henri IV to Messieur des Églises Réformées, May 25, 1593, Mantes, Berger de Xivery, vol. 3, pp. 779–780; *Avis aux français sur la déclaration faite par le roi en l'église Saint-Denis en France le 25e jour de juillet 1593* (Tours, 1593), p. 11; BN FF Mss 15909, fol. 421, Charles Faye d'Espesses to Bellièvre, September 16, 1593, Tours; IF CG Mss 262, fol. 75–76, Bellièvre to anonymous, July 10, 1593, np.

9. See BN FF NA Mss 7774, fol. 53–82, "Lettres des ministres du conseil du roy aux députés de la ville de Lyon aux estats de la Ligue," June 23, 1593, St. Denis.

10. BN FF Mss 15893, fo. 127, Bellièvre to anonymous, June 23, 1593, La Villette.

11. Laurens, *Discours et rapport véritable*, p. 110.

12. BN FF Mss 3631, fol. 19, Birague to Nevers, July 2, 1593, Mantes.

13. BN FF Mss 15893, fol. 129, Bellièvre to Belin, July 12, 1593, St. Denis.

14. BN CD Mss 500, fol. 174, Revol to Beaulieu-Ruzé, July 9, 1593, St. Denis; BN FF Mss 7773, fol. 362–364, anonymous to Madame de Nevers, May 21, 1593, Melun.

15. BN FF Mss 3631, fol. 6, anonymous to Nevers, May 24, 1593, Mantes.

16. BN FF Mss 16093, fol. 427, Revol to Maisse, July 15, 1593, Châlons.

17. BN FF Mss 3631, fol. 70, ville de Châlons to Nevers, June 3, 1593, Châlons.

18. BN FF Mss 3275, fol. 131, "Articles accordez par le roy aux habitans du citadel de Dreux," July 5, 1593.

19. IF CG Mss 262, fol. 61, Henri IV to anonymous, June 13, 1593, np.

20. See Michel Félibien, *Histoire de l'abbaye royale de St. Denis en France* (Paris, 1706); Félice d'Ayzac, *Histoire de l'abbaye de St. Denis en France,* 2 vols. (Paris, 1860), esp. v. 1; Aimé Bonnefin, *Sacre des rois de France* (Limoges, 1982), pp. 133–145; Jackson, *Vive le roi!* pp. 204–205.

21. BN FF Mss 15699, fol. 327–328; Estoile, *Registre-journal,* p. 18; Félibien, *Histoire,* pp. 410–411; L. Carolus-Barré, "Pillage et dispersion de la bibliothèque de l'abbaye de Saint-Denis, 1er octobre-10 novembre 1567," *Bibliothèque de l'École des Chartes,* 138 (1980), pp. 97–101.

22. Georges Duby, *The Europe of the Cathedrals,* trans. Stuart Gilbert (Geneva: Skira, 1966), pp. 13–34.

23. Margaret M. McGowan, "Les images du pouvoir royal au temps de Henri III," in *Théories et pratiques politiques à la Renaissance* (Tours: J. Vrin, 1977), pp. 301–320.

24. BN CD Mss 119, fol. 9, Nicolas de Thou to Cheverny, May 27, 1593, Chartres.

25. Gabriel de Lurbe, "Discours sur l'apparition des colombes blanches au haut de l'église Saint Denis lors de la conversion du roy," in *Chronique bourdelaise* (Bordeaux, 1616), pp. 57–60.

26. BN CD Mss 753, fol. 240–248, "Copie de certains mémoires dressés par ceulx de la religion réformée lors que le roy Henry le grand allant à la messe embrassa la religion papistique."

27. BN FF Mss 15591, fol. 268–269, "Relation de ce qui se passa à Paris et ès environs depuis l'expiration de la trêve jusqu'au 15 juillet."

28. BN FF Mss 3430, fol. 28–39, "Procès-verbal de l'absolution du roy Henri IVe lors de sa conversion à l'église catholique."

29. *Perroniana et Thuana,* 2nd ed. (Paris, 1668), p. 328.

30. BN FF Mss 5045, fol. 379–382, "Dialogue de MM de Rosne et Revol."

31. BN FF Mss 15893, fol. 137–141, Bellièvre to Nevers, August 24, 1593, Melun; BN CD Mss 119, fol. 2; BN FF Mss 3983, fol. 141, Desportes to the bishop of Lisieux, July 22, 1593, Rome.

32. BN CCC Mss 31, fol. 559–566, "Mémoires de ce qui s'est passé en l'armée du roy," June 8–August 1, 1593; BN FF Mss 15591, fol. 272.

33. BN FF Mss 3706, fol. 26–35, "Les sept preuves et tesmoignages rendus par ledict seigneur roy à la veue [*sic*] de tout le monde de la candeur et probité de sa foy et de sa conversion."

34. BN FF Mss 3706, fol. 17–21, "Définition générale représentée à sa

majesté de la pureté et vérité de la doctrine de l'église catholique et de l'erreur de la prétendue réformation."

35. BN FF Mss 3706, fol. 21–25, "Dernière preuve démonstrative de la faulsété de la prétendue réformation des calvinistes représentée à sa majesté dans laquelle se voyent de singulières remarques."

36. BN FF Mss 3706, fol. 1–17, "Raisons et preuves démonstratives contre les calomnies et faulses impressions . . . aux fins de rendre la conversion du roy Henry IV feinte."

37. BN FF Mss 4897, fol. 121; BN FF Mss 3430, fol. 34; Estoile, *Registre-journal,* p. 160.

38. Groulart, *Mémoires,* p. 560.

39. BN FF Mss 7774, fol. 258–264, "Relation des cérémonies qui furent faites à St. Denis à la conversion de Henry IV."

40. BN FF Mss 3997, fo. 66–141, "Journal des événements qui ont précédé et suivi la conversion du roy Henry VI" (May 17–November 6, 1593).

41. *Registres des délibérations du bureau de la ville de Paris,* vol. 10, pp. 357–358.

42. BN CD Mss 88, fol. 193.

43. Gueranger, *The Liturgical Year,* 2 vols. (Dublin, 1883), vol. 2, pp. 4–5.

44. Ibid., pp. 178–179.

45. Estoile, *Registre-journal,* p. 161; Boucher, *Sermons de la simulée conversion,* p. 224.

46. St-Denis AC Mss GG8, fol. 2234.

47. Oroux, *Histoire ecclésiastique,* vol. 2, pp. 244–246; Guillaume de Peyrat, *Antiquités de la chapelle des rois de France* (Paris, 1624).

48. Félibien, *Histoire,* p. 421.

49. BN FF Mss 3430, fol. 36.

50. BN FF Mss 2752, fol. 18.

51. BN FF Mss 15591, fol. 275.

52. BN FF Mss 17282, fol. 176.

53. Jules Formige, *L'abbaye royale de Saint-Denis: Recherches nouvelles* (Paris: PUF, 1960), pp. 85–86; Whitney S. Stoddard, *The West Portals of Saint Denis and Chartres: Sculpture in the Île-de-France from 1140 to 1190: Theory of Origins* (Cambridge, Mass.: Harvard University Press, 1952).

54. Duby, *The Europe of the Cathedrals,* p. 18.

55. BN FF Mss 1728, fol. 176; BN FF Mss 10198, fol. 91–92; BN CD Mss 119, fol. 12–16.

56. BN FF Mss 48907, fol. 121.

57. Palma Cayet, *Chronologie novenaire,* p. 496.

58. BN FF Mss 2751, fol. 17.

59. BN FF Mss 3997, fol. 102. See also Ernst H. Kantorowicz, *Laudes Regiae: A Study in Liturgical Acclamations and Medieval Ruler Worship* (Berkeley: University of California Press, 1946).

60. BN FF Mss 4897, fol. 121; Annie Baudry-Souriau, "Philippe du Bec

(1524–1605) ancien évêque de Nantes et le clergé nantais durant la Ligue," *Bulletin de la société archéologique et historique de Nantes*, 94 (1955), pp. 79–96.

61. BN FF Mss 2751, fol. 18.

62. BN FF Mss 7774, fol. 262.

63. St. Denis AC Mss GG8, fol. 2234; M. Pecquet, "Des compagnies de pénitents à la compagnie du saint-sacrament," *Revue du XVIIe siècle*, 69 (1965), pp. 3–36.

64. Lurbe, *Discours*, pp. 57–59; Boucher, *Sermons de la simulée conversion*, p. 207; Andre Grabar, *Christian Iconography: A Study of Its Origins* (Princeton: Princeton University Press, 1968), pp. 114–116, 122–123.

65. BN FF Mss 7774, fol. 263.

66. BN FF Mss 5755, fol. 14.

67. St. Denis AC Mss GG8, fol. 2234; AN K 1716 n. 7/18.

68. Palma Cayet, *Chronologie novenaire*, p. 597.

69. Pierre Pithou, *Traicté de la juste et canonique absolution de Henry IIII très-chrestien roy de France et de Navarre* (Paris, 1595). A Latin edition had appeared the previous year in Lyon.

70. *Les décrets du concile de Trente*, ed. A. Michel, session XIV, III, c. VII, "De la réserve des cas," p. 348.

71. BN CD Mss 119, fol. 2.

72. Marc Fumaroli, *Jésuites et Gallicans. Recherches sur la genèse et sur la signification des querelles de rhétoriques en France sous les règnes de Henri IV et Louis XIII* (Paris: H. Champion, 1983).

73. St. Denis AC Mss GG8, fol. 2234.

74. BN FF NA Mss 7761, fol. 6–21, "Oraison funèbre de Henry le grand IIII de ce nom roy de France et de Navarre"; AN K 1716 n. 32/1; Hennequin, *Henri IV dans ses oraisons funèbres*, pp. 55–60.

The Catholic King and Pacification

1. BN FF Mss 3985, fol. 200, Bellièvre to Nevers, September 7, 1593, Fontainebleau; M. de Rommel, ed., *Correspondance inédite de Henri IV, roi de France et de Navarre, avec Maurice-le-Savant, landgrave de Hesse* (Paris, 1840), pp. 4–6.

2. *Lettre de M. le légat cardinal de Plaisance* (Paris, 1593).

3. Estoile, *Registre journal*, pp. 161–174; AN K 1569 n. 214, "Pour prouver que malgré la messe de Saint-Denys Henry de Navarre est resté calviniste"; Barnavi, *Le parti de Dieu*, pp. 239–241.

4. Louis Dorléans returned to France in 1606 after writing a tract in favor of Henri IV's decision to readmit the Jesuits to the realm.

5. Peter Ascoli, ed., *Dialogue d'entre le Maheustre et le Manant* (Geneva, 1981), pp. 9–11, 3.

6. Jean Porthaise, *Cinq sermons esquels est traicté tout de la simulée con-*

version du roy de Navarre que du droict d'absolution ecclésiastique (Paris, 1594), pp. 19–20; BN FF Mss 23914, fol. 301, Saint-Belin to Henri IV, September 23, 1594, Poitiers.

7. Louis Dorléans, *Le banquet et après disnée du conte d'Arète, où il se traicte de la dissimulation du roy de Navarre, et des moeurs de ses partisans* (Paris, 1594), p. 14.

8. Ascoli, ed., *Dialogue d'entre le Maheustre et le Manant*, p. 7.

9. Dorléans, *Le banquet*, p. 69.

10. Boucher, *Sermons*, pp. 371–372.

11. Dorléans, *Le banquet*, p. 63.

12. BN FF Mss 23195, fol. 97, Guillaume de Bothéon to Henri IV, August 19, 1593, Romains; BN CD Mss 698, fol. 498, "Extraict des registres du parlement séant à Châlons," July 29, 1593; *Lettres clozes du roy envoyées à ses cours de Parlement touchant la conversion de sa majesté à l'église catholique* (St. Denis, 1593).

13. BN FF Mss 20153, fol. 641–701, "Affaires de Paris 1593."

14. See Père Apollinaire, *Les prières pour le roi en 1593* (Nîmes, 1892).

15. BN FF Mss 3948, fol. 199, Henri IV to Nevers, July 25, 1593, St. Denis; BN FF NA Mss 7774, fol. 146–148, Henri IV to Descars, July 25, 1593, St. Denis; BN CCC Mss 14, fol. 106–107, Henri IV to the Parlement of Paris in Tours, July 25, 1593, St. Denis.

16. Buisseret, *Henri IV*, plate 5, "Engraving of Henry IV Touching for the King's Evil."

17. BN FF Mss 2751, fol. 26, "Extraict du procez criminel faict à Pierre Barrière"; *Discours du procès criminel faict à Pierre Barrière . . . accusé de . . . assassinat par luy entrepris contre la personne du roy* (Chartres, 1593); Roland Mousnier, *L'assassinat d'Henri IV* (Paris, 1964).

18. Alexandre de Pont-Aimery, *Discours d'estat sur la blessure du roi* (Paris, 1595), p. 7; Duperron, "Sur la blessure du roy et le parricide attentat de Jean Chastel," *Les diverses oeuvres*, pp. 42–47; René Benoist, *Voeu et exhortation touchant la nécessaire conservation de la personne du roy* (Paris, 1597).

19. *Articles de la tresve générale conclue entre le roy et M. de Mayenne* (np, 1593).

20. BN FF Mss 3985, fol. 25, Jean de Pilles, abbé d'Orbais, to the commander of Diou, August 5, 1593, Paris.

21. BN FF Mss 15575, fol. 65–83, "Fragment sur l'histoire de la Ligue."

22. BN CD Mss 379, fol. 82–97, "Déclaration du roy sur sa conversion," August 4, 1593.

23. BN CD Mss 62, fol. 46, Sieurs de Crose and de Carces to the Parlement of Aix-en-Provence, November 19, 1593, Aix; Cl. de Pl., *Manifeste et déclaration de la noblesse de Provence contenant les causes qui l'ont meüe de prendre les armes contre le sieur d'Espernon* (Lyons, 1595).

24. Article II of the general truce, for example, reappeared as article V of the *Édit et déclaration du roy sur la réduction de la ville de Paris, soubs son obéissance* (Paris, 1594).

25. Yves-Marie Bercé, *Histoire des Croquants: Étude des soulèvements populaires au XVIIe siècle dans le sud-ouest de la France* (Geneva: Droz, 1972).

26. René Benoist, *Épistre consolatoire écrite au peuple de l'église St-Eustache en Paris* (St. Denis, 1593), p. 5; Claude de Morenne, *Épistre envoyée par M. Claude de Morenne, curé de S. Médéric aux catholiques de la ville de Paris* (St. Denis, 1593).

27. René Benoist, *Voeu et exhortation de continuellement . . . prier pour nostre roy* (Paris, 1597), pp. 3–8.

28. See also *Remonstrance aux françois sur la conversion de Henry de Bourbon III, de ce nom très-chrestien roy de France et de Navarre* (Paris, 1594).

29. BN FF Mss 15910, fol. 41, Perrot to Bellièvre, August 3, 1593, Chartres; IF CG Mss 262, fol. 75–76, Bellièvre to anonymous, July 10, 1593, np.

30. Bellièvre, *Advertissement*, pp. 6–8.

31. Sieur de Trellon, *Le Ligueur repenty* (Lyons, 1595), p. 14.

32. Bellièvre, *Advertissement*, pp. 11–14.

33. See also Alexandre de Pont-Aimery, *Discours d'estat où la nécessité et les moyens de faire la guerre en l'Espagne mesme sont richement exposez* (Paris, 1595), p. 9; M. M. Pelaez, "Los conceptos 'Franca' y 'Espanya' en el pensamiento literario y juridico-politico de Francese de Eiximedis (c. 1340–1409)," *Bulletin hispanique*, 82 (Bordeaux, 1980), pp. 353–361.

34. Arnauld, *Les fleurs de lys*, p. 18.

35. BN FF Mss 15909, fol. 421, Charles Faye d'Espesses to Bellièvre, September 16, 1593, Tours.

36. BN CD Mss 313, fol. 63–69, "Recueil de la harangue de M. Séguier faicte a Tours, le 13 novembre 1593."

37. Ibid., fol. 66.

38. BN FF Mss 3986, fol. 128–129, Sancy to Nevers, October 1, 1593, Nancy.

39. *Advis de quatre fameuses universités d'Italie sur l'absolution du roy* (Lyons, 1594).

40. Henri IV to Clement VIII, July 26, 1593, St. Denis, Berger de Xivery, vol. 3, p. 435.

41. *Discours de la légation de M. le duc de Nevers . . . envoyée par Henry IV envers le pape Clément VIII* (Paris, 1594).

42. Duperron, *Négotiations* (Paris, 1616), pp. 23–52.

43. BN FF Mss 2751, fol. 219–221, the Duc de Guise to Clement VIII, November 1594, np.

44. *Cérémonies observées* (Paris, 1595), p. 6; R. Chaplain, "Le cardinal d'Ossat (1537–1604)," *Société, Sciences, Arts de Bayeux*, 23 (1955), pp. 5–34.

45. Victor E. Graham, "Chartres ou les raison d'un choix: Le sacre et le couronnement d'Henri IV," *Pays Yvelines, Hurepoix et Beauce*, 24 (1981), pp. 42–44; BN FF Mss 3984, fol. 199, Henri IV to Nevers, July 25, 1593,

St. Denis; Maurice Jusselin, *Aménagements dans le choeur de la cathé-drale de Chartres pour le sacre de Henri IV* (Chartres: Imprimerie moderne, 1940), p. 2.

46. Jackson, *Vive le roi!*, pp. 138–156; Bonnefin, *Sacre des rois*, p. 142.

47. BN CD Mss 546, fol. 57–59, Achille de Harlay "A Chartres au sacre de Henri IV"; Alexandre de Pont-Aimery, *L'hymn du sacre du très chrestien et très victorieux prince Henry IV* (Tours, 1594); Claude de Morenne, *Les cantiques et quatrains spirituels . . . avec un panégyrique faict pour le sacre et couronnement d'Henry IV* (Paris, 1595).

48. Matthieu Giron, *Au roy, sur le sacre de sa majesté, avec l'épistre syn-odale des prélats de l'église de France assemblez en la ville d'Orléans* (Paris, 1594); Pierre Gasenault, "La Sainte-Ampoule de Marmoutier (Indre-et-Loire)," *Mélanges offerts à B. de Gaiffier et F. Halkin, Analecta bollandiana*, 100 (1982), pp. 243–257.

49. Nicolas de Thou, *Cérémonies observées au sacre et couronnement du très-chrestien et très-valeureux Henri IV, roy de France et Navarre* (Paris, 1594), pp. 3–4.

50. P. Feret, "Nullité de mariage de Henri IV avec Marguerite de Valois," *Revue des questions historiques*, 11 (1876), pp. 77–114.

51. BN FF Mss 3449, fol. 17, Charles de Bourbon, Comte de Soissons, to Henri IV, early December 1595, np; BN FF Mss 2751, fol. 252–254; *La conversion de la princesse de Condé à Rouen en 1596* (Rouen, 1596).

52. *Conférence tenue à Nancy sur le différent de la religion. A l'effect de convertir madame soeur unique du roy, à la catholique et romaine* (np, 1600).

53. BN FF Mss 2945, fol. 50, "Bref du pape Paul V à M. de Sully pour l'inciter à se faire catholique," Rome, October 9, 1605; fol. 51, "Responce de M. de Sully au bref du pape Paul V," Paris, November 27, 1605.

54. Jean de Sponde, *Déclaration des principaux motifs qui ont induict le feu sieur de Sponde à s'unir à l'église catholique. Adressée à ceux qui sont séparez* (Paris, 1595), pp. 27–28; Florimond de Raemond, *Le tombeau du feu sieur de Sponde* (Bordeaux, 1595); V. P. Palma Cayet, *Copie d'une lettre . . . contenant les causes et raisons de sa conversion* (Paris, 1595); *Discours de la conversion et mort du sieur de Morlas* (Paris, 1595); Agrippa d'Aubigné, *Confession catholique du sieur de Sancy* (np, 1597); Michel Perronnet, "Confession catholique du sieur de Sancy," *Réforme, Human-isme, Renaissance*, 10 (1979), pp. 24–33.

55. L. Grégoire, *La Ligue en Bretagne* (Paris, 1856), pp. 234–251.

56. BN FF Mss 5045, fol. 416, "Extraict des registres du Parlement de Paris," January 3, 1594.

57. BN FF Mss 3629, fol. 26–27, "Déchiffrement d'une lettre concernant les faits qui ont précédé et suivi la reddition de Meaux entre les mains de Henri IV en janvier 1594"; Nevers, *Mémoires*, vol. 2, p. 295.

58. *Édict et déclaration du roy sur la réduction de sa ville de Meaux à son obéissance* (Meaux, 1594); *Le manifeste de Monsieur de Vitry à la noblesse de France* (np, 1594), pp. 19–20.

59. *La proposition de M. de la Chastre . . . faite au corps et communautez de la ville d'Orléans, le 17 febvrier 1594* (St. Denis, 1594); BN FF Mss 15910, fol. 49, La Châtre to Bellièvre, August 30, 1593, Orléans; H. Le Charpentier, *La Ligue à Pontoise et dans le Vexin français* (Pontoise, 1878).

60. Palma Cayet, *Chronologie novenaire*, p. 508; A. Reure, *La presse politique à Lyon pendant la Ligue* (Lyons, 1898), pp. 143–147; Henri Hours, "Le 'conseil d'état' à Lyon pendant la Ligue," *Revue historique de droit français et étranger* (1952), pp. 41–50.

61. *Discours sur le dernier propos du duc de Nemours par lequel il advertit le Marquis de St. Sornin d'estre obéissant au roy* (Paris, 1595); Pierre Matthieu, "Discours des grand effets qui ont suivi la conversion du roi," in *Histoire des derniers troubles en France* (Lyons, 1594), pp. 3–27; Antoine de Verdier, *Discours sur la réduction de la ville de Lyon* (Lyons, 1594); BN FF Mss 23914, fol. 60–61, St. André to Henri IV, February 15, 1594, Lyons; BN FF Mss 23195, fol. 127, Épinac to Henri IV, May 13, 1594, Meulan.

62. Barnavi, *Le parti de Dieu*, pp. 239–255; Estoile, *Registre journal*, pp. 217–226; BN FF Mss 20153, fol. 541–710, "Affaires de Paris 1593."

63. BN FF Mss 3989, fol. 217, "Lettre du corps de la ville de Paris au party contraire," April 2, 1594.

64. Henri IV rendered special thanks to the Virgin Mary for the bloodless submission of the city. G. M. D. R., "Sommaire discours de la réduction de Paris," in Estoile, *Les belles figures de la Ligue* (Paris, 1608), pp. 308–311.

65. BN FF Mss 20153, fol. 693.

66. BN FF Mss 15591, fol. 336–339, "Déclaration du roy," (Paris, 1594).

67. Antoine Loisel, "Remonstrance fait en la grande chambre des édits et déclarations du roy sur la réduction de la ville de Paris soubs son obéissance, et restablissement du Parlement en icelle," in *Recueil des remonstrances* (Lyons, 1604), pp. 562–575; BN FF Mss 4391, fol. 194–198, "Interrogatoire faict à un conseiller de la cour ayant demeuré à Paris durant la Ligue," 1595.

68. BN FF Mss 20153, fol. 695.

69. *Advis, conseil et décret de l'Université de Paris* (Paris, 1594); *La daemonologie de Sorbonne la nouvelle* (np, 1594).

70. BN FF Mss 3989, fol. 203, Revol to Nevers, March 23, 1594, Paris.

71. See Bernard Chevalier, *Les bonnes villes de France du XIVe au XVIe siècle* (Paris: Gallimard, 1982); *La réduction de tous le pays de Normandie en l'obéissance du roy* (Angers, 1594); *Déclaration de la ville de Riom* (np, 1594).

72. BN FF Mss 13665, fol. 6, Henri IV to Sully, March 8, 1594, Senlis.

73. Antoine Loisel, *Homonoée ou l'accord et union des subjets du roy soubs son obéissance* (Paris, 1595), pp. 30–31; Jean Secret, "Sur la harangue prononcée par Antoine Loisel le 4 juillet 1583 à Périgueux," *Bulletin de la société historique et archéologique de Périgord*, 99 (1972), pp. 311–316; Jacques Clémens, "La renaissance de la fonction politique des villes de l'Agenais. Marguerite de Valois en la Gascogne (1578–1586)," *Revue Agenais*, 98 (1972), pp. 19–27.

74. BN FF Mss 20154, fol. 911, Boucher to Mayenne, August 27, 1594, Brussels.

75. René Benoist, *Remonstrance au roy de s'opposer à toutes hérésies* (Rouen, 1596), pp. 6–7.

76. *Édict sur la réduction de la ville d'Orléans en son obéissance* (Paris, 1594), p. 6.

77. BN CD Mss 62, fol. 104; *Édict sur la réduction de la ville d'Orléans,* p. 11.

78. Sutherland, *The Struggle,* pp. 324–326.

79. BN FF Mss, 5045 fol. 379–382.

80. See J. Garrisson, *L'Édit de Nantes et sa révocation: Histoire d'une intolérance* (Paris: Seuil, 1985); F. Baumgartner, "The Catholic Opposition to the Edict of Nantes, 1598–1599," *Bibliothèque d'humanisme et Renaissance,* 40 (1978), pp. 525–536.

81. Harding, *Anatomy,* pp. 105–107.

82. Guillaume du Vair, *Responce d'un bourgeois de Paris à la lettre de M. le légat, le 27 janvier 1594* (Paris, 1594), p. 7.

83. Antoine Loisel, *De l'amnistie ou l'oubliance des maux faits et receus pendant les troubles* (Paris, 1595), pp. 12–16; François Billacois, "Clémence ou justice: Un débat sur la fonction royale aux débuts de l'absolutisme," *Revue d'histoire du droit,* 24 (1960), pp. 444–450.

84. Loisel, *De l'amnistie,* p. 18.

85. Palma Cayet, *Chronologie novenaire,* p. 511.

86. *Édict et déclaration du roy sur la réduction de Paris,* pp. 5–6.

87. BN FF Mss 5045, fol. 417–418.

88. *Manifeste de M. le duc de Vitry* (np, 1594), pp. 3–14.

89. BN FF Mss 23194, fol. 109, Chillaud to Henri IV, April 2, 1594, Périgueux.

90. BN CD Mss 62, fol. 100, Hurtelou to Henri IV, April 10, 1594, Chevac.

91. *Édict et déclaration du roy sur la réduction de . . . Beauvais* (Paris, 1594), pp. 3–5.

92. BN FF Mss 3989, fol. 221, Revol to Nevers, April 2, 1594, Paris.

93. *Déclaration de la ville de Riom* (np, 1594), p. 4.

94. BN FF Mss 23194, fol. 114, Clergy of Lyons to Henri IV, March 15, 1594, Lyons; BN FF Mss 3629, fol. 26–27.

Bibliography

Primary Sources

MANUSCRIPTS

Archives Nationales Mss K 1569, KK 150–153, KK 1716.
Bibliothèque Mazarine Mss 20189, 22194, 24980.
Bibliothèque Nationale FF Mss 513, 1509, 1728, 2590, 2746, 2751, 2752, 2945, 3224, 3275, 3363, 3364, 3386, 3422, 3430, 3449, 3473, 3490, 3612, 3615, 3624, 3625, 3626, 3628, 3629, 3631, 3634, 3646, 3706, 3914, 3947, 3948, 3950, 3952, 3958, 3961, 3977, 3978, 3980, 3982, 3983, 3984, 3985, 3986, 3988, 3989, 3996, 3997, 4019, 4228, 4337, 4391, 4505, 4683, 4718, 4719, 4743, 4748, 4783, 4810, 4890, 4897, 5045, 5076, 5755, 5808, 6552, 7762, 7764, 7765, 7767, 7773, 7774, 7854, 10191, 10198, 13665, 14054, 15555, 15561, 15575, 15591, 15699, 15811, 15893, 15895, 15909, 15910, 16093, 16140, 17281, 17282, 17533, 20153, 20154, 23194, 23195, 23299, 23914; FF NA Mss 7761, 7774; FI Mss 851; CCC Mss 14, 31, 33, 397, 489, 500; CD Mss 61, 62, 88, 119, 313, 322, 379, 500, 525, 546, 549, 591, 698, 753, 770.
Institut Français CG Mss 262.
St. Denis Archives Communales Mss GG8.

PRINTED SOURCES

Over two hundred pamphlets printed between 1560 and 1600 were consulted and form a substantial portion of the evidence upon which this study is based. Most are currently held in the Bibliothèque Nationale and the Bibliothèque Mazarine in Paris. Citations of those principally used can be found in the notes, as can references to printed documentary collections of memoirs and letters.

Secondary Sources

Angers, Julien Eymard d'. *Recherches sur le stoïcisme au XVIe et XVIIe siècles.* Hildesheim: G. Olms, 1976.

Anquez, Léonce. *Histoire des assemblées politiques de la France, 1573–1622.* Paris, 1859.

Apollinaire, P. *Les prières pour le roy en 1593.* Nîmes, 1892.

Ars, Brémond d'. "Les conférences de Saint-Brice entre Henri de Navarre et Catherine de Médici, 1586–1587," *Revue des questions historiques,* 34 (1884): 41–43.

Aubin, Paul. *La problème de la conversion.* Paris: Beauchesne, 1962.

Aumale, Duc d'. *Histoire des princes de Condé pendant les XVIe–XVIIe siècles.* 2 vols. Paris, 1885.

Ayzac, Félice d'. *Histoire de l'abbaye de St. Denis en France.* 2 vols. Paris, 1860.

Babelon, Jean-Pierre. *Henri IV.* Paris: Fayard, 1982.

Barbiche, Bernard. "L'influence française à la cour pontificale sous le règne de Henri IV," *Mélanges d'archéologie et histoire de l'école française à Rome,* 77 (1965): 177–199.

Barnavi, Élie. *Le parti de Dieu: Étude sociale et politique des chefs de la Ligue parisienne (1584–1595).* Louvain: Nauwelaerts, 1980.

Barnavi, Élie, and Robert Descimon. *La Sainte Ligue, le juge et la potence.* Paris: Hachette, 1985.

Barnes, Andrew E. "Religious Anxiety and Devotional Change in Sixteenth-Century French Penitential Confraternities," *Sixteenth Century Journal,* 19 (1988): 389–405.

Baumgartner, Frederic J. "The Case for Charles X," *Sixteenth Century Journal,* 4 (1973): 87–98.

——— *Radical Reactionaries: The Political Thought of the French Catholic League.* Geneva: Droz, 1976.

——— "The Catholic Opposition to the Edict of Nantes, 1598–1599," *Bibliothèque d'humanisme et Renaissance,* 40 (1978): 525–536.

——— "Renaud de Beaune: Politique Prelate," *Sixteenth Century Journal,* 9 (1978): 99–114.

——— *Change and Continuity in the French Episcopacy: The Bishops and the Wars of Religion, 1547–1610.* Durham: Duke University Press, 1986.

——— *Henri II, King of France, 1547–1559.* Durham: Duke University Press, 1988.

Bayley, Peter. *French Pulpit Oratory, 1598–1650: A Study in Themes and Styles.* Cambridge: Cambridge University Press, 1980.

Beame, E. M. "The Limits of Toleration in Sixteenth-Century France," *Studies in the Renaissance*, 13 (1966): 250–265.

Benedict, Philip. *Rouen during the Wars of Religion*. New York: Cambridge University Press, 1981.

Bercé, Yves-Marie. *Histoire des Croquants: Étude des soulèvements populaires au XVIIe siècle dans le sud-ouest de la France*. Geneva: Droz, 1972.

—— *Fête et révolte, des mentalités populaires du XVIe au XVIIIe siècles: Essai*. Paris: PUF, 1976.

Bergin, Joseph. *Cardinal François de la Rochefoucauld, 1558–1645: Leadership and Reform in the French Counter-Reformation Church*. New Haven: Yale University Press, 1987.

Berriot, F. *Athéismes et athéistes au XVIe siècle en France*. 2 vols. Paris: Cerf, 1984.

Billacois, François. "Clémence ou justice: Un débat sur la fonction royale aux débuts de l'absolutisme," *Revue d'histoire du droit*, 16 (1960): 444–450.

—— "Du régicide: Matériaux pour une enquête sur la légimite dynastique," *Études réunies en l'honneur de Pierre Goubert*. 2 vols. (Paris, 1982), II, pp. 71–79.

—— *The Duel: Its Rise and Fall in Early Modern France*, ed. and trans. Trista Selous. New Haven: Yale University Press, 1990.

Bitton, Davis. *The French Nobility in Crisis: 1560–1640*. Stanford: Stanford University Press, 1969.

Bossy, John. *Christianity and the West, 1400–1700*. Oxford: Oxford University Press, 1985.

Boucher, Jacqueline. *Société et mentalités autour de Henri III*. 4 vols. Paris and Lille: PUF, 1981.

—— "L'évolution de la maison du roi des derniers Valois aux premiers Bourbons," *XVIIe siècle*, 34 (1982): 359–379.

Briggs, Robin. *Communities of Belief: Cultural and Social Tension in Early Modern France*. Oxford: Oxford University Press, 1989.

Bryant, Lawrence M. *The King and the City in the Parisian Royal Entry Ceremony: Politics, Ritual and Art in the Renaissance*. Geneva: Droz, 1986.

Buisseret, David. *Henry IV*. London: George Allen & Unwin, 1984.

Cameron, Keith. *Henri III: Maligned or Malignant King?* Exeter: Exeter University Press, 1978.

—— ed. *From Valois to Bourbon: Dynasty, State and Society in Early Modern France*. Exeter: Exeter University Press, 1989.

Cave, Terence. *Devotional Poetry in France, c. 1570–1613*. Cambridge: Cambridge University Press, 1969.

Cave, Terrence, and Michel Jeanneret. *Métamorphoses spirituelles: Anthologie de la poésie religieuse française, 1560–1630*. Paris: Gallimard, 1972.

Cazeux, Yves. "Les entretiens d'Henri IV avec le duc d'Épernon au cours de l'été 1584," *Bulletin de la société des amis du château de Pau*, 72 (1977): 41–50.

Chartier, Roger. *Lectures et lecteurs dans la France d'ancien régime*. Paris: Seuil, 1987.

Chaunu, Pierre. *Le temps des réformes: Histoire religieuse et système de civilisation. La crise de la chrétienté, 1250–1550*. Paris: Gallimard, 1976.

Chevalier, Bernard. *Les bonnes villes de France du XIVe au XVIe siècles*. Paris: Gallimard, 1982.

Chrisman, Miriam Usher, and Otto Grundler, ed. *Social Groups and Ideas in the Sixteenth Century*. Kalamazoo: Western Michigan University Press, 1978.

Church, William F. *Constitutional Thought in Sixteenth-Century France: A Study in the Evolution of Ideas*. Cambridge, Mass.: Harvard University Press, 1941.

Clark, Peter, ed. *The European Crisis of the 1590s*. London: Routledge & Kegan Paul, 1985.

Constant, Jean-Marie. *Les Guise*. Paris: Gallimard, 1984.

Crouzet, Denis. "Recherches sur les processions blanches, 1583–1584,"*Annales économie, société, civilisation*, 38 (1983): 511–563.

——— "La représentation du temps à l'époque de la Ligue," *Revue historique*, 272 (1984): 297–388.

——— *Les guerriers de Dieu*. 2 vols. Paris: A. Colin, 1990.

Crue, François de la. *Le parti politique au lendemain de la Saint-Barthélemy*. Paris: A. Michel, 1892.

Dampnier, B., ed. *La controverse religieuse*. 2 vols. Montpellier, 1980.

Davis, Natalie Z. "Strikes and Salvation in Lyons," *Archiv für Reformationsgeschichte*, 56 (1965): 48–64.

——— "The Rites of Violence: Religious Riot in Sixteenth-Century France," *Past and Present*, 59 (1973): 51–91.

Delumeau, Jean. *Le catholicisme entre Luther et Voltaire*. Paris: PUF, 1971.

——— *Le péché et la peur: La culpabilisation en Occident (XIIIe–XVIIIe siècles)*. Paris: Fayard, 1983.

Descimon, Robert. "La Ligue à Paris (1585–1594): Une révision," *Annales économie, société, civilistion*, 37 (1982): 72–111.

——— *Qui étaient les seize?* Paris: Hachette, 1984.

Desjardins, Arthur. *Les parlements du roi (1589–1596)*. Paris, 1879.

Desplat, Christian. "Le mythe d'Henri IV: Nouvelles approches," *Bulletin de la société des amis du château de Pau*, 72 (1977): 81–103.

Devyver, André. *Le sang épuré. Les préjugés de race chez les gentilhommes français de l'ancien régime, 1560–1720*. Brussels: Éditions de l'Université de Bruxelles, 1973.

Dewald, Jonathan. *The Formation of a Provincial Nobility: The Magistrates of the Parlement of Rouen, 1499–1610*. Princeton: Princeton University Press, 1980.

Dickerman, Edmund H. *Bellièvre and Villeroy: Power in France under Henry III and Henry IV.* Providence: Brown University Press, 1971.

—— "The Conversion of Henri IV: 'Paris is Worth a Mass' in Psychological Perspective," *The Catholic History Review,* 63 (1977): 1–13.

Diefendorf, Barbara. "Prologue to a Massacre: Popular Unrest in Paris, 1557–1572," *American Historical Review,* 90 (1985): 1067–1091.

Dreano, M. *La religion de Montaigne.* Paris: A.–G. Nizet, 1969.

Drouot, Henri. *Mayenne et la Bourgogne. Étude sur la Ligue en Bourgogne, 1587–1596.* 2 vols. Dijon: A. Picard, 1937.

—— "Les conseils provinciaux de la Sainte-Union (1589–1595)," *Annales du Midi,* 66 (1953): 415–433.

Duchêne, Roger, ed. *La conversion au XVIIe siècle: Actes du XIIe colloque de Marseille.* Marseilles, 1983.

Dumont, François. "La royauté française vue par les auteurs littéraires au XVIe sièle," in *Études historiques à la mémoire de Noël Didier* (Paris, 1960), pp. 61–93.

Eisenstein, Elizabeth L. *The Printing Press as an Agent of Cultural Change: Communications and Cultural Transformations in Early Modern Europe.* 2 vols. New York: Cambridge University Press, 1979.

Farge, James K. *Orthodoxy and Reform in Early Reformation France: The Faculty of Theology of Paris, 1500–1543.* Leiden: Brill, 1985.

Febvre, Lucien. *Le problème de l'incroyance au XVIe siècle.* Paris: A. Michel, 1942.

Feret, P. "Nullité du mariage de Henri IV avec Marguerite de Valois," *Revue des questions historiques,* 11 (1886): 77–114.

François, M. "La réception du concile et ses difficultés en France sous le règne de Henri III," *Revue d'histoire ecclésiastique,* 51 (1964): 236–257.

Franklin, Julian. *Jean Bodin and the Rise of Absolutist Theory.* Cambridge, Mass.: Harvard University Press, 1973.

Fumaroli, Marc. *Jésuites et gallicans. Recherches sur la genèse et sur la signification des querelles de rhétoriques en France sous les règnes de Henri IV et Louis XIII.* Paris: H. Champion, 1983.

Garrisson-Estèbe, Janine. *Tocsin pour un massacre. La saison des Saint-Barthélemy.* Paris: Le Centurion, 1968.

—— *Protestants du Midi: 1559–1598.* Toulouse: Privat, 1980.

—— *Henri IV.* Paris: Gallimard, 1984.

Gee, Adair. "The Abjuration of Henry of Navarre," *Journal of Modern History,* 5 (1933): 143–171.

Giesey, Ralph. *The Royal Funeral Ceremony in Renaissance France.* Geneva: Droz, 1960.

—— "The Juristic Basis of Dynastic Right to the French Throne," *Transactions of the American Philosophical Society.* Philadelphia, 1961.

Goubert, Pierre. "L'ancienne société d'ordres: Verbiage ou réalité?" *Clio parmi les hommes* (Paris, 1976).

Graham, Victor E. "Chartres ou les raisons d'un choix: Le sacre et couronnement d'Henri IV," *Pays Yvelines, Hurepoix et Beauce*, 24 (1981): 42–44.

Greengrass, Mark. "Dissension in the Provinces under Henri III, 1574–1585," in *The Crown and Local Communities in England and France in the Fifteenth Century*. Gloucester: University of Gloucester Press, 1981, pp. 162–182.

———— "The *Sainte Union* in the Provinces: The Case of Toulouse," *The Sixteenth Century Journal*, 14 (1983): 469–496.

———— *France in the Age of Henri IV*. London: Routledge & Kegan Paul, 1984.

———— "Noble Affinities in Early Modern France: The Case of Henri I de Montmorency, Constable of France," *European History Quarterly*, 16 (1986): 275–311.

Hanley, Sarah. *The "Lit de Justice" of the Kings of France: Constitutional Ideology in Legend, Ritual and Discourse*. Princeton: Princeton University Press, 1983.

Harding, Robert R. *Anatomy of a Power Elite: The Provincial Governors of Early Modern France*. New Haven: Yale University Press, 1978.

———— "Revolution and Reform in the Holy League: Angers, Rennes, Nantes," *Journal of Modern History*, 53 (1981): 379–416.

Harran, Marilyn J. *Luther on Conversion: The Early Years*. Ithaca: Cornell University Press, 1983.

Hauser, Henri. "François de la Noue et la conversion du roi," *Revue historique* (1888): 313–323.

Heller, Henry. *Iron and Blood: Civil Wars in Sixteenth-Century France*. Montreal: McGill-Queen's University Press, 1991.

Hennequin, Jacques. *La naissance d'un mythe: Henri IV à travers ses oraisons funèbres*. Paris: PUF, 1980.

Hoffman, P. T. *Church and Community in the Diocese of Lyon, 1500–1589*. New Haven: Yale University Press, 1984.

Holt, Mack. *The Duke of Anjou and the Politique Struggle during the Wars of Religion*. Cambridge: Cambridge University Press, 1986.

Huppert, George. *Les bourgeois gentilhommes*. Chicago: University of Chicago Press, 1977.

Hurtubise, Pierre. "Mariage mixte au XVIe siècle: Les circonstances de la première abjuration d'Henri IV à l'automne de 1572," *Archivum historicae pontificae*, 14 (1976): 103–134.

Jackson, Richard A. "Peers of France and Princes of the Blood," *French Historical Studies*, 7 (1971): 27–46.

———— "Elective Kingship and the *Consensus populi* in Sixteenth-Century France," *Journal of Modern History*, 44 (1972): 155–172.

———— *Vive le roi! A History of the French Coronation from Charles V to Charles X*. Chapel Hill: University of North Carolina Press, 1984.

Jedin, Hubert. *A History of the Council of Trent*, trans. Ernest Graf. 5 vols. St. Louis: B. Herder, 1957.

Jensen, De Lamar. *Diplomacy and Dogmatism: Bernardino de Mendoza and the French Catholic League.* Cambridge, Mass.: Harvard University Press, 1964.

Jouanna, Arlette. *Ordre social, mythes et hiérarchies dans la France au XVIe siècle.* Paris: Hachette, 1977.

Jusselin, Maurice. *Aménagements dans le choeur de la cathédrale de Chartres pour le sacre de Henri IV.* Chartres: Imprimerie moderne, 1940.

Kaiser, Colin. "Les cours souveraines au XVIe siècle: Morale et Contre-Réforme," *Annales économies, sociétés, civilisations,* 37 (1982): 15–31.

Kantorowicz, Ernst. *Laudes Regiae: A Study in Liturgical Acclamations and Medieval Ruler Worship.* Berkeley: University of California Press, 1946.

—— *The King's Two Bodies: A Study in Medieval Political Theology.* Princeton: Princeton University Press, 1957.

Kelley, Donald. *Foundations of Modern Historical Scholarship: Language, Law and History in the French Renaissance.* New York: Columbia University Press, 1970.

—— *The Beginning of Ideology: Consciousness and Society in the French Reformation.* New York: Cambridge University Press, 1981.

Keohane, Nannerl. *Philosophy and the State in France: The Renaissance to the Enlightenment.* Princeton: Princeton University Press, 1980.

Kettering, Sharon. *Judicial Politics and Urban Revolt in Seventeenth-Century France.* Princeton: Princeton University Press, 1978.

—— *Patrons, Brokers and Clients in Seventeenth-Century France.* Oxford: Oxford University Press, 1986.

—— "Clientage during the French Wars of Religion," *Sixteenth Century Journal,* 20 (1989): 221–239.

Kingdon, Robert M. *Geneva and the Coming of the Wars of Religion.* Geneva: Droz, 1956.

—— "Problems of Religious Choice for Sixteenth-Century Frenchmen," *The Journal of Religious History,* 4 (1966): 105–112.

—— *Geneva and the Consolidation of the French Protestant Movement, 1564–1572.* Geneva: Droz, 1967.

—— *Myths about the St. Bartholomew's Day Massacres, 1572–1576.* Cambridge, Mass.: Harvard University Press, 1988.

Kinser, Samuel. "Agrippa d'Aubigné and the Apostasy of Henry IV," *Studies in the Renaissance,* 2 (1964): 245–268.

Knecht, R. J. *Francis I.* Cambridge: Cambridge University Press, 1984.

Labitte, Charles. *De la démocratie chez les prédicateurs de la Ligue.* 2nd ed. Paris, 1865.

La Brière, Yves. *La conversion de Henri IV, Saint-Denis et Rome, 1593–1595.* Paris: A. Picard, 1905.

Lebigre, Arlette. *La révolution des curés.* Paris: A. Michel, 1980.

Leites, Edward, ed. *Conscience and Casuistry in Early Modern Europe.* Cambridge: Cambridge University Press, 1989.

Le Roy Ladurie, E. "Auprès du roi, la cour," *Annales économies, sociétés, civilisations,* 38 (1983): 21–41.

Love, Ronald S. "The Religion of Henry IV: Faith, Politics and War, 1553–1593." Ph.D. diss., University of Southern California, 1986.

────── "Winning the Catholics: Henri IV and the Religious Dilemma in August 1589," *Canadian Journal of History*, 24 (1989): 361–379.

Major, J. Russell. *Representative Institutions in Renaissance France*. Madison: University of Wisconsin Press, 1960.

────── *Bellièvre, Sully and the Assembly of Notables of 1596* (Philadelphia, 1974), *Transactions of the American Philosophical Society*.

────── "Noble Income, Inflation and the Wars of Religion," *American Historical Review*, 86 (1981): 21–48.

Martin, A. Lynn. *Henri III and the Jesuit Politicians*. Geneva: Droz, 1973.

────── "Une tentative ignorée de conversion de la veuve de Coligny par un Jésuite," *Bulletin de la société d'histoire du protestantisme français*, 126 (1980): 109–114.

────── *The Jesuit Mind: The Mentality of an Elite in Early Modern Europe*. Ithaca: Cornell University Press, 1988.

Martin, Victor. *Le gallicanisme et la réforme catholique: Essai historique sur l'introduction en France des décrets du concile de Trente (1563–1615)*. Paris: A. Picard, 1919.

Maugis, E. *Histoire du Parlement de Paris de l'avènement des rois Valois à la mort d'Henri IV*. 3 vols. 2nd ed. New York: B. Franklin, 1967.

Mechoulan, Henry, ed. *L'état baroque. Regards sur la pensée politique de la France du premier XVIIe siècle*. Paris: J. Vrin, 1985.

Mentzer, Raymond A. *Heresy Proceedings in Languedoc, 1500–1560* (Philadelphia, 1984), *Transactions of the American Philosophical Society*.

Mesnard, Pierre. *L'essor de la philosophie politique au XVIe siècle*. 2nd ed. Paris: J. Vrin, 1971.

Mousnier, Roland. *L'assassinat d'Henri IV*. Paris: Gallimard, 1964.

────── *La plume, la faucille et le marteau: Institutions et société en France du Moyen Age à la Révolution*. Paris: PUF, 1970.

────── "Les concepts d'"ordres,' d''états,' de 'fidélité' et de 'monarchie absolue' en France de la fin du XVe siècle à la fin du XVIIIe," *Revue historique*, 247 (1972): 289–312.

Nakam, Géralde. *Les essais de Montaigne: Miroir et procès de leur temps*. Paris: Nizet, 1984.

Neuschel, Kristin. *Word of Honor: Interpreting Noble Culture in Sixteenth-Century France*. Ithaca: Cornell University Press, 1989.

Nock, Arthur Doby. *Conversion: The Old and New in Religion from Alexander the Great to Augustine of Hippo*. Oxford: Clarendon, 1933.

Oestreich, Gerhard. *Neostoicism and the Early Modern State*, trans. David McLintock. Cambridge: Cambridge University Press, 1982.

Orlea, Manfred. *La noblesse aux États-Généraux de 1576 et 1588*. Paris: PUF, 1980.

Pagès, Georges. *La monarchie d'ancien régime en France de Henri IV à Louis XIV*. Paris: Hachette, 1928.

Pallier, Denis. *Recherches sur l'imprimerie à Paris pendant la Ligue (1585–1594)*. Geneva: Droz, 1976.

Pasquier, Étienne. *René Benoist, le pape des Halles*. Paris: A. Picard, 1901.

Patry, Raoul. *Philippe Duplessis-Mornay: Un huguenot homme d'état (1549–1623)*. Paris: Fischbacker, 1933.

——, ed. *La conversion religieuse (XVIe–XVIIe siècles)*. 2 vols. Montpellier, 1981.

Peronnet, Michel. "Confession catholique du sieur de Sancy," *Réforme, humanisme, Renaissance*, 10 (1979): 24–33.

Poirson, Auguste. *Histoire du règne de Henri IV*. 4 vols. Paris, 1865.

Powis, Jonathan. "Gallican Liberties and the Politics of Later Sixteenth-Century France," *The Historical Journal*, 26 (1983): 515–530.

Ranum, Orest. *Artisans of Glory: Writers and Historical Thought in Seventeenth-Century France*. Chapel Hill: University of North Carolina Press, 1980.

Richard, P. *La papauté et la Ligue française. Pierre d'Épinac, archevêque de Lyon (1573–1599)*. Paris: A. Picard, 1901.

Richet, Denis. "Aspects socio-culturels des conflits religieux à Paris dans la seconde moitié du XVIe siècle," *Annales économies, sociétés, civilisations*, 32 (1977): 764–789.

Ritter, Raymond, ed. *Lettres et poésies de Catherine de Bourbon*. Paris: H. Champion, 1927.

—— "Le roi de Navarre et sa prétendue fuite de la cour en 1576," *Bulletin philologique et historique*, 2 (1976): 667–684.

Roelker, Nancy L. *Queen of Navarre, Jeanne d'Albret, 1528–1572*. Cambridge, Mass.: Harvard University Press, 1968.

Rose, Paul Lawrence. "Bodin and the Bourbon Succession to the French Throne, 1583–1594," *Sixteenth Century Journal*, 9 (1978): 75–98.

Rothrock, George A. "The Constitutional Implications of the Bourbon Succession," *Canadian Journal of History*, 3 (1968): 34–51.

Salmon, J. H. M. *Society in Crisis: France in the Sixteenth Century*. New York: St. Martin, 1975.

Saulnier, Eugène. *Le rôle politique du cardinal de Bourbon, 1523–1590*. Paris: H. Champion, 1912.

Schalk, Ellery. *From Valor to Pedigree: Ideas of Nobility in France in the Sixteenth and Seventeenth Centuries*. Princeton: Princeton University Press, 1986.

Shortland, Michael. "The Figure of the Hypocrite: Some Contours of an Historical Problem," *Studies in the History of Psychology and the Social Sciences*, 4 (1987): 255–274.

Smith, P. *The Anti-Courtier Trend in Sixteenth-Century French Literature*. Geneva: Droz, 1962.

Stähelin, Ernst. *Der übertritt König Heinrich IV zur römischen katholichen Kirche*. Basel, 1856.

Strayer, Joseph R. "France: The Holy Land, the Chosen People, and the

Most Christian King," in *Action and Conviction in Early Modern Europe: Essays in Memory of E. H. Harbison,* ed. Theodore K. Rabb and Jerrold E. Seigel. Princeton: Princeton University Press, 1969, pp. 3–16.

Sutherland, N. M. *The French Secretaries of State.* London: Athlone, 1962.

—— *The Massacre of St. Bartholomew and the European Conflict, 1559–1572.* New York: Barnes & Noble, 1973.

—— *The Huguenot Struggle for Recognition.* New Haven: Yale University Press, 1980.

—— *Princes, Politics and Religion, 1547–1589.* London: Hambledon Press, 1984.

Tentler, Thomas N. *Sin and Confession on the Eve of the Reformation.* Princeton: Princeton University Press, 1977.

Thompson, Martyn P. "The History of Fundamental Law in Political Thought from the French Wars of Religion to the American Revolution," *American Historical Review,* 91 (1986): 1103–1138.

Turchetti, Mario. *Concordia o tolleranza? François Bauduin (1520–1573) e i "moyenneurs."* Geneva: Droz, 1984.

Tyvaert, Michel. "L'image du roi: Légimité et moralité royales dans les histoires de France au XVIIe siècle," *Revue d'histoire moderne et contemporaine,* 21 (1974): 521–547.

Vaissière, Pierre de. "La conversion d'Henri IV," *Revue historique de l'église de France,* 14 (1928): 43–68.

Varachaud, Marie-Christine. "La conversion au XVIIe siècle," Thèse du Troisième Cycle. Paris-Sorbonne, 1975.

Viller, R. "Aspects politiques et juridiques de la loi de catholicité (1589–1593)," *Revue d'histoire de droit,* 37 (1959): 196–213.

Weill, Gaston. *Les théories sur le pouvoir royal pendant les guerres de religion.* Paris, 1891.

Wolfe, Michael. "Piety and Political Allegiance: The Duc de Nevers and the Protestant Henri IV, 1589–1593," *French History,* 2 (1988): 1–21.

Yardeni, Myriam. *La conscience nationale en France pendant les guerres de religion.* Louvain: Nauwelaerts, 1971.

Yates, Frances A. *The French Academies of the Sixteenth Century.* London: Warburg Institute, 1947.

—— *Astraea: The Imperial Theme in the Sixteenth Century,* Boston: Routledge & Kegan Paul, 1975.

Index